hindus Awake!

Book 1: The Foundation

Two Harbors Press
212 3rd Avenue North, Suite 570
Minneapolis, MN 55401
612.455.2293
www.TwoHarborsPress.com

Website: www.HindusAwake.com
Author Email: DrK@HindusAwake.com
Editor Email: SmitaK@HindusAwake.com

While every effort has been made to painstakingly reference our work, it is entirely possible that we may have inadvertently overlooked, misquoted or misreferenced something. We humbly request that you forgive any such errors or omissions, and address these to Krishna Kripa, LLC at www.krishnakripa.net. We genuinely welcome all suggestions or comments from readers, and will try to implement these in future revisions, if any.

ISBN - 978-1-935097-00-6
ISBN - 1-935097-00-8
LCCN - 2008905358

Book sales for North America and international:
Itasca Books, 3501 Highway 100 South, Suite 220
Minneapolis, MN 55416
Phone: 952.345.4488 (toll free 1.800.901.3480)
Fax: 952.920.0541; email to orders@itascabooks.com

Cover Design by Deepak N. Kotecha, O.D.
Typeset by James Arneson
Edited by Smita D. Kotecha, R.Ph.

Printed in the United States of America

hindus Awake!

Book 1: The Foundation

by

Deepak N. Kotecha, O.D.

Aum Shri Ganeshai Namaha

There are not enough words to describe Hinduism,
The Magnificent treasure we take for granted -
Cherish it and Relish it or you may soon Relinquish it!

- Deepak N. Kotecha, O.D.

...Bhagvan tells Arjun in the Gita that it is He who
Is the Source of all Strength, wisdom, knowledge, ability...

- His Divine Holiness Pramukh Swami Maharaj

(Excerpted & Translated
from a speech given in Gujarati)

December 13, 2007
BAPS Swaminarayan Shatabdi Mahotsav
Ahmedabad, India

True dharam founded on vidya, the correct knowledge,
always unites.
It is only avidya, the lack of this proper knowledge,
confounded by arrogance that divides.

- Deepak N. Kotecha, O.D.

The Sands of Time
And the Doot of Yam
Wait for No-One.
The Time to Act is Now!

- Deepak N. Kotecha, O.D.

hindus Awake!

Dedication

Advaitam Achyutam Anadim Anant-Roopam
Adyam Puranna-Purusham Nava-Yauvanum cha
Vedeshu Durlubhum Adurlubhum Aatma-Bhaktau
Govindam Adi-Purusham Tam aham Bhajami

- Sri Brahma-Samhita (5:33)

The significance:

I worship Govind, The Original Purush, The Supreme
The One without a second,
Who is Eternal,
Without a beginning, and of infinite beautiful forms,
The One Who is the beginning Purush and yet Who is eternally youthful, and Who
Though Unobtainable by the Vedas,
is easily obtainable
by an Aatma's pure devotion

Dedicated First & Foremost to the Lotus Feet of Shri Krishna

& Thereafter
To His Selfless and Humble Devotees,

& To
My dear Grandmother,
(Late) Diwaliben Vanravan Kotecha,
The treasure house and foundation
of our spiritual knowledge & devotion

As well as To
The worthy Repository for that
spiritual knowledge & devotion,
My Wonderful Parents,
& My Family, too,
Who selflessly give all
Asking for nothing in return

Table of Contents

Editor's Note

Aum, Shri Ganeshai Namaha

I am sure you have all heard the story of a little boy who went to the temple one day with his parents, where he saw everyone praying in a high language that he could not even understand, let alone recite. He felt a little down, therefore, that everyone was praying to God except him. After everyone was done praying, the little boy started reciting the alphabet, A, B, C, D, and so on. His father asked the little boy why he was saying his A, B, C's. The little boy answered simply "Popa, I don't know the prayer that all of you just said, but I do know it was made out of A, B, C, D and so on. So I just asked the Lord that 'Oh God I don't know the prayer that everybody was just singing but I do know A, B, C, D. Will you please make a prayer that you like the most out of these on my behalf?' " A touchy little story, huh? It is obvious that when someone talks innocently and from the bottom of the heart about the Lord, it is always going to be touchy.

There is a reason for telling you or reminding you of this little story. It is because I truly think that this little book-set is *our* offering of our A, B, C, D, to the Lotus Feet of Shri Krishna. It is a simple look into the complicated concepts contained within the vast ocean of treasure that is Hinduism, from our concepts such as our lunar-based calendar, to death and beyond. Most importantly, I believe it deals with the most complicated and crucial concept, the one of our *Aatma,* in an elegant and simple way that makes it much easier to understand. Understanding the foundations of Hinduism makes it easier to see why we must always treasure it.

First of all, I am truly blessed and thank Shri Krishna for putting me in a religious, loving and caring family in Bhaarat, or India. Furthermore,

He gave me an even more caring and religious family as my in-laws. My father-in-law is truly a *gyani*, truly knowledgeable, and I have learnt a lot from him, my mother in law who is very devoted and religious, my brother-in-law, whom I absolutely adore, who, though younger than I, shelters me through many storms, and sisters-in-law who I deeply love and respect. He also blessed me with my little babies lalo and budhu-ram, and last but not least a wonderful husband who loves me truly; My husband who wrote this book and gave me the opportunity to critique and edit it, which became a crucial turning point in my spiritual and personal life. Quite frankly, my dear friends, my true understanding of God and our true purpose of this precious human life has become crystal clear after reading and editing this book.

I was fortunate enough to be born in Bhaarat and being raised there for the important first twenty years of my life. Bhaarat is where *Adhyat-mikta* is in every atom of our pure Bhaarat bhoomi. Coming from a strictly vegetarian Hindu family, I was also very religious to start with. However, I know now that I was also then without *vidya*, the true *gyan*, or *real* knowledge. Are you Surprised? Let me begin to tell you why I am saying this.

It started with the birth of our first son, our little lalo, Avi. He was a gift to us when we had given up hope. He came after a lot of *tap* to Shri Ram, Shri Krishna, and Maa Aamba. When he joined us, I decided against career advancement to become a full-time mother and wife instead. We are of the firm belief that a baby needs a mother, not a caretaker, especially for the first few years, and especially up to age five. It is a decision we have not regretted and have come to regard as a blessing. My little lalo has always been very curious about anything related to God. He started asking me some hard questions at the age of four, especially when he saw deities. He loved to hear stories from the *Ramayan*, *Mahabharat*, and so on, and would not get tired of hearing them. I was able to answer some of his questions, but others I wasn't able to. I would tell him we would ask his *popa*, his father, when he would get home. And so started our little *ghar-sabhas*, our home-satsangs, begun by our little lalo! One day he asked a question that made his father become very quiet. After some thought, his father answered the question, but also said that he was going to write some simple thoughts and guidelines on Hinduism for him.

And so it went for a few weeks or months. One day, his father came up to me and said he was going to start putting it all on a computer. I didn't say much to him at the time, but I laughed on the inside. What difference would that make? But, as he started to do this, I noticed it was taking a lot of time away from the boys, along with the rest of the family and me. I was very much engraved with the idea that chanting Hari's name is the only way to achieve God in Kal-Yug. This began to bother me, so I finally said something. I told him that he was wasting his time and he should be chanting Hari's name instead! He completely ignored me, and went on typing late into the nights, for he worked by day.

Then, one day, I saw his diagram on *Creation* and saw how nicely he had simplified this very complicated subject dealing with birth and death. This diagram was very easy to understand and self-explanatory to me. So I started asking more questions which he clarified very nicely and in a very easy to understand language, using the example of children and playground. All of a sudden, something inside me just lit up. Things suddenly fell into place and were much clearer now. As I looked more and more at his work, my love and devotion for Krishna rose to a whole new level. I realized that this happened because I was more aware of the *correct* knowledge of Krishna. The more I read, the more interested I became.

And then I told him that he should write this as a book so that we could share it with not only the children but also the rest of our family and perhaps even a few close friends! He was very surprised. First I tell him to stop wasting time, and now I am asking him to put more into it! He said he would do it if I helped to edit the book, and we had a deal. I want to share some more personal experiences with you as I went through this process with him.

I truly believe that this book was 'divine driven' right from the very beginning. It started with our little lalo asking all the right questions sending his father into deep thought and typing away at the keyboard, to little things like titles, phrases and ideas simply 'falling' instantly into place by 'themselves.' For example, one night, after we both came home from work, finished dinner and put the kids to sleep, we started wondering what name we should word the website for the book as. Amazingly, the words *Krishna Kripa* were out of my mouth before my brain could even entertain the question or the response! My husband had 'thought' of the title to the book in exactly that way – it just happened.

It truly has been Krishna's kripa all through. And the name of the book and the website was simple, spiritual, appropriate and perfect. The other thing that happened was that as the last chapter of the book was being written, my work for editing started to pile up. My schedule was completely full, with full-time work, mothering children and husband, and so on. Suddenly, I became very ill with congestion, fever and a sore throat, and lost my voice! I could not speak a word! I was sent home from work, and my schedule quickly became clear! Well, I lay in bed all day and finished editing this book within a mere five or so hours, for I could not sleep. In the process, I even forget I was ill to begin with, as no talking was required! As soon as the editing was finished, we began to consider the order in which the book would proceed from start to finish, and title or sub-title the remaining sections that needed it, and finish the Chapter on *The Final Analyses*, which is critical from our stand-point to invoke thought in and unite the *bhole-bhale* Hindus and devotees that are being torn apart and misled both from within and without.

Surprisingly, the titles, sub-titles and the remaining final comments fell into place amazingly quickly, literally within minutes! We were shocked! There had to be an intelligence much stronger than ours that was driving it on, my dear friends, for I know for a fact that we were not that efficient! There are many instances such as these, but we won't get too detailed. The project was immense, and we decided to split it into easy to take-with-you-and-read volumes, rather than one huge volume that everyone would be afraid to haul around! As we continued to wrap this multi-book project up, we debated briefly what size and form the books should be, and whether they should be as a paperback or hardcover. I decided on hardcover for the durability point of view, even though it may slightly raise the final production cost. Most of us have books we treasure or use regularly, and we prefer these in the durable hardcover option. I hope that this set is useful enough for you to keep in your library to either refer to it, or to save it for the family, especially for little ones who may someday also want to explore Hinduism for what it can *truly* do for them rather than just dogmatically and superficially following it like I did.

I know that I have changed after working through this entire project of multiple volumes. Something significant and beautiful in me has lit up. *Should I say I have awakened?*

This project has affected me personally and professionally. It is a change that is hard to describe. I look at things quite differently now. I now am able to see the world and appreciate it more innocently and without judgment, just like my little ones. Though I have always worked hard, I am now able to give my very best to my family, work and most of all, my Supreme, my Krishna, for whom I have a whole new appreciation. I now understand with true clarity what my real purpose in life is, and that this human form is absolutely precious.

I am truly devoted to Krishna, but now with even greater appreciation for all He has done for me, especially this book set. I am truly glad my husband ignored me and continued to write. I know he has changed in the process, just as I have. It is a wonderful change that we both welcome and are grateful for, and it is not possible without Krishna Kripa. Who says Grehasthis can't truly strive towards Krishna? We now realize the *significance* of shastra's position that *Grehasth Ashram* is best positioned for spiritual enlightenment and Krishna consciousness.

I still chant today, but my chanting is now different and much more meaningful. It has a depth and dimension that has not existed for me before, and I know it is the same for my husband. And it all started with our little lalo and his difficult questions. I feel that I am now a giant step closer to Krishna because of him, and because of my husband.

Even though this entire discussion was really meant to be a private family dialogue for our children, I insisted on putting these thoughts in writing, for they may help others as well. You decide if they do help you or not.

I am truly thankful for my little lalo and his father. I now have a sense of urgency and a level of devotion that I did not have before. I had a lot of knowledge, but it was dormant, for I know I was asleep. I believe that I have awakened, and have had the privilege of receiving Krishna Kripa by reading, contributing to, and editing this book set.

Are you ready to Awake too, my friends, and receive Krishna Kripa?

Jai Shri Krishna!

Smita D. Kotecha, R.Ph.
\- Editor

APPRECIATION

This little set of books, a project that has been several years in the writing, is my humble *seva*, my way of serving those that I wish to serve. It is a simplistic representation of the culmination of my deepest thoughts, contemplations and reflections. These, however, are based on concepts that were formulated by the selfless rishis of Bhaarat who are the true and rightful founders of Vedantic or Sanatan dharam for us. Therefore, the appreciation and gratitude starts at their *Shri charnarvind,* their lotus feet. It is through their immense efforts *for us* that we enjoy the magnificent philosophy that has become known to the world as 'Hinduism.' Our sincere and humble obeisances to them as we get started on exploring Hinduism.

Although it is not possible to thank everyone that has made this little *seva* possible, I would at least like to begin to try.

Hindus have a common saying that one will need even a pinch of sand in time. That may be true in many ways for many people, and I know it is certainly true for me. This little project has had a lot of help along the way. It is a life-long project, for one doesn't learn overnight, and one continues to learn till the end of life. Learning is a gradual process, and mine certainly is. One must learn what one can at any given opportunity. According to Hindu philosophy, one that teaches one something valuable in life becomes one's guru. My list is long and growing, and for that, I am always thankful.

It is my little one that initiated this little project, and it is *him* whom I first thank for asking the questions in the *first* place. My lalo, my little *bubu, my* little *pranah* (life force) outside my body, my son *Avi*. Whether he or my other little ones (my Kishna-ben, my Bhuddhu-Ram, my Shai-

Baba, or my little Wali) ever get anything out of this work or not is not the issue that strikes me. What *does* is that *I* got a lot out of it! *Dhanya dhanya, mara wala*, for asking. *You* are the one who made me do this! Little did I know where this little project would lead, and how it would affect me! You made my thoughts clearer! You made me lay awake for many a night pondering and asking, reading and debating, smiling and crying, but ultimately for realizing, beyond a shadow of a doubt, of what *I* must do, now and forever! You made me realize that the sands of time are indeed running out. Without you, this sense of urgency would not have been possible. And for that, I am eternally grateful, for it has affected me deeply. And I don't use *eternally* lightly. *Dhanya dhanya, mara lala, mara wala*, for asking in the first place! One day you will hopefully realize how much *you* have helped *me*! You, too, are my little *guru*, for I have learned a lot just by observing you.

I also want to humbly thank my parents for the many, many things that they have done. Shastra says that making shoes out of one's own hide for your parents will not even *begin* to repay one's debt to them! Most of all, however, I want to thank you for going the great distance with such patience and instilling in me the treasure of Hinduism from a very young age. You lead by example and sacrifice, which I shall remember to my pyre. I am truly blessed to have parents like you! Putting up with me has never been easy. I am the first to realize that! How? Because I don't have a choice in putting up with me! You do! I especially want to thank my mother, publicly and openly. You are always there for me *inspite* of me! For better or for worse, you, *mama*, molded me! Someone has said it right – God did put mothers on earth because He could not be everywhere! However, soft as mums are, God had to also interject Himself, as a protector and an enforcer, as fathers! Discipline is essential, and fathers have to set the correct boundaries. Without the appropriate boundaries and without border enforcement, young impressionable minds are easily led astray. Therefore, it has to be teamwork, and teamwork is what I was blessed with. Whether I appreciated it then is not important; that it is valued at some point in life is really what counts. And not a day passes when I do not count my blessings for being blessed with parents like you.

Thanking the rest of my family is no less significant. They are the ones that help silently and unhesitatingly *without* even being asked. My brother and his family, my sisters and their families. You, too, always have a choice. Yet you choose to *always* be there for me! You will *always* have my deepest gratitude, but mere words fail me now. How can I ever thank you for everything you have always done?

I also need to thank my wife, *my better half*, first for saying *yes* to me (for reasons clear only to her) and second, for *making* me write this book, helping to critique and edit it, contributing to it in so many other wonderful and significant ways, and for taking over a lot of my responsibilities to allow me the additional time needed to devote to this book set. It started out as a hodge-podge of handwritten notes and outlines for my children, but she *made* me write this in a more structured form (from which it evolved by *Krishna Kripa* into this little book set, albeit conversational and informal) for *she* said it might help others. *That* is for you to decide. I did her bidding to preserve peace and harmony in *my* life. For, in all great homes, the real power *is* the woman, be it a mother, a wife, or a sister and, in my case, *all* of the above! Lucky Me! Truly! However, if these books help you in any way at all, no matter how small or insignificant it may seem, we will have considered our efforts worthwhile and are grateful for you having given us the opportunity to be of humble service to you in the first place.

There are many extended family members and close friends whom I also thank for you, too, have always been there for me, and I know you always will. You know who you are, and you should know that you are appreciated, whether it is verbalized or not.

Ultimately, I also humbly and sincerely want to thank the *sadhus* and devotees who have given me the privilege of their association now and throughout my life. I consider myself to be truly fortunate to have even been in your presence, what to speak of your kind association. *You* have touched me in ways that can never be repaid, and for every moment that you have ever spared me, I am eternally grateful. All I can do is to offer my humble and respectful obeisances to each and every one of you. I fully realize that this work may or may not be what meets with your full approval. A thousand apologies if you feel that I may have failed you in any way. I pray that you continue to bless me with your association, nonetheless, so that I may return to, or continue on, a path that *is* appropriate.

Shastra says that when we cannot repay a great debt, when we are left speechless and words seem meaningless, we should join hands and bow with respect to acknowledge that debt, and thus begin to be relieved of it.

To *all of you,* who have touched my life so meaningfully in one way or another, with my hands joined and my head silently and respectfully bowed, my *humble* and *heartfelt* gratitude, and my Jai Shri Krishna!

- *Deepak N. Kotecha*

RESPECTFUL OBEISANCES

Puja, Prayers & Recitals

Aum Shree Ganeshai Namaha

Aum Gan Ganapataye Namah

Aum Namo Bhagavate Vasudevạì

Aum Namo Bhagavate Vasudevạì

Aum Namo Bhagavate Vasudevạì

ॐ

Aum

The most auspicious, most sacred, most revered and holy of *all* Hindu sounds and symbols.

Shri Krishna says in the *Shrimad Bhagwat Gita* that *He* is *Aum*[1]

Rig Ved proclaims *Aum* as the *Supreme*[2]

Aum

Vasoode-Vasutum Devum
Kansa-Charoor Namar-danum
Devaki Param-Anandum
Shri Krishnam Vande Jagat-Gurum

Aum Bhur Bhuvaha Svah
Tat Savitur Varenyam
Bhargo Devasya Dheemahi
Dhiyo Yo Nah Prachodayat

- *Rig Ved*

The significance:

We meditate upon Aum (the Supreme)
Creator of the Three Worlds,
Who is Transcendental and Eternal,
Whose brilliance is Brighter than
untold Suns,
and Whose Knowledge
Removes Ignorance and Sins
(To Lead us from ignorance and
darkness to knowledge and truth)

Hari Bol!

Hare Krishna
Hare Krishna
Krishna Krishna
Hare Hare

Hare Ram
Hare Ram
Rama Ram
Hare Hare

Jai Sia Ram

Shri Ram Jai Ram Jai Jai Ram

Shiv

Aum Namah Shivai

Buddh

Buddham Sharanam Gacchami

Swami Narayan

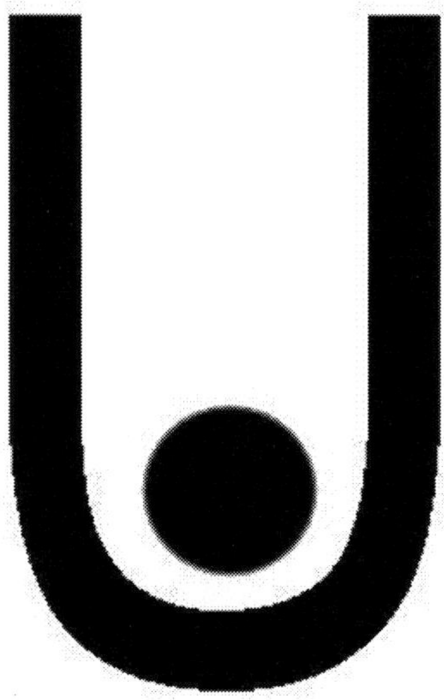

Jai Swami Narayan

Om Shri Sai Nathai Namaha

Jai Jai Sai Ram

Jalaram Bapa

Jai Jalaram
Ramji no bhakta Lohano

Satchitandanda Rupaya
Vishvotpatyadi Hetave
Tapatraya Vinashaya
Shri Krishnaya
Vayam Namaha

- *Shrimad Bhagwat*
(Mahatmay Shlokh)

The significance:

Oh Eternal Truth, Consciousness
and Bliss
Creator of the Universes
Destroyer of Ignorance,
Shri Krishna
We bow and pay homage to You

Achyutam Keshavam Rama Narayanam
Krishna Damodaram Vasudevam Harim
Shridharam Madhavam Gopika Vallabham
Janaki Nayakam Ramachandram Bhaje

- Shankar Acharya

The significance:

Krishna, the Eternal One Who Never Fails
His devotee,
The One Whom the Gopies Worship, and
Ram who is Janki's husband and is also Narayan,
You, Who are One and the Same,
We Worship You

PREFACE

Hinduism, or more correctly *Vedic* or *Sanatan Dharam*, is totally scientific in its approach, beliefs, teachings, practices, knowledge and indeed even customs. Therefore, contrary to popular or current belief, Hinduism and Science are not a dichotomy and are certainly not diametrically opposed.

Science is, in fact, derived from the teachings contained within the Vedantic knowledge. Modern 'discoveries' merely re-state these 'findings' as 'new discoveries' and present them as such. Interesting, though, as the 'scientific' basis of Hinduism is, our basis of discussion proceeds with the firm knowledge that our religion, our culture, or Hinduism, *is* indeed totally scientific.

Therefore, we will not spend any time on addressing the 'scientific basis' of Hinduism, as we already know it is solidly rooted in it! We will focus our energies on loftier discussions and even loftier goals, seeking thoughts and answers on questions of real significance to Hindus and indeed all human beings ultimately.

This guide, an insider's guide to Hinduism as well as a brief and occasionally even blistering commentary on it, is the first in a mini-series, and is presented in an outline form in a highly simplified manner. It is purposefully written in an easy to read conversational style of English. Little attention has been paid to the exact formality of grammatical and other rules as the emphasis of the entire discussion is on the easy and informal delivery of the intended message. Therefore, please forgive grammatical and other such mistakes.

There is also accompanying commentary, most of which has been deferred to either the *Background* section, or the *Closing* and *Parting*

Thoughts section of the material. This commentary is not necessarily directed just to a neophyte but also to one better versed with Hinduism. You are highly encouraged to read these commentaries and to contemplate these at your leisure, for it may contain pearls or alternative insights that even a native Hindu may find thought provoking or even enlightening.

The presentation of this outline is a logical progression of how one might approach the vast ocean of treasure that is Hinduism. Its purpose is to attempt to prepare merely a groundwork or a framework of reference. It is hoped that this groundwork shall serve as a springboard to investigate desired topics in greater depth and start to build on this foundation.

For a reader well versed with Hinduism, it serves as a handy guide to topics that may not be ordinarily or easily accessible all in one place, especially if one is presented with the responsibility of educating a child or a neophyte.

Even if you are well versed in Hinduism, you are still urged to read the chapters or sections of *The Need to Return to Basics,* with emphasis on *The Present Predicament*, *Ahinsa & Vegetarianism*, and *The Final Analyses*. These sections deal with issues that are highly relevant today.

The *approach* to the subject is focused on one goal and one goal only. It is to acquire the most useful information in the simplest way possible and in the shortest amount of time that will lead to the path of spiritual salvation while maintaining cultural and spiritual integrity. The approach is to distill our complex ideology into highly simplified concepts to achieve this purpose. Therefore, it is *not* inundated with data and references, scientific, spiritual or otherwise, that do not meet this single criterion and test. Throughout the discussion, the *only* objective is the focus and goal of exiting creation with the specific purpose of going back home to our maker through spiritual and cultural integrity.

As you read the suggested or any of the sections, it is naturally implicit that your opinions, ideas, thoughts and conclusions may differ from those presented here, and that is always welcome. That is what makes us each human. The final opinion that matters is *yours*.

The style of this book is meant to be candid, simplistic, and closer to a conversation or a narrative, rather than a formal text. There is frequent and non-translated use of non-English terms, especially Gujarati or Sanskrit ones. As you read on, it may seem to ramble a bit, and at other times, take on a more formal tone, and yet again take on a mischievous tone. The reason is that *this discussion* is a father's conversation (albeit one-sided) with his children in their tender *baal-avastha* in an attempt to answer some of their questions, and to further prepare them for others they may not even thought of.

The inspiration for this project is my five children (two mine, really, and three my little brother's whom I also love dearly). There are lots of other wonderful little ones on my sisters' and other sides as well but, according to Hindu custom and tradition, I cannot claim them as mine.

Here, then, is an attempt at organizing the various fundamental and basic (but essential) ideas and concepts that comprise the cornerstones of Hinduism in a somewhat orderly fashion. As the objective of any language should be to communicate with a goal to *lower* rather than *raise* barriers, the language is kept deliberately simple. This is not meant to be work of reference to be put away on some shelf and forgotten. Quite to the contrary, it is meant to be a simple and practical approach in a summary fashion to understanding this complex and wonderful philosophy, and is designed to provoke thought and inquisitiveness in the reader.

The other objective is to unite several thoughts and concepts into one, easy to understand outline to *begin* to lay the foundation for what is Hinduism. Its purpose is not to be an in-depth analysis of what *is* or *should* be, but rather *my* understanding of what *is*. Concepts are presented in an abstract fashion to simply provide a broad understanding of *some* of our fundamental beliefs and teachings. In other words, it is a summary to unite my many thoughts, concepts, rituals, customs, and significance of symbolism. The focus is more on understanding 'why' rather than merely 'what' one does as a Hindu.

The *Bhagwat Gita*, the *Shrimad Bhagwat*, and the *Ramayan* serve as the fundamental basis and underpinnings for the concepts and ideas in here. The two main scriptures when directly quoted out of are *Bhagavad-Gita As It Is* and the *Shrimad Bhagavatam* by His Divine Holiness A.C. Bhaktivedanta Swami Prabhupad, the founding Acharya of ISKCON; the other sources of information include my father's daily recitations from the *Ram Charit Maanus* by Goswami Tulasidas, and out of the *Shrimad Bhagwat* by Donghre Maraaj. I have had the distinct privilege of having grown up with these through my wonderful parents and my grandparents, family and friends, and through the many teachers, books and various discourses and associations I have experienced throughout my life.

Therefore, understand that the ideas are not mine, but are a culmination of these flows of ideas and *manthan* in me.

Let us start by making an observation of a common issue dogging Hindus. A derogatory term 'ABCD' is used by non-American-born Indians to describe or denote American-born Indian-descent children. The acronym ABCD may stand for many things, but as used in this context, stands for 'American Born Confused Desi.' This acronym has a negative connotation and, unfortunately, rightfully so.

An American and a *Desi* may sound like an oxymoron, but it does not have to be. It is true that some youngsters shy away from decism and adopt western features, customs and cultures, to the point of hiding their desi or bhaaratiya origin, and even preferring to adopt 'western' names under the pretext that their name may be hard to pronounce, or worse yet give their ethnicity away! 'Harit may become popularly known as 'Harry,' or 'Mukesh' as 'Mike, and so on. Remember, we are not talking about nicknames or pet names. We are talking about truly *adopting,* for everyday use, western names and shying away from using their given Indian names even amongst other Indians! Hence the acronym - born a desi here, but (thoroughly) confused as to his (or hers) root identity. The other similar acronym is OBCD, or *Overseas* substituted for *American.* The pressure and the need to belong or blend in can be tremendous, which explains why many American-born desi children shed desi attributes and hastily adopt prevailing ones.

However, maybe its because I've always been *mindfully rebellious* and *non-conformist*, *my* position has always been don't say *Me Too* but say *Only Me!* We are each individual, and should maintain that individuality for the betterment of mankind. Politicians may invite crowds, but true leaders must always walk alone. And with arrows in their backs, if need be! One *must* learn to think outside the box. However, one should *not* rebel against the status quo just for the sake of it. Do not give up what you have in hand till you are sure that what you are about to be served with has been proven better in every respect than what you are proposing to give up.

A culture that teaches respect for elders and society, balance and harmony of all of creation, and the concept and practice of *simple living and high thinking* should command admiration and respect, not the cowering behind an adopted name just because yours is too ethnic, different or difficult to pronounce!

You can be a proud American or a Citizen of your country, and serve your country well without giving up your cultural lineage, heritage, and treasure. This is what our great country, the United States, is made of – diverse ethnic and cultural goals working in unison – the so-called "melting pot" for the common good of all mankind.

This confusion however, meaning ABCD, does not have to be. And, if this confusion is allowed to propagate, the entire culture will be lost in a mere generation or two. What then to speak of *your* grandchildren's *Pitru Roon*!

My children are American born and we are extremely proud of it, I am happy to say. However, they are also proud of their *Bhaaratia Sanskriti*, or Indian heritage, thanks to their tireless grandparents and their wonderful *acharyas* and teachers. This combination of proud American heritage combined with proud Bhaaratia Sanskriti will ideally serve the nation of United States and indeed the world to make it a more noble place, a more peaceful place and indeed an even stronger place for generations to come.

At the age of five, my son inspired me to *read* the *Shrimad Bhagwat Gita*, and the *Shrimad Bhagwat,* among others, even though I had *heard* them many times.

How did he do this? He was asking me "why" questions as to some of our ideas, rituals and concepts. Questions that were highly appropriate, but to which I was able to give only stuttered and simplistic answers as I understood them. The concept of *karma*, or deeds, and mystical powers of sages that defy laws of nature, for instance. Or the concept of *death* and why that must occur, and what would happen after that. Why we celebrate *Diwali*, the beautiful festival of lights, or *Janmashtmi*, and when in the year they generally fall. Why our calendar is so different than the Roman or current calendar. And many more.

Thankfully, I had sufficient knowledge to answer a five year old, but that got me thinking. How much did I *really* know? How deep was my understanding of the *fundamentals* of our culture and religion? I, too, knew a little of this and a little of that. My wonderful parents are devout *Vaishnavs*, and have taught me a great deal over my life. Mum's position (as most mums go) is you must do this ritual or that *puja* based on faith and *bhakti* alone and *without* question even if one's understanding may be limited. My father's position, however, has always been to probe deeper and understand the meaning or significance of it. His mindset is that one can ask and debate as long as one's question and the need to *want* to know is genuine, rather than merely for debate or cheap rhetoric.

The *inquisitiveness* and the *desire* to know is termed *Jignasa.* One must have unyielding *Jignasa* to attain the Ultimate Truth, the Supreme. One is highly fortunate if the desire to know The Supreme stirs at a young age. The *Brahma Sutra* starts *Athato Brahma Jignasa,* which loosely translated means let us begin the inquiry into the *Brahm*, or the *Supreme Personality.* It is highly desirable, then, at *any* age to have a yearning or desire to know Brahman, the *Supreme* Personality.

Subsequently then, the question arose, how do I pass what little knowledge or information I had to my son? Would he continue searching for this knowledge when I was gone? There really is no single structured guide, outline, or book that I could leave for him to study to get him started. As I searched, only scattered parts of the ideas were available, but none to bring together our basic concepts, the very fundamentals, as a whole.

So, here it is. A little of this and a little of that as I, a proud *Hindu* and a *Vaishnav*, see it. It is not a thesis but, rather, a simple and straightforward first guide to understanding our amazingly rich and truly magnificent heritage. It is not meant to provide a complete education by any means. Rather, it is meant to answer some simple questions that my five beautiful children have already asked or will ask someday and want to look up. Then, with this outline in hand to take that difficult first step, the proverbial journey of a thousand miles shall hopefully begin.

So forgive me, friends, if this work may be a little simplistic. It is meant for *my* little ones, really, but I hope that it may someday also benefit *yours*.

I do not claim or pretend to be an expert or an authority in Hinduism. – only that I *am* a Hindu *and* a Vaishnav. If there are truths in the ideas and concepts presented here, they are simply *my* take on the collection of some wonderful thoughts of great rishis, acharyas, scholars and parents of Bhaarat that hopefully shed some light on issues you may not have known, or perhaps illustrate them under a different light. Therefore, if the concept is correct, bear in mind it is *not* mine – I am merely re-stating these great and ancient yet timeless and wonderful thoughts and reflections.

The ultimate goal of our discussion is to return back home, and information deemed to be important in the eventual attainment of this goal is the consistent focus of our discussion for the remainder of this work.

On the other hand, though, if there are any errors or blunders in the material presented, the blame is singularly mine in that I have failed to grasp that idea or concept. When this occurs, my learned brothers and sisters, please forgive me. My intention is to inform, and not to misinform. My goal is to impart knowledge and not misconceptions to my little ones. I humbly request that any errors be pointed out at once and without reservation or hesitation so that I may correct them.

Moreover, remember I am conversing with *my* little ones, and have absolutely no interest or desire in locking horns with theologians, theorists, sampradays, sadhus, katha-kaars, esoterics, or the like.

Lest you rush to judgment or criticism bear in mind that *I* am entitled to *my* opinion just as much as *you* are entitled to *yours!*

This project is my little *seva*, my way of serving those that I wish to serve. It is a simplistic representation of the culmination of my deepest thoughts, contemplations and reflections.

These pages, then, represent my thoughts, feelings, opinions, ideas and reflections. They may not represent yours. Nevertheless, we should always agree to disagree, for that is our human God-given right.

Be that as it may, I urge you to contemplate and reflect on my thoughts, simple as they may be. It is after all, your life, your after-life, and your *peddhi* and *vansh,* your future generations and your lineage, that depend upon your decision.

Remember, the final word is *always* yours.

Jai Shri Krishna!

Deepak N. Kotecha, O.D.

CHAPTER 1

Hinduism:

Setting The Stage for Discussion

Contrary to popular and naive belief, Hinduism and Science are not a dichotomy and are certainly not diametrically opposed. All science is, in fact, fundamentally derived from the teachings that are contained within the Vedantic knowledge base.

1.1: Setting the Stage for Discussion A Brief Introduction

Hinduism! Wonderful, colorful, mystical, spiritual, magical, romantic, passionate, beautiful, eloquent, poetic, powerful, and many more such words fall short of even coming close to describing Hinduism, or better yet, *Vedic* or *Sanatan Dharam* and *sanskar*. This wonderful, deeply philosophical and highly intellectual *religion* (if we may be so bold if somewhat *incorrect* to use this term) and the magnificent culture that goes with it is beyond simple words and defies easy description.

For our discussion at present, we will use the terms *Hinduism*, *Vedic Dharam* and *Sanatan Dharam* interchangeably even though we should realize that there *is* a technical difference, which we will address later.

Although the *approach* used here is highly distilled and deliberately simplistic, the subject matter, *Hinduism*, is not. It is an *aseem* and vast treasure that is difficult if not impossible to corral. The very depth of this magnificent treasure is difficult to fathom, and mere words do it little justice. Even though Hinduism defies words, for it is deeper than the depths of the Universe, it is indeed words that one must use to initially get any message across. So here goes.

Hinduism is an intricate and intertwined, immensely complex and diverse system of faith, culture, customs, duty and indeed even religion. It can be difficult to comprehend some of even the simplest basics or underpinnings, but without this basic or fundamental conceptual foundation of core knowledge, the journey to discovering its treasures is akin to sailing a ship that is rudderless – swept where the oceanic current (or current thinking) goes. Therefore, an attempt even as rudimentary as this at organizing this knowledge in a systematic way would be a good first start for any young person or neophyte interested in this amazing treasure that Hinduism has to offer. It also, however, serves to provide a culmination of several flows of thoughts and reflections, distilled down to the very basics, which would probably benefit even a seasoned Hindu by challenging him to think outside the box, so to speak.

Hinduism, or more correctly *Vedic* or *Sanatan Dharam*, is totally scientific in its approach, beliefs, teachings, practices, knowledge and indeed even customs. Therefore, contrary to popular or common and naive belief, Hinduism and Science are not a dichotomy and are certainly not diametrically opposed. Science is, in fact, derived from the teachings that are contained within the Vedantic knowledge, be it astronomy to medicine, aviation and communication to surgery and medicine, agriculture and construction to politics, or even the science of war and destruction, and so much more. It is *all* in the Hindu or Vedantic scriptures.

Tragically then, when 'modern' Hindus shy away from Hinduism as a culture and religion with 'mythical' beliefs, nothing could be further from the truth! Awake, my Hindu friends! Ignorance is *never* bliss! Hinduism, based on Vedantic knowledge, *is* totally scientific, and is in fact the real *mother* of all scientific knowledge, if you will.

Interesting, though, as the 'scientific' basis of Hinduism is, *our* basis of discussion and our ultimate goals are unique, and our discussion rests on the foregone conclusion and knowledge that our religion, our culture, or Hinduism, *is* totally scientific.

Therefore, we will not spend time on addressing the scientific basis of Hinduism, as we already know it fully rests on it! Instead, we will focus our energies on loftier discussions and even loftier goals, seeking great deliberation, thought and possible answers to questions of *real significance* for all Hindus and indeed, ultimately, all humanity.

Tragically, some 'modern' Hindus also shy away from Hinduism because of the stigma from ancient and 'weird' customs and rituals such as the 'caste system' or the 'dowry system' and the like. The resultant stigmatization and stereotyping of Hindus from such issues has caused some Hindus to abandon Hinduism entirely and jump across to perceived 'safer' and more western social and cultural environments. However, this is akin to throwing the baby out with the bath water, to quote an old adage! This is not just sheer folly but absolute madness!

Indeed, Hinduism is the only 'culture' on the face of this planet that historically and currently not only equates men to women but actually cherishes and idolizes them, be it in the form of a sister, a wife, a mother, or even a deity! Where else, and in what other culture, have women traditionally received such glorious reverence and protection? And where else is the multi-generational, close-knit family unit cherished and so fiercely protected? Only in Hinduism, and only in the *vishaal* and humble hearts of Hindus! A glorious precedent and tradition established by none other than Shri Krishna Himself!

If you research 'religions' of the world, you will quickly realize that 'organized religion' is the *root* cause of major issues, and not necessarily the spiritual platform on which such 'religion' may be based. The same is true of 'Hinduism' if you dig deep into its history. While certainly not flawless, the majority of 'issues' and 'stigmas' are truly of the 'imported' variety, whether from Europe, Persia, Eurasia, or elsewhere. What is even worse is the fact that we 'Hindus' are a peaceful and docile people has worked *against* us in this respect.

Therefore, my Hindu friends, you must awake! Do not be naive and throw 'the baby' out with the bath water! Your *vansh*, your *peddhi*, is finished if you do! We will address some of these concerns in a little more depth in the final two chapters as we conclude our discussion.

With these foregoing notions in mind, please note that *our* entire discussion is fully a spiritual one and not a 'religious' one. Hinduism is not a religion *per se*, but is a term that encompasses the beliefs, customs, rituals and cultures of the people it labels. However, these are for the most part based upon a foundation of knowledge rooted in its underlying scriptures, which include primarily the *Veds*, the *Purans* and the *Upanishads*. These magnificent scriptures, then, form the spiritual foundation upon which 'Hinduism' is based, and their *distilled* knowledge and teachings is what *we* shall focus all our energy on.

Consequently, our discussion has nothing to do with organized 'religion' of any sort, and seeks to implement the *cream* of the Vedantic wisdom, which should be more correctly thought of as *the foundation* of 'Hinduism,' into our otherwise mundane and meaningless *human* life. The word 'dharam' as we use it here correctly means 'duty,' and the application and execution of that duty correctly should be guided by one's *spiritual* wisdom. Hence, the use of the word 'dharam' in our discussion means *duty* and not *religion*, and the use of the term 'Hinduism' is intended to mean its *spiritual* foundation and the concepts related to and derived from it.

You will notice that as we proceed through the discussion, our emphasis will be focused on the 'why' questions addressing some of our ideas, rituals and concepts rather than the 'what' questions or even mere dogma. These *why* questions are very significant and highly appropriate at any age, but are issues to which answers are not easily discernible. For example, the concept of *karma*, or deeds, and mystical powers of sages that defy laws of nature, for instance, or the concept of *death* and why that must occur, and what would happen after that. Or, w*hy* we celebrate *Diwali*, the festival of lights, or *Janmashtami*, and when in the year they generally fall. Why our calendar is so different from the Roman or current calendar. And many more such as these may be addressed as we proceed with our discussion.

The other issue is *who* our intended audience is for our discussions. It is initially our children, our immediate Hindu family, and the Hindu community that wishes to read these discussions, and please allow us to elaborate on why we are focusing initially on this limited audience.

To stay focused, grounded, realistic and practical, one must start any attempt at spiritual education first with the self, then include the family or loved ones at home, and only expand outside the family if it is merited in any way. Our goal, therefore, is humble and simple - start only with the immediate family, and others are welcome to join in if they find the subject matter interesting or deem it worthy of further thought. Furthermore, the discussions herein indeed require and assume *some* knowledge of Hinduism already of the reader. Therefore, please do not mistake the title or the intention of this series of discussions to be polarizing or narrow-minded, for it is truly not meant to be. It is really in keeping with the age-old Hindu tradition of merely starting with what we consider to be a realistic and reasonable goal, a small and focused target audience - our Hindu immediate or extended family, and not 'pushing' or 'imposing' our views on those not of a similar spiritual background.

However, even this reasoning is merely academic, for what we truly discuss and attempt to highlight is eternal and timeless, and belongs not just to 'Hindus' but to any human being who questions his true and genuine purpose in life. We will revisit this last observation again just prior to closing our initial discussion in *The Final Analyses*.

As we proceed through our discussion, you may also find the tone a bit stern and perhaps even harsh in some places. This is neither intended nor shied away from. Since our entire discussion is aimed initially at *our* children, this is almost unavoidable in some respects; parents can be a bit stern at times, and we are no different. We will call *a spade a spade*, so to speak. The rationale of our entire effort here is to present what *is*, without watering down or sweetening the language and thereby risk altering the true and intended message or indeed its gravity and importance.

The *intention* of this entire series, our efforts and the heartfelt message contained within, is meant to unite *all* Hindus *as Hindus* in the first place and then to awaken Hindus and, yes, perhaps even you *if it applies*, from your slumber to your magnificent treasure as a human *and* as a Hindu. If that takes some mental 'jolting' or 'shaking' to achieve, then so be it. There is no ulterior motive – just the desire to be completely candid, sincere, honest, and truthful to those we wish to serve.

If these discussions help jarr *you* from your spiritual *non-chalance* or dormancy by introducing an element of a *real* sense of urgency, and by helping define a *definite* spiritual goal and direction to attain to, in any way at all no matter how small or insignificant it may seem, we will have deemed our efforts worthwhile.

In any case, whether you find our discussions useful to you or not, we are nevertheless grateful for *you* having given *us* the opportunity to be of humble service to you at all in the first place.

Aum Tat Sat
(Bhagwat Gita, 17.23)

1.2: Hinduism: Where do we Begin?

Hinduism addresses important issues and questions. But where and how should we begin? Well, the answer is not an easy one, but one that must be attempted nevertheless. The path to *Hindu consciousness* and *Hindu dharam* must begin with the fundamentals.

We have to begin at the beginning, and we must begin with the basics. Our children are the future leaders of our samaaj, wherever they may be, and that is where we must start in order to achieve stability and continuity in the future.

One must start instilling knowledge and virtues at a very young age. The analogy of being able to guide and mold a seedling rather than waiting till it becomes a tree is truly applicable here. We must achieve this purposeful education and goal one child and one person at a time. Therefore, we may start with the children, but we must also educate ourselves as needed. We, too, must grasp the fundamentals firmly in order to achieve any real progress ourselves in our own lifetime.

However, *our* generation for the most part, and especially the one prior is the do-it-don't-ask generation out of great respect for our tradition, our culture, and the deep reverence and love for our parents and elders. The dilemma, then, is how can we impart what we ourselves may not posses?

In stark contrast to our (current or past) generations, the "me" and "I" generation now, though, is very different from its previous two. It always responds with "why?' while *silently* thinking "what's in it for me?" almost as if by Pavlovian conditioning. Not that there is anything necessarily wrong with their questioning, motives aside. Confronted by such attitudes, we struggle with answers that we ourselves may not fully comprehend.

Nevertheless, we should not be afraid of their questions. Our religion *is* totally scientific if understood and presented correctly. All the answers are there for us to unearth. But, with the vast treasures Hindus posses, how do we cherry pick what we should give them?

The answer is, we don't. At least, not initially. We start with the basics. We present a structured approach to our vast and *aseem* treasure, and let the individual decide what path to eventually undertake when their understanding matures. If the fundamentals have been correctly laid and the foundation solidly built, the rest shall come naturally by divine grace.

There are four questions that we raise that *must* remain at the center of our thought processes as we proceed with our discussion. Only enough detail sufficient to *comprehend* and *answer* these questions will be given as we proceed with our discussion. These are,

1. *who am 'I,'*
2. *'how' did I get here,*
3. *'what' is my purpose here*, and
4. *'how' do I get back home?*

These questions are so powerful that they must always remain at the forefront of our thought process as we proceed not just with this discussion, but also with life itself. Therefore, one must raise and then ask these very questions consistently and constantly to one's self in life.

These questions will challenge *you* to change your very life *if* you let them. They are exactly *that* important!

CHAPTER 2

From the Perspective of Hinduism:

Man In the Overall Scheme of Creation

Why on Earth is Man on Earth?

Let us start with a simple fact. The *only* two constants in all of creation are the Creator and Change.

Whether one believes in the Creator or not, change is an obvious and ever-present fact. However, realize that change is dependent on the Creator. Thus, the *creation* is subject to change but the *Creator* is not.

Change is inevitable. It is also natural. In science, one *process* of constant change, called entropy, is the idea that all systems tend to disorder over time. However, what may appear superficially as disorder may not actually be disorderly at all. It is more correct to say that the term disorder as used in *this* context is a label that man has applied scientifically to a process that appears to causes a change from a seemingly ordered system to one that appears disorderly to man.

In nature, a system undisturbed by man tends to be highly ordered in just about every respect. Highly structured in terms of function and purpose, these are superb examples of perfection of micro and macro ecological systems in perfect natural balance and harmony.

Even a sandstorm from a desert blowing into an ocean or a natural forest fire is highly beneficial, for instance. In this example, a sandstorm or a forest fire is a random and unwanted occurrence to man, but is really a brilliant and functional element in the overall design of nature. We may call this disorder, but nature is purposefully at work – we are just ignorant of the fact at the outset. In nature, therefore, everything has a purpose, and every creature has a role to play. Having learned the benefits from a seemingly unwanted and unwelcome element of nature, we realize that in the grand scheme of things, *man* is the one and only *real haram-khor*, the monkey wrench that upsets the perfection that is nature. Where does man fit in all of this?

Man has tremendous abilities but equally tremendous shortcomings. If harmony is to be maintained, there has to be a structured approach to society, with each structure contributing correctly and gainfully to achieve a balance with each other and with nature. Great sages of the past with the proper knowledge from the scriptures realized this. They also realized that although man shares the planet with other creatures, the *true* purpose of man is quite different than that of any other creature on the planet. There had to be a way Man could fit into the *sansar chakra*, the circle of creation and life, be *eco-sensitive* and achieve *that* purpose without disturbing or hindering the rest of creation.

To this end, from the scriptures was derived a social and religious system that would maintain peace and harmony while preserving Vedic knowledge and advancing Vedantic wisdom. This system would be least likely to impact the rest of creation while at the same time allowing man the pursuit of his true purpose in the human form.

One must realize that the force behind this socio-religious system devised by our sages of yore is the very same force that designed all of creation. So it should be of little surprise that we create misery when we go against what our sages devised for us. Thus, it is best to accept its broad structure with the best of intentions and work diligently to learn and implement their teachings. Only then can we begin to fulfill our mission in life while maintaining harmony with all of creation.

Alas, we work diligently to break down the structure thus created by Vedic knowledge and act like animals superficially as we enjoy with our senses and live for mere sense fulfillment. But unlike the animals we emulate, we do not at the same time contribute to nature. We serve no such useful purpose, unlike the creatures we copy who dutifully and purposefully contribute to the planet in one way or another.

Therefore, to say we are behaving like animals is truly doing injustice to those animals! Whereas we merely enjoy, they purposefully contribute in everything they do!

Remember, we only create misery for *all* when we work against nature. *Even ours.*

Bear in mind that the purpose here is not to be a man-basher, but to illustrate a point. The idea that we share this planet with other living creatures and that we have a responsibility and an obligation to them as well.

This concept will be repeated and elaborated on later on. However, suffice it to pose a question of supreme importance here. If every creature in all of creation serves a purpose and contributes to the rest of creation *by design*, what then is Man's purpose, and how can he achieve this purpose without harming the rest of creation?

Which gets us back to our first question, which is *where in the overall scheme of Creation does Man fit?*

It is a question that only man, in his supreme arrogance, fails to ask. That is, until, you run into a humble and unassuming Hindu rishi. A rishi that not only raises this question but ponders long and hard over it, attempting to seek the truth. Why on Earth is Man on Earth? He really serves no useful purpose, yet he is here! He plunders and he destroys, yet he is here!

Why?

Well, enter magnificent Hindu philosophy, from the unassuming and selfless rishis and sages of ancient India.

Read on, and start to discover for yourself. Be sure to strap your cerebral seat belts on, open your eyes to your mind and heart and soul, and be truthful and honest to yourself.

CHAPTER 3

The Fundamentals of Creation

Although Creation and Dissolution may initially appear convoluted on the surface, it really is not all that complicated. It is, however, absolutely essential that you understand this process, for it can truly change your life for eternity! Yes, eternity!

The Fundamentals of Creation 3.1: Background

There are multiple and differing theories to the beginnings of the Universe, both from the East and the West.

The West has put forward many interesting theories, both of scientific and divine premises. Of the theories that they have advanced, some conflict with each other. Some are unable to set timelines that do not contradict each other.

These theories have wonderful presentations and fancy vocabulary, with amazing mathematical derivations to attempt to validate the proposals. However, these proposals still are inconclusive to say the least, and if one was to elaborate slightly, have glaring holes that entire universes could slide through, if you pardon the pun.

Please understand, there is no intent to disrespect any one proposal or theory. Obviously, man is entitled to individual opinion, and opinions can be as numerous as there are individuals who care to render them.

However, scientific space research and calculations as opposed to mere theories, speculations and proposals are an entirely different issue.

Amazingly, the 'secrets' to the beginnings of the Universe are all cleverly *hidden* in the Vedic and Hindu Scriptures. They are 'hidden' in plain sight for all to unearth that care to know the truth.

Man will never have all the tools, technological, mathematical, or otherwise, that he needs to know all the secrets to the Universe. There have to be some *gimmes* so that he can at least get a clue as to the magnitude of the problem. These gimmes are in Hindu scriptures courtesy of divine mercy. He put them there so that we would appreciate the complexity and magnitude of creation and thereby recognize the value of our true purpose and mission in life.

Having said this, what is even more astounding is that as the West, with its powerful technology and immense resources begins to explore the secrets of the universe, is coming to conclusions that are becoming glaringly similar to the revelations in our ancient but *timeless* and eternal Hindu scriptures!

3.2. Origin of The Universe

The origin of our own and other universes (yes, shastras say that there are other universes) is a timeless and contentious question.

Obviously there is more than one side to a story, and as many opinions as there are people who care to render one. When the dust clears on the debate, however, fundamentally only two camps are discernible, each of which have multiple proposals in multiple formats. The two camps essentially represent those that believe in a Creator and those that do not.

The first camp, regardless of religious affiliation, believes there is a superior personality that has created this and other universes. The other camp believes that creation simply 'happened' by chance alone, and do not believe in a Creator.

Logic entails that for there to be a *product*, there must be a *producer* that prepared it. Things simply do not 'appear' from nothing. Science also supports the notion that *something* cannot be produced from *nothing*. Raw material is required before *any* product can be made.

Therefore, logic is what we shall follow.

Let us turn to our scriptures to help answer some fundamental questions of creation of the Universe. Remember that the approach used here will be with the objective of understanding creation from a *spiritual* point of view with the specific *goal* of exiting creation and returning back home. It is not our intent here to attempt to piece together 'what' happened over what timeline or dimension.

Our focus, then, will be on 'why' rather than merely 'what.'

There is a general consensus among *our* scriptures on how the Universe (and others) came into being. Although atheists and foolish and ignorant people split hairs on the exact methodology and timelines, the *fundamental* concept of creation that finally emerges from our scriptures is essentially the same.

Apologetics would have us believe that Kapil Bhagvan's *Sankhya* philosophy is basically different and denies a Creator. However, such mundane thinkers skew and manipulate His teachings to attempt to deliberately show this. To the contrary, His philosophy, with one exception, is almost analogous to *Vedic* philosophy and differs only in terminology, numerology and approach.

A *combined* approach is used here and further simplified greatly for ease of conceptualization. Again, our goal is to understand who we are, how we got here, what our purpose should be, and how we exit this marvelous but *nashwant* creation, a temporary one, that is ultimately destroyed. Everything else we will leave to theologians and 'thinkers' to argue over and waste precious human time and resources over.

Initial Discussion

Creation and the origin of our universe (and other Universes) is understandably controversial.

When we look at information from space exploration and researches in modern times, the most interesting thing that we see emerge is *how similar* the modern concept of origin is getting to what has been described in the ancient Hindu scriptures already. There are multiple parallels and similarities in timelines, magnitudes and distances, concepts, and so on.

Having said that, we are going to step out of mundane *mechanical* details, and simply explore that what is *necessary* for comprehending the underlying *fundamental* concept of origin and annihilation, with the specific goal of understanding how we may *exit* it.

Sure, how it all originated, whether from a big bang or not, how long it took to 'cook', how the different parts of creation settled slowly into their orbits, how violent it all may have been, how many light years this or that may be apart, how this universe is still expanding, how there may be other universes with multiple suns, and so on is all very fascinating if that interests you at all. For our purpose, though, it is completely immaterial.

For, all this data will only wow and bewilder you without actually answering the fundamental four questions we already raised, which are *Who am I, How I got here, what I should do here,* and *how I may return safely home. That* is what is important. For therein lies the secret to *true* freedom and happiness. The other details are, well, just details. Technical and absolutely non-essential to *mukti* or *moksh*, true liberation, or the return home to our maker.

Let us review the basics of Creation, or Genesis, from a *spiritual* rather than from a *mechanical* viewpoint.

In the beginning there is only one – the Creator. The Supreme thinks *eko hum bahu syami*. The one Supreme decides to be many from *One*.

Therefore, both the *advait* and *dvait* theories attempting to define our relationship to the Supreme are ostensibly correct (but not fully) in their own way, depending on how far up the creation ladder you go. For our purpose, we are a multitude of steps from the *initial* creation, so *dvait*, or *duality*, is more *applicable* to us.

The Supreme Personality is Shri Krishna, and *Maya* or *Prakriti* is the dormant and unmanifested creation *within* Him and *from* Him but only initially. Maya is dormant within the Maha Tatva when creation starts anew. Aatmas are the 'souls' that also reside *within* Him prior to creation, but lay dormant in the *Maha Tatva* outside of Him thereafter until creation starts anew.

If this sounds complicated, don't worry. We will address this in greater detail later.

For now, let us assume that there are three 'permanent tatvas' in re-creation: the Supreme, *His* Maya, and the aatmas.

Let's proceed to Genesis.

The Creation

Although Genesis and Dissolution may initially seem convoluted on the surface, it really is not all that complicated. It is, however, absolutely essential that you understand this entire thought process completely, for it can really *change* your life literally for eternity! Yes, eternity! Grasping this concept is *key* to understanding *how we got here* in the first place, *what* our intended purpose and goal should be, and *how we may be able to get out of here* and safely back home.

According to *Vedic knowledge*, and for our purposes here, there are essentially three 'permanent' *tatvas,* or entities, in the *process* of material re-creation. These are the *Supreme Personality*, *His Maya*, and *Aatmas*. Everything comes into existence from these three.

We will refer to the Supreme Personality as *Brahm*, who is not to be mistaken for Brahma, the creator in the Holy Trinity of Brahma, Vishnu and Mahesh. Brahm, the Supreme, is also referred to as Brahman, the Purush, and so on in the scriptures.

Brahm, the Supreme, chooses to be many from One.

He chooses to be many from the One, from His eternal and transcendental form, that of the Supreme Personality, Shri Krishna. From Him come His abodes too, the islands of *Nitya GoLok*, and other Loks, of which *Vaikunth Lok* is the lowest. All *Avataars* come from Vaikunth Lok via the Supreme's second expansion, except when Shri Krishna descends personally as Himself. Mind you, the use of the word *lowest* in describing Vaikunth Lok is merely a *physical* descriptor of position, not of importance!

From the *second expansion* of the form of the Supreme Personality, two *shaktis*, or divine energies emanate into creation. These are the *Akshar Purush*, and the *Kshar Purush*. Akshar Purush, also known as *Akshar Brahm*, is *shaswat* or permanent, and His abode is *Akshar Dhaam*. The Kshar Purush is *nashwant*, or temporary and destructible, but the divine energy within it, the *chetna* or aatma, is not.

Refer to *Illustration 1: Creation of the Universe* as we proceed.

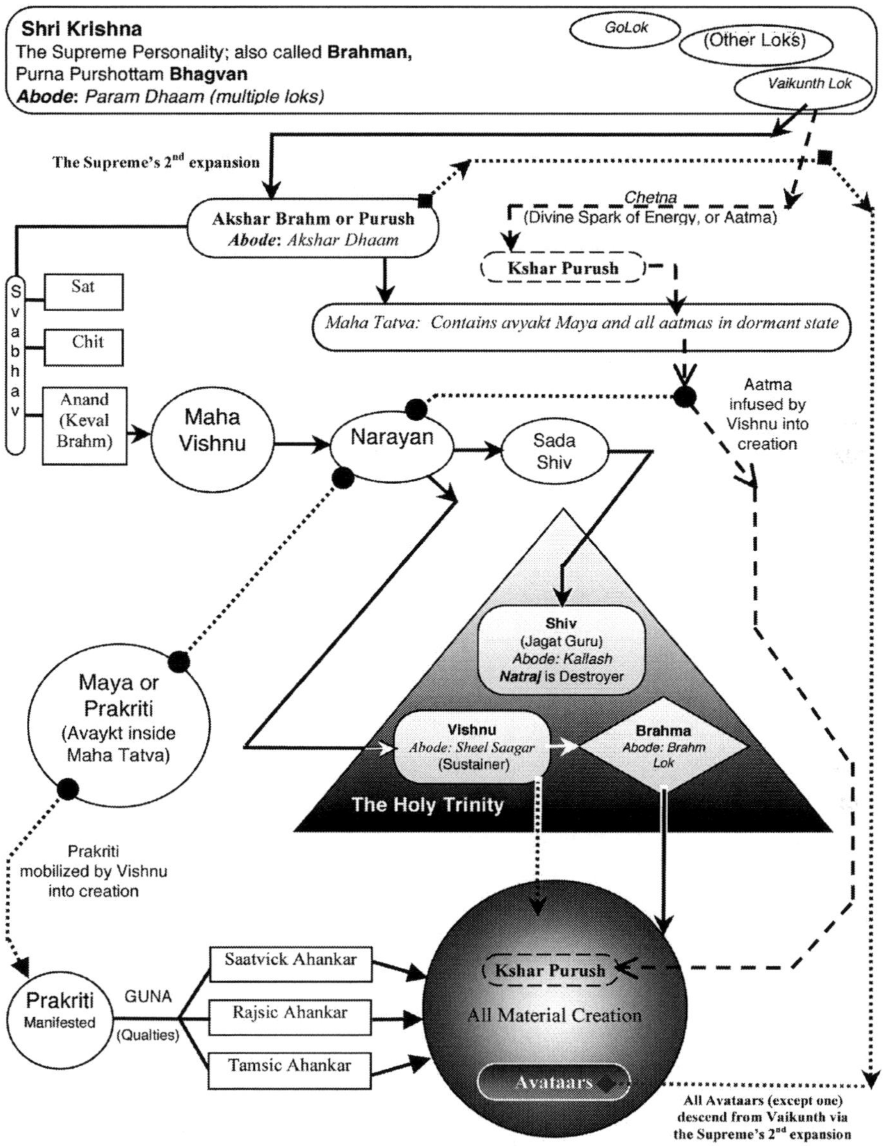

Illustration 1: Creation of the Universe (Highly Simplified rendition, with gaps)

Akshar Brahm is also referred to as *Maha Vishnu*, and as *Bal-Ram*, from which come three other types of *Vishnu*. Although technically *slightly* off, we will accept this definition to simplify our concept, allowing for our purposes the equating of Bal-Ram, Maha Vishnu and Akshar Brahm as perfectly acceptable. These forms or expansions of the Supreme are also non-material, or transcendental.

The Akshar Brahm has three *swabhavs* or qualities, namely *Sat*, *Chit* and *Anand*. These are combined in spoken language and vocalized as *Satchitanand*, meaning Akshar Brahm, or even meaning the Supreme Personality, Shri Krishna. *Sat* means truth, *Chit* is consciousness, and *Anand* means bliss. Again, 'bliss' doesn't fully mean or represent 'anand' but we will allow it for our discussion here. We will clarify this point much later. Referring to the Supreme, these are *eternal* qualities of the Supreme. Therefore, the Supreme is also referred to as SatChitAnand roop, meaning a form of eternal truth, eternal consciousness and eternal bliss.

From the *superior* energy of *anand swabhav* of Akshar Brahm, which is also known as *Keval Brahm*, comes *Narayan*, the wakeful state of Maha Vishnu. *Maya* or *Prakriti* also emanates from the *inferior energy* of Keval Brahm. It is important to note that Maya is in a dormant state in the Maha Tatva in subsequent creations, and not in Keval Brahm. Maya or Prakriti are essentially the same entity with two names.

From *Narayan* comes the transformation into *Sada Shiv* and *Vishnu*. From Sada Shiv comes *Shiv Shambhu* or *Shiv Shankar* who resides on Kailash, and from Vishnu's *nabhi*, or navel, springs forth a lotus that is said to have the brilliance of untold suns, on which sits *Brahma*, the 'creator' of the universe. Together, Vishnu, Brahma, and Shiv Shambhu (also called Mahesh) form the Hindu Holy Trinity.

Brahma, the 'creator' in the Holy Trinity, is really an assembler and *not* a creator. He assembles the parts supplied by *Maya* in the form of the transformation of *Prakriti*. However, Brahma is Supreme *shakti*, or energy, and only with Him as the Chief Engineer is the Creation of the Universe even possible. Consequently, even though Brahma is the *first* created being, He is the highest of all created beings in addition to being the *Secondary* Creator of the Universe, and really represents the *creation shakti* of the Supreme Himself.

The metaphor of Brahma being produced from Vishnu's navel and supported by a cord from it is *supremely* significant, for this signifies an *umbilicus*, thereby making Brahma the first (and most intelligent) *created* being in the Universe. This metaphor makes Vishnu feminine first, purush second, and hence when one chants *Tvamewa Mata, Ch Pita Tvame Va*, one pays respects *first* to the *feminine* Vishnu, the *first mother* of all creation with Brahma as the child, the first *created* being.

The *Aatmas* are a divine shakti, one of the two to emanate from the *Supreme* at initial creation. The lotus flower Brahma sits on is said to contain *all* the *aatmas* of this Universe, which helps explain the extreme brilliance of the lotus, for a separated portion of brilliance is still absolutely brilliant. *How can it be otherwise?*

A highly significant point to note in creation is that *our entire universe*, according to the scriptures, is said to be contained *within* the stem of the lotus on which *Brahma* sits, with *Brahma Lok* being the highest, our earth in the middle, and *Patal loks* or loks on which *rakshas* and *asurs,* the demons, reside being on the bottom. Now, read this last bit of information again. If *our entire universe* is contained *within the lotus stem* springing forth from Vishnu's navel, can you even *begin* to imagine the size and opulence of Brahma, Vishnu and Mahesh? Absolutely magnificent and completely stunning!

Backtrack a moment and let us catch up the other side.

Recall that we said that *Maya* or *Prakriti* is really the same entity with two words. Vedic knowledge calls this (creation) entity *Maya*, and Kapil Bhagvan's *Sankhya* philosophy calls it *Prakriti*. Simple.

Maya, or Prakriti, comes from the inferior energy of *Keval Brahma* or *anand swabhav* of the *Akshar Brahm* residing in Akshar Dhaam. Note that this Prakriti or Maya is now *inside* a storage entity called the *Maha-Tatva* that is now *separate* from Maha Vishnu, but remains fully under His control in subsequent creations. This entity remains dormant until creation becomes a reality only by *Maha Vishnu glancing* at Maya.

Maya or Prakriti is a real *material* entity and has three real and material *properties* or qualities called *Gunas*. These properties are intertwined, interdependent and intrinsic, and cannot be separated. These gunas are *Sat*, *Rajas*, and *Tamas*.

All of creation will have these three properties, and living entities shall have a preponderance of one over the other as a varying mixture of the three. Merely coming into contact with Maya will necessitate the acceptance of these three properties.

Brahma of the Holy Trinity now assembles the raw material supplied by Maya or Prakriti, and creates the environments and also the forms or bodies that will enentually spring to life.

Referring to *Illustration 1*, note again that from the Supreme also emanates an infinitesimal *chetna* or energy, representing the *aatma*, or the divine spark of life that will animate the lifeless bodies created by Brahma. These chetnas, or aatmas, reside in a *dormant* state within the Maha Tatva *outside* of Maha Vishnu until creation is initiated.

Once physical creation starts and the time for life is imminent, *Maha Vishnu* glances at the *Maha Tatva* and infuses these dormant aatmas into creation, and these aatmas bring 'life' to the lifeless bodies created by Brahma.

Once these bodies come to life, it is *Vishnu's* job to sustain that life. Vishnu is really the life force behind *all* life, as illustrated in this verse in the *Shrimad Bhagwat Gita*,

Gam avisya ca bhutani
Dharayamy aham ojasa
Pusnami causadhih sarvah
Somo bhutva rasatmakah[3]

Vishnu enters into each heavenly body, initiates and maintains their orbits, and becomes the life-sustaining force of *everything*. It is Vishnu's energy that is in the vegetables, the fruit, the grains, and so on that we eat that sustains the very basis of all life.

Sustenance of life, therefore, is not possible without Vishnu's energy in these food sources. This is also the reason that Hindus view food as *divine*, because food *is* divine, and should be treated with the utmost respect, paying particular attention to wastage, spillage or spoilage. In other words, eat what you need, but waste not a morsel or a drop.

Think of Creation and complete Annihilation as a play, and creation to the point of partial annihilation as only a scene in that play. Once a scene in the play is over, *Natraj*, the destroyer form of Shiv Shambhu, annihilates almost all life as necessary, save a precious few. This destruction is known as *Prahalay*. The ones saved will then be allowed to start anew, and the cycle repeats as a new scene in the play begins. Once the whole play is over, entire Universes are annihilated, and this is termed *Maha-Prahalay*, and Maya or Prakriti returns to dormant or unmanifested state inside the Maha-Tatva.

Creation & Re-Creation

So, in the *initial* creation, Prakriti is dormant *within* the Supreme till mobilized. This dormant Prakriti is known as *Avaykt*, or *unmanisfested.* Once mobilized, creation starts to occur and spring forth and is *manifested.* The *Mundak Upanishad* proclaims that the Universe emerges from the Supreme much as a spider projects or retracts its thread.[4] This same description is also found in the *Shrimad Bhagwat.*[5]

In the *subsequent* creations, dormant *Prakriti*, along with dormant *jiv-aatmas*, is stored *inside* the *Maha-Tatva* but really *outside* of the Supreme.

The Maha-Tatva contains and stores all the jiv-aatmas and annihilated universes in a dormant state until the next cycle of creation begins.

However, this is merely academic, as nothing truly exists outside of the Supreme!

See *Illustration 2: Creation & Re-Creation of the Universe,* for our final points. This illustration elaborates and highlights what happens during the initial creation and then the subsequent re-creations with the aid of the Maha-Tatva complex in the spiritual *physical* plane.

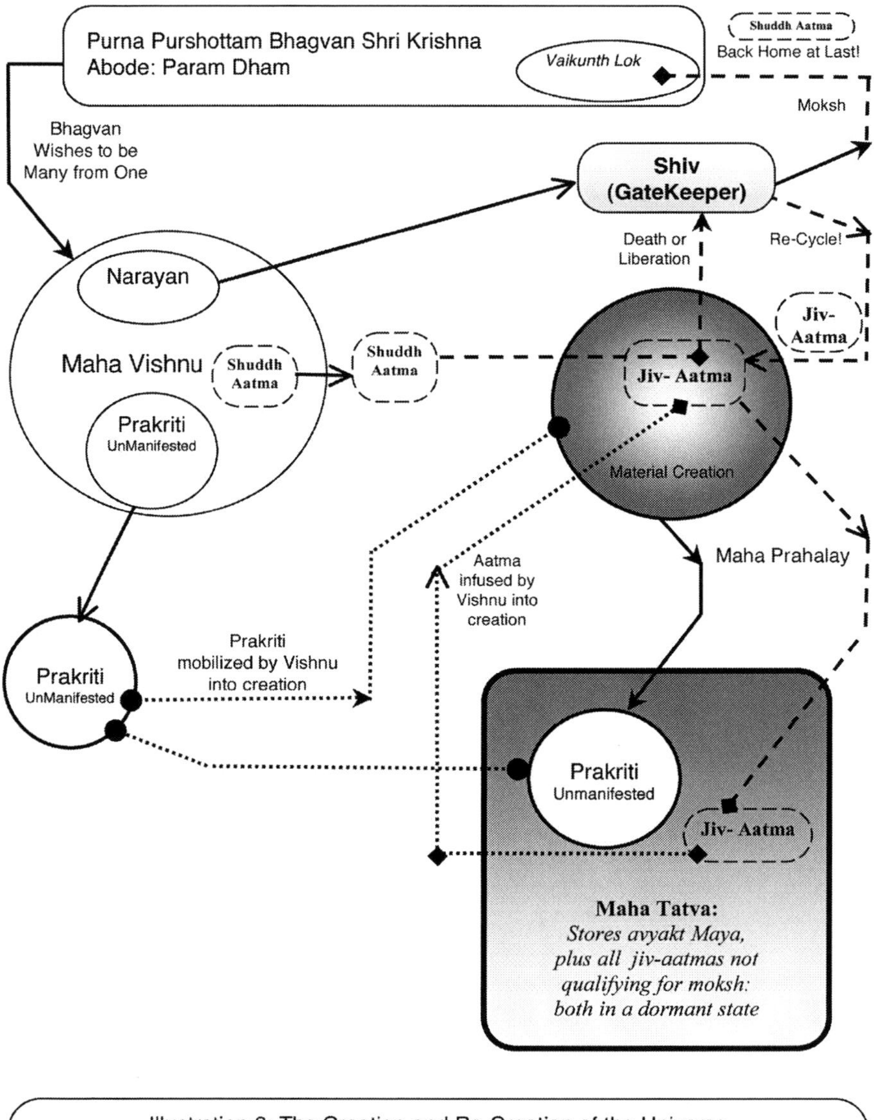

Illustration 2: The Creation and Re-Creation of the Universe

After reviewing *Illustration 2: Creation & Re-Creation of the Universe,* two final points should become completely evident.

This illustration shows how second and subsequent Creations are slightly different *in origin* only, but are the same in all other respects. Herein lies the confusion as to how many 'permanent' tatvas there are in Creation.

It should be clear, now, that there really is only *One permanent tatva*, and everything else is His energy, expansion, or creation. Therefore, how many 'permanent' tatvas depends on far up the ladder one goes to get to the ONE source of all creation - *Shri Krishna.*

The second and more important clarification that should become apparent is between the top half and bottom half of the illustration with respect to us - the aatma.

We can each elect to spend an *eternity* on the bottom half 'enjoying' ourselves *foolishly*, or spend *this* lifetime *wisely* earning our way back to the top half and having an even better time while at it.

The choice is *yours*.

Closing Thoughts

The *Maha Tatva* when initially formed is pure and *shuddh*. The *aatmas* when initially formed are also pure and *shuddh*, and are called *shuddh aatmas*.

Once the shuddh aatma comes into contact with manifested *Maya*, or creation, almost all aatmas, save a rare few, will become tainted and soiled due to their desires, and will now become *jiv-aatmas*. At annihilation, these jiv-aatmas will come to be stored in a dormant state alongside Maya within the *shuddh Maha Tatva*. This Maha-Tatva containing the now-tainted jiv-aatmas and Maya is no longer considered shuddh, and it really should now be thought of as the Supreme's *insignificant* storage bin.

A simple analogy is the holy Ganges river in India. When it first originates from Vishnu's Lotus feet, it is *shuddh* and pure. When it goes through Shiv and Kailash, it remains untainted, shuddh and still pure. As it flows down the Himalayas where man resides, it starts to accumulate junk and crap from what man puts into it, and it becomes soiled and tainted. It is shocking and appalling to see what the cities and people are doing to the holy Ganges at the present time! The cities and the people responsible for soiling the holy Ganges and other rivers should be ashamed! And then do something about it!

Anyway, to return to our analogy, both the aatma and the Maha Tatva are shuddh when they are on the Creator's side, such as the holy Ganges leaving Vishnu's Lotus feet or Shiv's jatta. The aatma and Maha Tatva only get soiled on the *created* side, with the jiv-aatmas being the real culprits, just as we are soiling and spoiling the holy Ganges! Is there no limit to how *low* we can go?

Therefore, if you are reading this, *you* are a jiv-aatma returning from the Maha Tatva's storage, and will also be hurled back into it one day at annihilation. Unless, of course, *you* decide to do something about it! And that something is nothing short of figuring out how you *re-attain* your former status and glory as a *shuddh aatma*, for that is how we all started.

In short, looking at creation and genesis, Ishwar, Paramaatma, Vishnu, Maha Vishnu and so on are, in fact, just small expansions of the *ParamIshwar* or *Parmeshwar* for short, the *second* expansion of the Supreme Shri Krishna. Yet entire Universes and galaxies pour from the pores on the skin of *Maha Vishnu*. Some have one sun like our solar system, and one moon around a planet like our earth. Other universes could have more than one sun, or multiple suns, at their centers according to our *shastras*. This is not hard to imagine, for if you look within our own solar system, we see the existence of planets with even multiple moons.

Now, let us revisit another point again for it is worth emphasizing. Our Brahma sits on a lotus, and His lok is the highest, called Brahma Lok or Satya Lok. If our *entire universe* is contained *within* the lotus stem springing forth from Vishnu, can you even *begin* to imagine the size and opulence of Brahma, Vishnu and Mahesh? Absolutely magnificent and mind-blowing! And if there are innumerable Brahmas and indeed Vishnus, meaning innumerable Universes, all emanating from Maha-Vishnu, can you even *begin* to imagine the grandeur of Maha-Vishnu, who, though an expansion of the Supreme isn't even His *fragmental portion?*

So, *what* to speak of the Supreme? Unlimited in every way imaginable and beyond 'magnificent' or, in fact, simply beyond *any* terminology at all. Now there's food for thought! Actually, you should very quickly realize the incredibly rapid appearance of the *seema*, the very limit, of even *our* over-active imaginations and cerebral abilities. It is, quite simply, beyond mere human comprehension.

In the invocation *Aum Purnam Adaha Purnam Idam*, the *Isha Upanishad* points out to us that even with entire and perfectly complete galaxies, universes and life forces emanating from Him, *The Supreme* still remains perfect, complete and whole with no depletion. And at annihilation, all is retracted back into Him, with no addition. How is that for mathematics and physics? Simply put by our shastras and our humble bhaaratia rishis, Infinity plus or minus Infinity is *still* Infinity!

That is *the* Supreme! Jai Shri Krishna!

3.3. The End of Life on Earth Our - Maha Prahalay

Everything is cyclical. Therefore, the Universal cycle starts with creation and concludes naturally with destruction and dissolution.

At the conclusion of a cycle, all living souls return to the Supreme and lay dormant for eons awaiting the next cycle of creation. These souls are dormant in the Supreme yet are separate from Him. This separation is by way of the Maha-Tatva, which is distinct and separate from the Supreme. These souls shall then be infused into the *next creation* according to their *karma,* or deeds, and *vaasnas*, or desires.

There are cataclysmic events that affect all life on our planet earth on a periodic basis. These events cause most human life to be destroyed, but not all. This particular destruction of life, especially human life, is termed *Prahalay*.

At the termination of the partial destruction, life starts anew, and *sanatan dharam* is re-established. Each such period, from one cataclysmic event to the next, is called a *Manvantar*, according to the scriptures. The progenitor for each such period is called *Manu-Maharaj*, or Manu, and through him life, society and civilization is renewed. *Manusmriti* is a detail of rules and regulations that would govern such new civilizations, established by each Manu.

At the conclusion of the fourteenth *Manvantar*, which is further explained in *Chapter 4*, there is complete rather than partial destruction of our Universe. According to our scriptures, our Solar system was created from the Sun, and shall be destroyed by that Sun at the time of our annihilation, or the *Maha-Prahalay,* of our Universe.

There are wonderful descriptions in the scriptures of Creation, Prahalay and Maha-Prahalay. However, details are details.

The fundamental concept is one of creation, partial destruction, and, after a few such rounds, absolute obliteration of our universe, with storage in the Maha-Tatva.

Till the creation of the next Universe, that is.

Shri Krishna tells us in the *Shrimad Bhagwat Gita* that,

Prakritim svam avastabhya
Visrjami punah punah
Bhuta-gramam imam krtsnam
Avasam prakrter vasat [6]

Creation, annihilation and re-creation of *everything* in the Cosmos originates from Shri Krishna, and occurs *under* His will and *by* His energy.

Closing Thoughts

If you clean your latrine, where will you store the soiled and used brushes and soaps and cleaners and miscellaneous supplies? Will you store them in your fabulous living room, or even in your china cabinet? Or, will you store them in the garage or out-house storage, where they belong?

And where do you think the Supreme is going to store all the soiled jiv-aatmas, prêt-aatmas, and so on, along with Prakriti and its gunas? You got it! The Maha-Tatva, incredibly spiritual as it may be, is the soiled and *insignificant* storage can of the Supreme, with *us* in it!

And yet Man, in his supreme arrogance and folly, still thinks *he* is signficant.

3.4. Darwin and Evolution

It is necessary to visit the theory of evolution advanced by Charles Darwin when discussing human habitation of the planet. It is a brilliant theory, but one with a serious flaw.

Simply put, the theory postulates evolution of life from non-living matter, regardless of the fancy names used for such non-living matter. It goes on to elaborate how a species may adapt to its environment, and then evolve with such adaptations to new forms of life as entirely new species.

However, in spite of fancy vocabulary, the simple and *final* truth of the matter is that only *life* can bring forth life, and irrespective of the verbiage, language or discussions by multi-lettered literary individuals, non-life cannot bring forth life. How can it? For there to be an offspring, a parent (or two, in most cases) is necessary. Modern medical science, with all its advances in science and technology, has failed to produce life from non-living broths or matter. Therefore, only life can bring forth life. Period. End of discussion.

Now examine evolution and adaptation. Evolution would signify or represent changes of a species with reference to specific characteristics over multiple progeny or generations through their genetic make-up, or genes. Adaptation on the other hand would imply changes over the relatively short-term period without necessarily having to modify the genetic code or sequence, meaning over the same lifetime, and not necessarily subsequent lifetimes. If we blend the ideas, adaptation could lead to evolutionary changes in subsequent offspring, hence the concept of natural selection and the idea of the survival of the fittest.

Let's dissect these ideas and look deeper.

To illustrate, let us look at a herd of deer that were the potential targets of a lion hunt. The deer that gets caught is not able to pass on its genes, so it is the end of the line for that gene sequence. The ones that got away get to live another day and pass on theirs. If the deer that got away have specific traits (features or abilities) that allow it to keep surviving the lion attacks their genes would be represented in greater numbers in the subsequent offspring. The proponents of the theory of evolution would call this natural selection. Or, in other words, survival of the fittest. The one that got caught was not fit enough and so fell to the process of natural selection, where only the fittest survive. However, there never will be a time when the lions will not be able to catch one. They will always be able to catch one. If evolution was perfect, the lions would die off. However, the evolutionists will argue, the lions will also simultaneously evolve to keep pace, and so, they will always catch one. Lets look at it from a different angle. Look at laws of nature, where there is a delicate balance and harmony to everything (save what man has touched – the Midas touch, so to speak).

The food chain is stacked as a pyramid *by design*, not by accident. There are always more prey than predators to ensure balance and harmony. The vegetation would be the most plentiful, and so would form the base of the food pyramid or chain. There are also enough prey grazing (in our example of deer and lion) to ensure a balance between plant life and animal life, where a balance of all is essential. The deer would form the next smaller block, or middle block, of the pyramid. The predator, or lion in this case, would number the fewest and sit on the top of the pyramid. If the deer were allowed to graze unchecked, the plant life would eventually cease, and if that happened, the deer would cease to exist, as would the predators. The pyramid would crumble. The vegetation would suffer, too, as it would have no deer to pass on its seeds through the dung and spread the plant life.

This is a model so advanced and perfect in its function, and yet so simple and elegant in its process, that it could *never* have happened by chance alone. It *is* by design, and no accident. Completely thought through, and nothing left to *chance*, really.

Let's examine the design of the animals while we are thinking about design. Consider the design of the lion. This beast is a carnivore, with the proper tools of trade for survival. It has large angled incisors, called fangs, with the ability to bite deep, rip and tear flesh. Its digestive system is very well suited to the rapid processing of the meat and the rapid disposal of waste. Its powerful and well-designed body is well suited for bringing down prey, small and large. Lions have the ability to hunt in unified groups.

Look at these qualities! Every detail *is* by design, and no accident. Look at a baby lion – a cub. Who taught a lioness how to care for her very *first* cub? This ability is *innate*, right? The cub initially suckles on its mother's milk, and later joins the ranks of the hunters when old enough. Innate, or built-in, again. By design or accident?

There is simply no way a soup or a broth held the blueprints for such magnificent designs, regardless of how much time elapses. And the architect and engineer behind every design of everything, living or not?

Any way you slice it, the undeniable fact remains that only life can bring forth life. And proponents of the theory of evolution even today are at a loss to explain that stumbling block of how life appeared in the first place!

Shri Krishna Himself answers this simple but fundamentally important question:

Yac capi sarva-bhutanam
Bijan tad aham arjun
Na tad asti vina yat syan
Maya bhutam caracaram[7]

Lord Krishna says in the *Gita* that *He* is the *primordial* seed, the beginning seed of all life, the *sarva karan karanum*, the source of ALL things, moving and unmoving. Period. End of discussion. End of debate.

3.5: The so-called Big Bang & Black Hole Theories

The West has poured massive resources in an attempt to answer the most basic questions to the creation of the Universe. Knowing how we came into being could help us answer many questions. One burning question given the current global geo-climatic change is *if* it could one day end, and if so, *how* it may end, how one might delay or prevent such an ending, and so on. The value to knowing how it all came into being could be priceless.

Many technological advances have been made in the past two decades aiding in the gathering of data that could help answer these questions and, based on such data, the Big Bang theories arose.

There are many that believe in the *Big Bang* theories for the creation of the Universe. There are many opinions and ideas that fall under this now umbrella term. And though they cannot explain "a few details" as they put it, the rest is easily explained by mathematics, or physics, and so on. The proponents are completely at a loss to explain the most glaring question of what existed *prior* to the Big Bang. And *from where* all the material came to supply the components of this Big Bang and the resulting Universe.

A relatively new realization now in modern science is that the Universe is still expanding, and the realization that this may not be the *only* universe. These ideas, along with the various derived intricate and excruciatingly complicated mathematical models depict the various ideas and parameters of our galaxy and stars with respect not only to creation but size, timelines and positions as well that are amazingly similar to what Hindu rishis have known from the scriptures all along.

How very interesting!

Closing Thoughts

The 'west' has come to realize in recent times that our universe is 'still expanding' instead of 'as is,' in a fully cooked or static state like it had pre-supposed originally. The west also suggests a 'black hole' phenomenon that is the 'anti-matter' phenomenon that annihilates all matter it encounters or that falls into it.

Let us turn to our rishi scientists and the scriptures to see what their opinion on this matter is.

Since the scriptures tell us that *we* are in a mid-phase of the cycle of creation, *obviously* the Universe is *still* expanding. And the Maha-Tatva will swallow everything at dissolution, and *there* is your so-called 'black hole' phenomenon. *So What?* Our rishis have known this all along. And so much more!

While we are on the subject, let us elaborate on one interesting phenomenon, re-creation and dissolution of the Universe.

Realize that our shastras point out that our Maha-Tatva, the so-called 'black hole' as referred to by the west, stores everything in a dormant and unmanifested state. As such, the theory of 'anti-matter' describing the 'black hole phenomenon' is therefore explained away, and is technically incorrect because the storage of Maya and jiv-aatmas in the Maha-Tatva still exists even in an *unmanifested* state and could not do so if the western proposal of 'anti-matter' was correct, for *anti-matter* implies complete *annihilation* instead of temporary warehousing or storage.

Laws of physics would also support our shastra's viewpoint because matter or substance can only be *re-arranged* and not completely *annihilated* in the true sense of the word.

For example, let us take water. As a liquid, it flows and is in the fluid shape of its container. As ice, it expands, solidifies, occupies more volume and is no longer fluid or dynamic. As water vapour, however, it occupies the least space, and is also the least visible to gross human senses.

Now think of the *water* as the actual physical element or 'guna,' the *ice* as 'material creation,' and the *vapour* as the final resting and 'storage' medium. In this analogy, turning ice into water vapour would be analogous to dissolution of the universe, turning manifested maya into unmanifested maya. Since the water vapour still exists, albeit in a miniscule space, you cannot define its storage container as 'anti-matter' although you could call it whatever you fancied, such as a 'black hole.' Note that 'storage' or unmanifested time scales are cosmic and extremely lengthy!

If the West had taken the time to talk to our rishis, they would have been saved a lot of headaches and resources, for the answers are already there. *In our scriptures!*

It is high time we stopped asking *unintelligent* questions like *Is there Intelligent life out there*, and started worrying about not squandering away the only life we have at our disposal - *ours!*

3.6: Parting Thoughts

Creation is subject to interpretation and manipulation by foolish and unscrupulous persons and sects. Splitting hairs and playing fancy vocabulary games don't change facts.

It is becoming increasingly popular to say that there are three (or even more) 'permanent' tatvas. Proponents of these notions say that these 'tatvas' are the Supreme, the Maya, and the aatmas. Some add the Supreme's abode as an additional 'permanent' tatva. They then specify that although the Supreme may control the other tatvas such as 'Maya,' He did not actually *originate* these.

Well, let us see in just one verse where it *all* really originated. Shri Krishna tells Arjun in the *Gita*,

etad yonini bhutani
sarvanity upadharaya
aham krtsnasya jagatah
prabhavah pralayas tatha[8]

In other words, Krishna says that He is both the origin and the dissolution of all, whether material or spiritual. He goes on to say in the next verse,

mattah parataram nanyat
kincid asti dhananjay
mayi sarvam idam protam
sutre mani-gana iva[9]

Shri Krishna says that everything rests upon Him, just as *pearls on a string*, and there is no truth superior to Krishna.

Hence, it is immaterial if one *thinks* that there are three permanent tatvas or five. How far up the ladder of creation did one *really* go to make this or that claim? And having made this or that claim, how does that help *you* with *mukti* or *moksh*, the liberation of your *aatma* or soul? Playing fancy games and skewing facts does, however, give rise to entire cultish and clannish sects and sampradays, a manipulation that we must end *quickly* and *decisively* for it is eroding and dividing our *dharam*, our culture and indeed even *us* as a people!

Obviously, first there was only *One*. That is the Supreme. From *Him* came the so called 'Big Bang" when *He* mobilized Creation from Maya.

And upon His command comes dissolution. The ultimate reality is, there is only *One* in the beginning. Then there were three. Then five. Then infinite!

Shri Brahma Samhita says that Krishna *is* the *sarva karan karanum!* Shri Krishna tells us in the Gita that *He* is the source of simply *everything*[10].

Case closed. Mundane and foolish thinkers go home.

CHAPTER 4

Hindu Concept of Time

Time exists only in our dimension, the created dimension. It simply does not exist in the divine abode where the Creator, the Supreme, resides for He is sanatan and eternal. He creates, sustains, annihilates, and starts the cycle again and again.

4.1: Background

The Hindu concept of cosmic time may seem strange at first to a neophyte, but on closer examination, is more descriptive, more accurate, and of a longer or greater duration.

For example, if one was to represent a large sum of currency or measure in a much smaller unit, the zeros at the end start to look almost meaningless or overwhelming, and the unit of measure seems unable to quantify it in a manner that we can easily comprehend. For example, if you want to write the physical number down in dollars to represent the amount of 10 trillion, the numbers of zeros following the one would be almost overwhelming. Linear time, then, as we see it represented today, fails to approximate our specific time with respect to *universal* time, and makes it almost incomprehensible.

The Hindu concept is based on a *cyclical*, rather than a linear measure of time. It allows for better perspective of time as a whole, rather than the linear concept of taking a small piece or "chunk" out of overall time and subdividing it.

As Hindus, we know that there are cyclical patterns to everything. Take re-incarnation, for example. We know that a soul attains various body forms through a huge multitude of generations, until finally achieving the thinking, or human form. This human form is the ultimate body form, allowing for free will and the ability to realize God. The *cycle* then from one form of the body to the next depends on ones deeds which leads to the selection of the next body after the "death" of the first body, and so on. Time, represented in cycles, is a more understandable, and easier to comprehend.

Please note that *all definitions* of time in the ensuing pages are from the *Shrimad Bhagwat (3.11)*.

4.2: Cosmic Time

Cosmic time, when conversed about in linear time such as in years, becomes almost meaningless because the numbers become immense.

Therefore, Hindus talk about Cosmic time with different descriptors, where time is cyclical, and is divided into portions.

The easiest relationship to understand with respect to time is that smaller cycles or periods of time combine to make a bigger cycle, which then combine to make yet a bigger cycle. This is the fundamental basis of time.

For example, twenty-four hours make a day, seven days make a week, fifty-two weeks make a year, ten years make a decade, and ten decades make a century. In archeological terms, for instance, it would be more useful to use centuries rather than weeks or years when discussing time to make it more comprehendible, and even then, 'ages' or 'periods' are used to describe large blocks of time when referring to certain events.

Similarly, *universal time,* or cosmic time, makes more sense if we use other descriptors rather than years or even centuries. Unlike archeology, however, Hindu Cosmic time descriptors are more precise, more accurate, and most importantly, cyclical rather than linear.

We will start from the largest period of time that affects us and progressively divide and get smaller. We will then return to the biggest portion. The definitions herein are from the *Shrimad Bhagwat.*

To understand time as it affects us, we have to start with Brahma, the secondary Creator, of the Holy Hindu Trinity, who is divine *shakti* that 'lives' for a hundred years. Brahma's life span is a hundred years, and at the end of a hundred Brahma's years (not human years!), even our Brahma must go.

A daily cycle of Brahma is divided into one day and one night. Brahma is 'awake' by day, and 'sleeps' by night. When Brahma is 'awake' creation and life exists, and when Brahma 'sleeps' Creation and life is 'dormant' and non-existent. Of importance is that when Brahma 'sleeps' so do the demi-gods associated with that creation! The partial destruction, however, that occurs when Brahma 'sleeps' does not involve all planets, just those lower than Brahma Lok, and earth is included, as are the planets of the demigods.

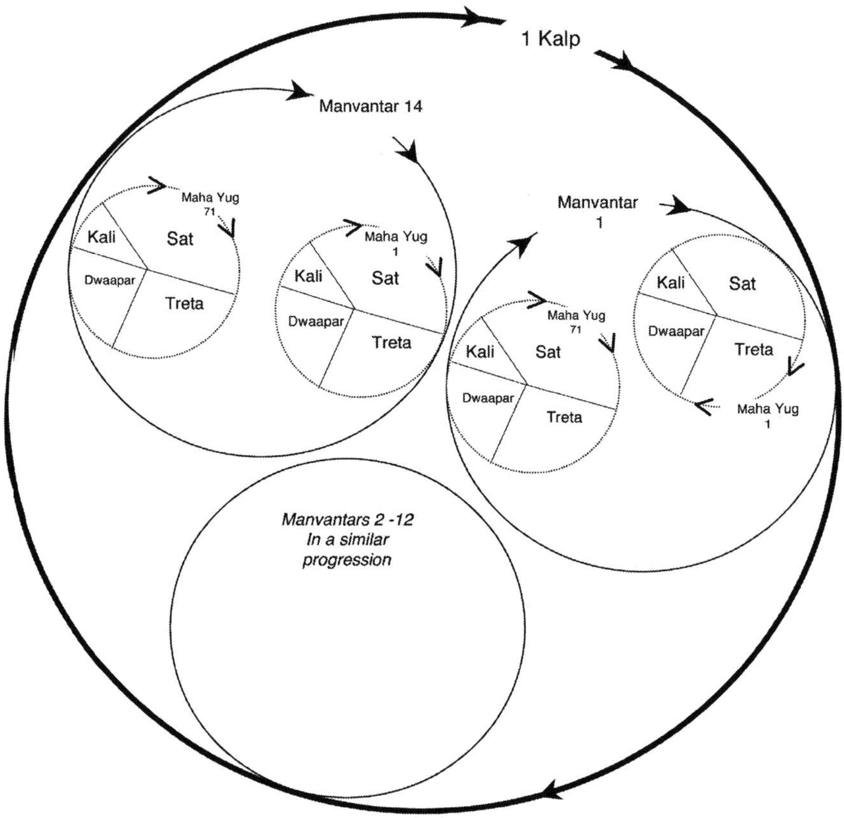

Illustration 3: Cosmic Time Cycle (Highly Simplified rendition)

When Brahma's *day* starts, a new cycle starts on Earth. It is called a *Kalp*. When Brahma's day ends and His night begins, the Kalp ends also. A Kalp is the largest cycle for Earth.

A Kalp is represented two different ways, for reasons that will become evident.

The first relationship is that each Kalp is divided into a thousand cycles, and each of these cycles is called a *Maha-Yug* or *Chatur-Yug*. Each Maha Yug is further divided into four uneven *portions,* but not cycles, called a *Yug*.

The second relationship is that each Kalp *also* has fourteen cycles, and each cycle is called a *Manvantar*. If you do the mathematics, dividing a thousand Maha-Yugs by the fourteen Manvantars, each Manvantar will have approximately seventy-one Maha-Yugs, with a transition period between each Manvantar.

Therefore, some scriptures will refer to a Kalp as fourteen Manvantars, and some will refer to a Kalp as seventy-one Maha-Yugs. The relationship is what is significant, the absolutes are not.

The other significant thing is that each Manvantar starts with a progenitor called Manu. There is a different Manu for each period. Therefore, at the conclusion of each Manvantar, there is destruction.

Okay, so each Maha-Yug is further divided into four uneven portions called *Yugs*. The four Yugs are Sat Yug, Treta Yug, Dwaaper Yug and Kal Yug.

For our purposes, the Yug is most important. It is an uneven portion of the divine cycle that is a Maha Yug. The cycle begins with the longest yug, and ends with the shortest, with a transition period between the last and first yugs.

Refer to *Illustration 3: Cosmic Time Cycle.*

The Yugs

The first yug is the age of 'goodness' or *Sat-Yug*. It is the longest period, supposedly over a million years in duration, with human life-span reaching a hundred thousand years. It is a time when *sanatan dharam* is established, and dharam stands on four pillars.

Next is the age of 'three' or *Treta-Yug*, where dharam stands on *three* legs, and bad deeds start. It is a little shorter in duration. A 'zero' is stricken from human life span, which decreases it to ten thousand years.

The age of 'two' or *'dvi'* called *Dwaaper-Yug* follows next, and dharam only has two legs. It is a little shorter than Treta-Yug, bad deeds increase, and another zero is lost from the human life span, now reduced to one thousand years.

The last is the age of ignorance or darkness, *Kali-Yug*, which we are in. Dharam now stands on one leg only. It is the shortest and most horrible of the four, with horrific events punctuating this period. This period is supposed to last a few hundred thousand years, with human life spans starting at just over a hundred years in the beginning, and decreasing from even that. Maximum life-span in this age starts at just a little over a 100 years at the beginning of this yug, and progressively shortens as this period matures, and it may shorten to just a few decades by its conclusion.

There are four pillars to dharam in Hindu religious philosophy: *Tapashchary* or austerities, *Pavitrata* or purity in thought and deed, *Daya* or Compassion, and *Satyam* or Truth.

The cycle starts with Sat Yug, standing on all four pillars or legs of dharam. People of Sat Yug perform tapascharya, are pure of mind and deed, are very compassionate to all of creation, and are honest and ethical.

One leg, Tapascharya, is lost at the close of Sat Yug, so dharam only has three legs in Treta Yug. Next, Pavitrata is lost, so dharam stands only on two legs in Dwaaper. Finally, Daya is lost also, and dharam stands on one leg only in Kali Yug.

Dharam cannot stand on one leg, and so starts to collapse. The ensuing chaos intensifies, as the Kali Yug gets more mature, reaching finally to the point that Krishna is obligated to descend to Mrityu Lok to fulfill what He ordains in the *Shrimad Bhagwat Gita.*

Lord Krishna promises in the *Gita* that,

Whenever righteousness is lost,
whenever there is unrighteousness,
then I shall descend,
for the destruction of evil,
and to re-establish purity,
righteousness and dharam,
I will descend in every Yug[11]

Therefore, at every Yug, when dharam collapses, Shri Krishna descends to set the balance right and to re-establish dharmic principles. However, we will explore these and other purposes when we discuss His Descensions *in Chapter 7.*

To Re-Cap, refer to *Illustration 3: Cosmic Time Cycles*

Night of Brahma: Annihilation and storage

Day of Brahma: Creation and Sustain Creation

One day of Brahma (12 hours): One Kalp

Kalp: A cycle consisting of a thousand Maha-Yugs

Kalp: A cycle consisting of fourteen Manvantars, with a transition period between each.

Manvantar: Seventy-one complete cycles of Maha-Yug, with a transition period after Kali Yug.

Maha-Yug or Chatur Yug: One divine cycle consisting of four uneven portions called Yugs.

Yug: A small and uneven portion of Maha-Yug. Smallest component of the divine cycle. Sat is the longest period, followed by Treta, followed by Dwaaper, and finally Kali, which is the shortest.

4.3: Fundamental definitions and conversions

Only the commonly used time units are given here. These are directly from *Shrimad Bhagwat, 3.11.* Some not so common are also presented to show the relationship.

Nimesh: A blink of an eye. It is also a third of a *kshan.* Approximately half a second.

Kshan: 3 *nimeshas*

Ghadi: 24 minutes

Prahaṛ or Yamah: 3 hours
1 human day or 1 human night = 4 Prahar = 12 hours

1 human day and 1 human night = 8 Prahar

Muhurat: is equal to 2 ghadis, or approximately 48 minutes.

Usha: Pre-Dawn, marked by change from darkness of the night to a multi-colored sky

Prabhaat: Dawn, follows Usha. Indicates Sunrise

Sandhya: Dusk, marked by the multi-colored sky just prior to nightfall

1 Paksh = 1 fortnight, or 15 days

2 Paksh = 1 month or maas. Each maas has 2 fortnights, or 2 paksh, one dark, one bright.

Mahino or Maas: A Hindu month. A complete lunar cycle from new moon (Ekam) to full moon (poonam) and end of the full moon again (amaas or amaavus). This is approximately 30 days.

Rutu: is 2 months. There are six Rutus, or seasons, in a year

Ayane: 6 months, or 1 solar movement from the North to the South

1 year: 2 Ayanes

1 divine year = 360 days of Brahma

24 divine hours = 1 day and 1 night of Brahma

1 day of Brahma = 1 Kalp

1 day of Brahma = 100 dev years (DemiGod years)

1 Dev year = 360 human years

1 day of Devs = 1 human year, or 360 days

The life-span of the Devs is 100 years of the Devs

1 Maha-Yug = 12,000 Dev Years

Sat Yug = 4,800 Dev Years

Treta Yug = 3,600 Dev Years
Dwaper Yug = 2,400 Dev Years

Kal Yug = 1,200 Dev Years

(See Shrimad Bhagwat, 3:11, for more information)

4.4: The Hindu Calendar – A Brief Introduction

The Hindu calendar is lunar-based rather than solar-based (which is really what most of us are used to.)

The lunar month is based on a 30-day month, so there is over-lap and mathematical difference with the solar month, which fluctuates. Additionally, the lunar cycle also fluctuates some, and there may be an increased day or *teethi* every once in a while. Therefore, there is not a neat tie-in. The solar calendar in use today starts the new calendar day at midnight, whereas the lunar calendar begins at sunrise rather than midnight.

Important Hindu dates, events, festivals, and so on are based on this lunar calendar, which is more precise and predictable than the solar calendar. The *only* exception to this rule is the solar-based day of *Makar Shankrati*, which always occurs on January 14th of every calendar year.

The lunar-based calendar is called a *panchaang*, a lunar month is called a *mahino* or a *maas*, and a lunar phase or day is called a *teethi*. There are two *pakshas* to represent the increasing and diminishing cycles of the moon. The increasing cycle, causing increasingly brighter nights, (*ajwaaria*) is called *Sud* or *Shukla Paksh*, and there are fourteen teethis or days, followed by the full moon on the 15th day called *poonam*. After this, the moon cycle becomes a diminishing one called *Vud* or *Krishna Paksh*, causing darker nights (*andhaaria*). The last night after this is called *amaas* or *amavas,* with no moon.

The 15th and 30th days, or poonam and amaas respectively, have no teethis. The acceptable date format when referring to the panchaang is month first, followed by paksh, and then teethi. The general rule is auspicious activities are done in the rising phase (Sud), although there are major exceptions to this rule.

Refer to *Illustration 4*: *The Hindu Lunar based Month,* and it will become clearer.

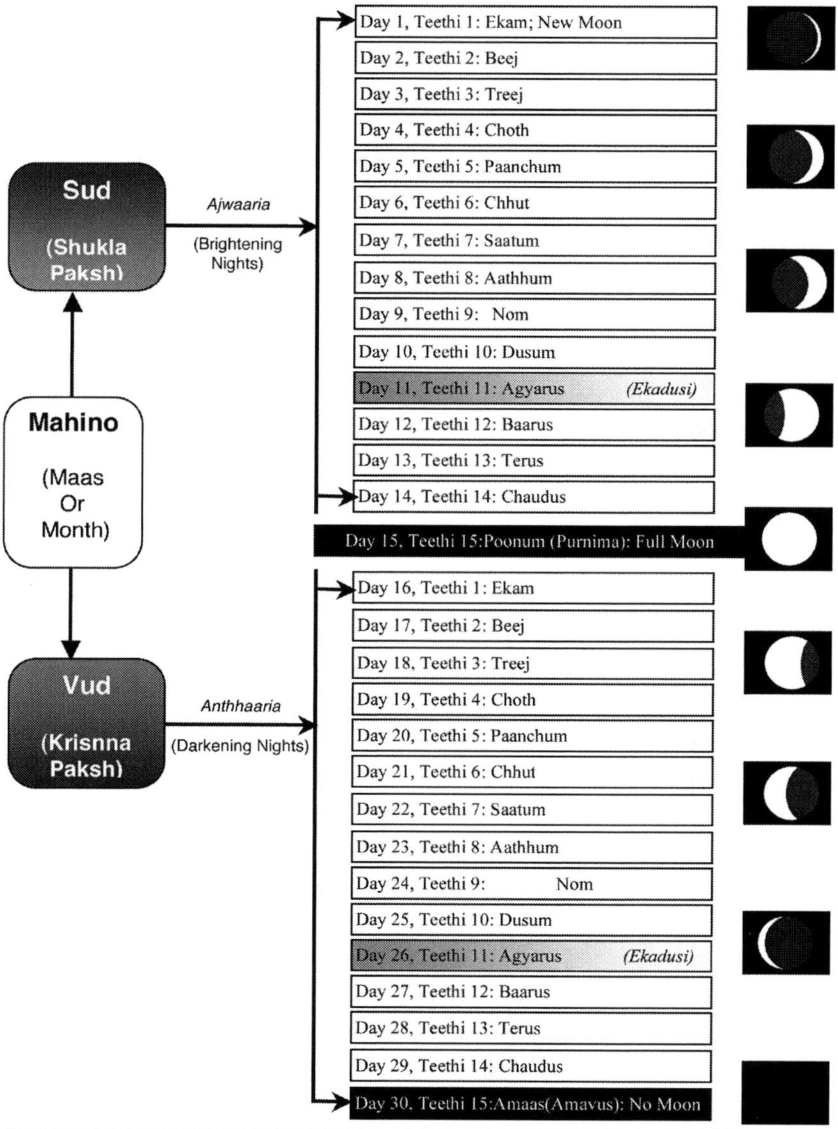

Illustration 4: The Hindu Lunar-based Month

Teethis

It is an age-old custom to perform good events on auspicious teethis. This custom is not just a mere religious ritual or custom, but is also highly scientific.

For those of you that are skeptical, hold your snickering for a minute. Let us explore this concept with a few simple examples. These are no-brainers, really. We will look at it from three different angles.

Examine tides. There is high tide on one end, and low tide on the other. While there are several factors at work, the easiest concept for most people to relate to is the gravitational pull of the moon. We accept the role of the moon in influencing tides, then, right?

Examine the traditional but practical and satvick *kisaans*, or farmers, of rural India. They lay down seed in their fields on what they call an auspicious teethi, but which coincides with the best planting season naturally. Sheer coincidence, faith or science?

Examine our History. When maa *Devhuti* wanted a meaningful child, teethis were kept for conception. Though all daughters are divya, *maa Ansuya* comes quickly to mind, for she is the mother of *Durvasa Rishi*. Sheer co-incidence, faith or science?

Get the picture?

Heavenly bodies will influence everything, from tides and climates, to moods and mental well being through life and, yes, even conception and children!

Awake, my Hindu friends! Teethis are extremely important! Just because you didn't know or didn't care, will not excuse you. If you are going to do something meaningful, do it right the first time! If there is an auspicious event planned, performing it under the most auspicious teethi, or time, should be of paramount importance.

Closing Thoughts

Life is punctuated with important and life-changing events. Plan for them!

4.5: A Loose Approximation of the Hindu Calendar

The Hindu version of the calendar with approximations is presented below.

Remember, this may fluctuate slightly as leap years are added, or Hindu calculations add an extra maas (adhik maas) every three or so years to make up for lunar cycles. Also, there can be extra teethis, or reduced teethis as well.

Nutan-Varsh / New Year:	Kartak	October-November
	Magshar	November-December
	Paus	December-January
	Magh	January-February
	Fagun	February-March
	Chaitra	March-April
	Vaisakh	April-May
	Jyesth	May-June
	Asadh	June-July
	Sravan	July-August
	Bhadervo	August-September
	Asho	September-October

The important religious festivals that occur during the period, along with the Hindu dates that they fall in, and a more detailed description of some of the important festivals is summarized in *Chapter 9.*

4.6: Parting Thoughts - The *Relative* Concept of Time

Time is a *relative* concept. It is not an absolute. Having said that, however, there are two final juxtaposed thoughts one must consider with respect to time.

One, on the created side, time *is* finite. The clock is *always* ticking, as the old adage goes. Time is precious and priceless. It cannot be purchased, bartered for, or even bargained for. For us, time goes, never *ever* to return. Therefore, waste not a moment of it, not a *kshan*.

Second, there are numerous mentions to the Supreme as *Maha-Kaal*, or the *Kaal of the Kaal*. Both of these *sound* great but are *incorrect*.

Let's examine the concept of *Kaal* or time. Whether time is measured in solar or lunar units, realize both of these luminaries are *nashwant*. At a certain point in time, they will be annihilated and cease to exist as we know them. Obviously, entire new planetary systems will subsequently arise at another point in time. Therefore, time *even in these terms* becomes merely a *fleeting point* on the 'overall' cosmic time frame. Can you imagine the beginning through the end of *our* sun being only a meagerly fleeting point in cosmic time?

The most important apprehension should be the fact that time *only* exists in *our* dimension, the *created* dimension. Time simply does *not* even exist in the divine abode where the Creator, the Supreme resides for He is sanatan and eternal. *He* creates, sustains, annihilates, and starts the cycle again. And again.

Hence, there is no beginning, no middle, and no end if one applies the concept of time to the Supreme. When all else is gone, including the planetary abodes of Brahma the creator in the holy trinity, *only* the Supreme remains. And He shall be there again when He creates anew. And this will go on ad-infinitum. At the risk of applying cyclical-sounding logic, where then is the beginning, the middle or the end when dealing with the Supreme? The final answer is, there just isn't.

The Supreme is, therefore, *sanatan*, beyond *kaal*, beyond time, and beyond simply *everything*.

CHAPTER 5

Ahinsa and Vegetarianism

For humans to simply take lives of defenseless creatures, whether for 'sport' or 'food' or 'business' is appalling, atrocious, reprehensible, arrogant, counter-productive to natural harmony and order, and comes with dire consequences.

5.1: A Few Opinions on Non-Violence & Vegetarianism

Non-violence leads to the highest ethics, which is the goal of all evolution. Until we stop harming all other living beings, we are still savages."

- **Thomas Edison**

I have no doubt that it is a part of the destiny of the human race, in its gradual improvement, to leave off eating animals.

- Henry David Thoreau

As long as there are slaughterhouses, there will be battlefields

- Leo Tolstoy

Nothing will benefit human health and increase chances for survival of life on Earth as much as the evolution to a vegetarian diet.

- Albert Einstein

For as long as men massacre animals, they will kill each other

- **Pythagoras**

A man of my spiritual intensity does not eat corpses.

- George Bernard Shaw

Flesh eating is unprovoked murder.

- Benjamin Franklin

I am in favor of animal rights as well as human rights. That is the way of a whole human being
- Abraham Lincoln

Truly man is the king of beasts, for his brutality exceeds theirs. We live by the death of others: we are burial places!
- Leonardo da Vinci

The highest realms of thought are impossible to reach without first attaining an understanding of compassion.
- Socrates

The time will come when men such as I will look upon the murder of animals as they now look upon the murder of men.
- Leonardo da Vinci

The animals share with us the privilege of having a soul.
- Pythagoras

The love for all living creatures is the most noble attribute of man
- Charles Darwin

We manage to swallow flesh only because we do not think of the cruel and sinful thing that we do.
- Rabindranath Tagore

The greatness of a nation and its moral progress can be judged by the way its animals are treated
- Mohandas Karamchand Gandhi

To become vegetarian is to step into the stream which leads to nirvana
- **Lord Buddha**

It is very significant that some of the most thoughtful and cultured men are partisans of a pure vegetable diet.
- Mohandas Karamchand Gandhi

He who permits the slaughter of an animal, …cuts it up…kills it… buys or sells it… cooks it … serves it … eats it …is to be considered as the slayer of the animal

- Manusmriti, 5.51

As many hairs as the slain beast has so often indeed will he who killed it … suffer a violent death in future births

- Manusmriti, 5.38

One who partakes of … flesh … of another animal, and … cows, O King, if such a fiend does not desist by other means, then you should not hesitate to cut off his head.

- Rig Ved, 10.87.16

You must not use your God-given [human] body for killing God's creatures, … animal or whatever.

- Yajur Ved 12.32

Ahimsa is not causing pain to any living being at any time through the actions of one's mind, speech or body.

- Sandilya Upanishad

One is dearest to God who has no enemies among the living beings, who is nonviolent to all creatures

- Bhagwat Gita

5.2: Ahinsa and Vegetarianism: Not just a Philosophy

'Hinsa' is violence, so 'a-hinsa' is opposite. Ahinsa literally translated means non-violence. But the concept of ahinsa is not just a mere translation. It is a holistic perception, a total view and philosophy, a complete outlook to life and creation itself.

The original true *activist* of this whole philosophy of non-violence was Lord Buddha, an *avataar* or a manifestation of the Supreme who came at a time when the world was filled with terrible violence and cruelty. Lord Mahavir further elaborated and championed this philosophy.

This philosophy was brought to light again in modern times in India by Mahatma Gandhi, and successfully duplicated and implemented in the United States by Dr. Martin Luther King. Ironically, Gandhiji's life was brought to a brutal end *by hinsa* by an extremist Hindu brainwashed by a non-Hindu, and Dr. King's life was also brutally brought to an end in a similar violent fashion.

Most people start to equate vegeterianism and ahinsa. However, that is not correct because the philosophy of ahinsa is not merely limited to vegetarianism. The treatise of Ahinsa really deserves an entire discussion on its own which could take up volumes. Suffice it to note that Ahinsa really has a very broad outlook, and is a process that unifies the mind, body and soul in its outlook and approach towards rest of creation with the utomost in compassion *and* by deed.

The idea of vegetarianism is really a separate and distinct subject matter, yet it is also a subset of, or a product of, the philosophy of non-violence. Although these two concepts are different and really should be treated separately, they are so intertwined in their *karam* that they will be treated almost as one in our discussion here.

Vegeterianism, then, is a small but integral part of the overall philosophy of Ahinsa. Hence, simply being a vegetarian does *not* guarantee non-violence or compassion, but being rooted in the philosophy and practice of ahinsa almost certainly does.

Vegetarianism to a Vaishnav refers to a diet of food from the Plant Kingdom, plus milk products from the cow. Krishna's favourite was *makkhan*, especially if 'stolen' from the Gopis, derived from cow's milk, hence His name *makkan-chor*. Therefore, milk products are acceptable to a Vaishnav because in no way is the cow harmed. Krishna went so far as to say that only milk left after the calf's feeding should be accepted.

Some would call this lacto-vegetarianism, but we are not here to get into nomenclature.

The purpose of vegetarianism is many-fold, but as a general rule, vegetarians shun cruelty to other animals and, indeed, all of creation. Now we specifically said earlier the Plant Kingdom. Not the Animal Kingdom and not the Kingdom of Fungi, which are neither plants nor animals. Fungi demonstrate a few characteristics of both, hence the separate Kingdom. Fungi then are forbidden food as much as animals are. In *Manusmriti*[12], for instance, mushrooms are expressly forbidden.

There is an age-old saying that goes *you are what you eat*. This does not stop at the external body, however. This also reflects on your thought process, your demeanor and nature, your compassion, and your spirituality as well. If one consumes spicy or intoxicating foods, most certainly being *rajsi* or *taamsi*, one's mind becomes agitated, the body becomes agitated, and the balance and mood swings to where there is less calm and less overall alertness.

In the *Upanishads*, the ancient rishis clearly state that quite literally, *you are what you eat*. The *Chhandogya Upanishad* specifically details how food is the basis of and affects the formation of everything, from the mind to the speech, from the flesh to the feces, and quite simply, *absolutely everything*.[13]

Note carefully, however, eating through the mouth is but one inlet into the body. Multiple other inlets via your *indriya* also exist. Hindus and Vaishnavs must be careful, then, of what they consume, whether by way of eating, drinking, inhaling, hearing, seeing or touching. For instance, seeing violence will lead to agitation of mind and loss of inhibition. Hearing violence will also diminish inhibition and lead to a numbing effect toward violence. One can extrapolate over other indriya and arrive at similar conclusions.

See, hear, and speak only what we truly know is correct. Taste or eat without hinsa or killing. If you eat non-vegetarian, you eventually become numb to the violence of killing, and this will lead to propagation and escalation of more agitation and violence in one's own life. The simple presumption is that unless one can *generate* life, one should not *extinguish* it!

In short, ahinsa is truly the practice of not causing pain to *any* living being by *mind, speech or body*.

The repercussions of extinguishing a life are tremendous. There are very few, specific and rare exceptions to this, such as a *Kshatriya* on a battlefield in a fair fight and under orders can take lives of others, or in self-defense or in defense of another victim. This is called *'Sva-dharam'* or self-duty. But for humans to simply take lives of defenseless creatures, whether for *'sport'* or *'food'* is appalling, atrocious, reprehensible, arrogant, counter-productive to natural harmony and order, and comes with dire consequences, according to Hindu shastras. Besides, where is the sport in harming or killing a defenseless creature?

Be vigilant over your other inputs into the body also. If you ingest alcohol or drugs or intoxicating perfumes for instance, your mind shall go down that path and may cause an outcome that you may be ashamed of later. However, if you inhale incense, hear the *ghhant* or bell at *aarti*, or hear the sound of a conch-shell blown, your senses are immediately directed to Krishna, your mind calmed, your thoughts at once purified, and your mind and thoughts clearer and more focused. You are much less likely to fight or quarrel if your mind and heart are filled with bhakti, let alone kill.

Lord Krishna says that our indriya cannot and should not be suppressed, only re-directed. One who merely suppresses the senses is a *mithyachari* or liar, because sooner or later, the power to suppress will fail, and he will fall.[14] Therefore, we must redirect our senses to Krishna rather than merely attempting to suppress them.

There is an old story I have heard that someone once said that when asked what the difference was between a Hindu and a westerner, Swami Vivekanand replied that it all starts at dusk when Hindus light little *deepaks* in their homes with the family, while the westerner lights up with big cold ones down at the local pubs alone or with similar lonesome friends.

What a striking difference there is in the two scenarios presented above! Obviously, the rhythm that subsequently follows from each as the evening progress (and certainly as life itself progresses) is simply worlds apart. Remember, seen as the bigger picture, this would start to affect not just family units, but societies and ultimately nations as a whole.

5.3: The Human Design: A Dilemma that Shouldn't Be

Now, if that alone is not compelling enough, let's also examine the magnificent human body from an *elementary* design perspective.

Let's examine basic differences *in design* between carnivores and herbivores, and we'll also detail a few human traits or features as we go along.

Carnivores, or meat-eating creatures, have tools *by design* that aid in the capture of its prey, the efficient shredding of its flesh, and its rapid digestion and disposition of waste.

Carnivores are predatory animals, meaning they have to hunt what they eat. If they are somehow hurt to a point where they are not able to catch prey, they will die. Let us look at just a few obvious clues to their carnivorous nature.

Predatory animals have features that allow them to seek prey and get close without being easily detected. For example, big cats have fur coats with patterns and markings that allow them to blend into their environments to avoid detection. Lions on the plains of Africa for instance have patchy golden coats that allow them to blend into the usually dry plains, or the sand, and 'disappear' into the background. Indian tigers on the other hand have vertical stripes on their golden coats to blend in with the tall grassy and bushy elements of their backgrounds and help break up the lengths of their bodies. Big cats also have better night vision by design that allows them to see incredibly well in even poor light. These big cats have a reflective layer where the sensory retina ends to help redirect available light back to the sensory retina. This allows maximum use of any available light, giving the cats phenomenal night vision. By contrast, humans have a *darkly* pigmented non-reflective layer just posterior to the sensory retina to help *absorb* light after exposing the sensory retina, rather than reflect it. This design makes for poor night vision for the humans.

The predators are usually much stronger one-on-one than the prey that forms their dinner. They usually have sharp claws if they are land predators. This allows them the ability to grab and hold their prey. They have the ability for rapid speed in short bursts. Both land and aquatic predators, such as the big cats on land and sharks in the oceans, illustrate this incredible phenomenon. They have sharp and elongated teeth that sink into and rip flesh efficiently. Again, big cats and sharks illustrate this 'point' nicely, if you pardon the pun. The size of the predator's jaws are much larger to allow for larger and longer teeth, and their jaws move up and down in a scissors fashion rather than also side to side to allow chewing. Hence, predators are able to rip but not chew. The massive jaws are powered by massive muscles that provide tremendous bite pressures compared to non-predatory animals. The digestive juices in their stomachs allow for a rapid breakdown of flesh, and are usually extremely acidic. Lastly, the lengths of their overall digestive tracts are small to enable rapid passage and disposal of waste. The most important thing to note about carnivores is that, almost without exception, they only hunt when they are hungry, and do not strike mindlessly when they are not.

Herbivores are grass eaters, and also have tools *by design* that help them digest and extract what they need from plants and fruits. They are usually prey animals, so usually have the ability to distance themselves from their predators, and have usually better stamina, pound for pound. They stay in larger groups, for there is indeed strength in numbers. Large herds allow for more eyes to keep vigil for predatory animals. They have no claws, for they have no need for them. They are not as strong or as well muscled as the predators. They do not have sharp front teeth, fangs or incisors, like the big cats or sharks, but in fact have flattened teeth (molars) to help grind rather than rip and tear. The digestive juices in their stomachs are less acidic than carnivorous stomachs, and their digestive tracts are extremely long to allow for slow passage of food through them.

And what design do humans have?

Biologically, the human is designed as a herbivore, not a carnivore. We do not truly have the teeth to rip flesh, let alone posses the ability to digest it. Our incisors are equi-length and un-extended. Our jaws are relatively small, we have a decent set of molars, and our jaw design is optimized for side-to-side movement for chewing. This means we *chew* our food, not simply shear it off and swallow the chunks. The digestive juices in our stomach are not as acidic as those inside of a carnivore. The extended length of our gut also says we are biologically a herbivore rather than a carnivore. There are other features as well, but I think we have made our 'point.'

Remember, the underlying basis and goal of digestion is the absorption of useful nutrients, and the rejection of that which is not or cannot be absorbed. Meat in our extra, extra long digestive system tends to rot and ferment during its prolonged passage through the long digestive tract. What good is such rotting or fermented material? What good can come of its absorption? Why, then, should modern medical science be surprised at the alarming increase in all types of cancers and ailments?

Sure, modern science 'convinces' us that primary protein and certain other trace elements can only be had from meat. If that is the indeed the case and these are the only ways we can survive and thrive, explain the many multiple and healthy generations of Hindus on strict vegetarian diets.

Let us look at another issue.

No one voluntarily wants to die, right? This includes all creatures, human or otherwise. Even a unicellular or one-celled organism is known to react to adverse stimuli or pain! Therefore, all creatures want to live, and do not wish to suffer infliction of pain in any way, let alone die!

All animals come with a response system to stimuli. We want what gives us pleasure, and we attempt to get away from that which gives us pain. To this end, animals come equipped with built-in mechanisms that allow us to get to or away from something. When we wish to get away from something very quickly, such as in panic situations or facing imminent death, we have a set of events that occurs within the body to help achieve this quickly, which is universally called the *fight or flight* system.

This sequence of events rapidly prepares the body to either fight or run away. Among the things that happen is that a series of hormones such as epinephrine get released, blood pressure goes up, heart rate goes up, muscles get affected to aid in quick moves or exit, and so on. All these things happen extremely rapidly, and it takes a much longer time for the hormonal and other components to dissipate.

Well, to no surprise, animals also have this fight or flight system too, and it works! What do you suppose happens when animals are getting slaughtered? Yup, theirs hormones have been released, and they don't want to die either, without a fight, whether they show it or not. Once released, these hormones and chemicals end up where, do you think? Correct again, in their organs, and muscles, and so on. The meat that gets eaten in other words.

To add insult to injury, modern food has added chemicals to animal diet that humans consume. Antibiotics, steroids and hormones, and so on.

Does common sense not tell one that *these very things*, now more appropriately called toxins or carcinogens, will end up in one's own blood when such flesh is consumed? Does this not explain accelerated aging, obesity, hypertension and cardiovascular disease, diabetes and Alzheimer's, increased mental agitation, mania and depression, organ failures, cancer, decreased immunity, to name just a few?

Yup, its controversial, but makes sense doesn't it?

And we aren't even going to talk about the abominable, cruel and atrocious conditions that humans put the animals through in their short and horrific life!

5.4: Parting Thoughts

Although the preceding section on vegetarianism is brief, a few things should be immediately apparent from the discussion:

1. Humans *by design* are herbivores, not carnivores or meat-eaters
2. By design, eating meat is unnecessary for human survival and flourishment
3. You are what you eat, physically, mentally and emotionally. Eating meat may not be the best for you physiologically or psychologically.
4. There are consequences to eating non-vegetarian, both personal and national. Eating meat will numb you to a degree to violence, which may not be the best for personal, social or national harmony.
5. Eating non-vegetarian will definitely be a serious obstacle to your spiritual advancement in pursuing pure consciousness or Hinduism.
6. Eating non-vegetarian (or the trade of animal or meat products) is cruel and barbaric, and contributes to and propagates abominable animal cruelty and slaughter. Remember that the shastra holds *you* responsible for not just every animal abused, but by *how many hair* on *each one* harmed, maimed or slaughtered!
7. Eating non-vegetarian (or the trade of animal or meat products) contributes significantly to global climatic changes and indeed global climate collapse through intensive animal agriculture. We will revisit this concept in *The Final Analyses*.

Recall that we have discussed that we humans are herbivores *by design*, not carnivores or meat-eaters. When we go *against* nature's design, there is usually a price to pay, and it is one that is paid multiple times and in multiple ways.

Are *you* ready to pay this horrible price? What's going to be on your plate?

CHAPTER 6

Hindu Symbolism

Two Magnificent Hindu Symbols

The very existence and daily routine of a Hindu is punctuated with symbols that serve to remind him of his position in life, family, society, country, universe and God.

6.1: Background

Hindu symbolism illustrates and consolidates wonderful ideology and thought based entirely on the Hindu scriptures. What may appear to be meaningless gestures or simple symbols superficially are actually powerful portrayers and representations of deep and meaningful philosophy.

The very existence and daily routine of a Hindu is punctuated with and centered around such markers and reminders. It is a philosophy that serves to remind one of one's position in life, family, society, country, universe and God. It teaches deep respect for parents and elders and their acquired wisdom, respect for the acharyas and sages, respect for especially women and the children. This leads to social harmony, respect for country and the Creator, and respect for all of creation. The philosophy encourages plowing and not plundering, rejuvenation and not tribulation, tolerance and not torture, patience and not haste, temples and not retirement homes, and one that especially places great emphasis on the unity of people rather than the modern-day isolation and *me'ism* represented by I, me and mine.

Religious *yagnas* and gatherings that seek to unify people to bring peace and harmony, and cause de-centralisation of wealth for improvement and upliftment of society as a whole rather than the individual. Modesty and humility are cherished and encouraged in all and in every way, from gestures and greetings to clothing and posture.

It is not possible to cover it all, so we will attempt to merely highlight it with just two of our most important symbols of divinity and harmony.

6.2: Symbols and their Cultural & Religious Significance

There are many cultures that have symbolic representations of their faith and belief. These symbols signify to their followers a sense of belonging to their faith and belief, and provide a continual source of comfort and joy.

For instance, Christianity has a Cross that signifies the sacrifice that the son of God, Jesus Christ, made for all mankind. It is a symbol that brings great comfort and joy upon visualization. It reminds one of the divine presence, and allows one to make the appropriate choices in life for spiritual upliftment. Such is the power of the symbol.

A symbol can also be misused, however, as in the case of the cross, or the Hindu swasthik. If a cross is held upside down, it denotes the exact opposite of divinity. Unfortunately, the madman that stole the second most important Hindu symbol did not turn it upside down – he merely rotated it a little in some cases, and not at all in others. Tragically, most modern historians associate the cherished Hindu swasthik, better called the *saathio*, with a madman's brutality and do little to investigate its true purpose or, in fact, even its correct and rightful origin!

However, simply because someone insane decides to use an upside down cross to represent him or his culture does not mean that entire Christianity abandons the cross itself! So why should Hindus abandon what has always been rightfully theirs? Why indeed should Hindus abandon the sacred saathio?

Hence, in Hinduism and indeed for Hindus worldwide, the *saathio* remains Hinduism's second most important symbol, however, and no madman can rob a people of their treasure forever! The saathio, or swasthik, always has been and always will be a cherished, revered and holy Hindu symbol regardless of what a madman (or any man, for that matter) says or does! For, it represents the ultimate balance in life to create peace and harmony. It is rightfully the Hindus' and shall always stay ours! Next time you see a saathio, think peace and harmony, *not* a madman.

6.3: Two Magnificent Hindu Symbols

i. Aum:

Aum is the single most important symbol, bar none.

Shri Krishna in the *Shrimad Bhagwat Gita* says that He *is* Aum. Therefore, Aum is *the* sound of the Creator, *the* sound of all Creation. It is *the* beginning sound in the Universe, and the culmination of all sounds divine.

Aum symbolizes God in His totality, purity, and everlasting and eternal state.

The symbol, Aum, and the sound, Aum, are an auspicious and holy representation of the omnipresent and omnipotent All Mighty, Shri Krishna.

The sound Aum is eternal, it is transcendental, and at once produces bliss and peace. It is thus meditated upon and meditated with. It has the power to reach at the very core of a human, the *aatma*.

Aum is the most auspicious, the most sacred, the most revered and holy of *all* Hindu sounds and symbols.

Shri Krishna says in the *Shrimad Bhagwat Gita* that *He* is *Aum*[15]

Rig Ved proclaims *Aum* as the *Supreme*[16]

ii. Saathio

Perhaps the second most significant Hindu symbol. A very auspicious symbol, with religious connotation and denotation.

The *saathio*, or swasthik as it is sometimes referred to, represents the four balanced goals in life. These are *dharam* or self-duty, *arth* or the acquisition of material wealth and prosperity, *kaam* or desires, and *moksh or absolute* salvation. It teaches and signifies the paramount importance of balance in one's life. This balance in life, or the ability to strive for it, represents the crux of Hindu philosophy and is the main pillar in all ashrams of life except *sanyaas* or *tyaag* ashrams, which carry different denotations and expectations of the term *balance*. Man must be an asset to society, not a parasite upon it. Therefore, man must have goals to flourish, prosper, and finally pursue and attain moksh. However, which goals to pursue? What should be sought after more? What portion of life to devote to each?

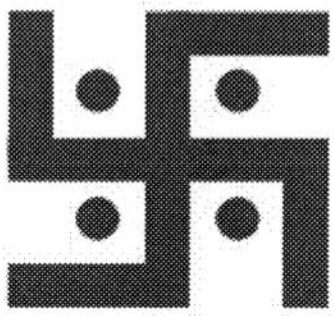

In a simple way, the saathio brings together the very basis of Hindu philosophy on the importance of balance in *simply everything* in life. To implement this simple but elegant philosophy in one's life would be tantamount to starting the journey in the correct *disha* or direction towards attainment of peace and God. This balance of life and the ensuing harmony is what the sacred Hindu symbol of saathio captures so brilliantly and so completely.

The saathio is a symbol stolen by a madman and sacrilegiously so twisted that Hindus are even afraid to use what is rightfully theirs in the correct and appropriate context! Hindus Awake! That stops now!

Closing Thoughts

The transcendental Aum, without a question, stands on its own. It is the first sound, the first syllable in the Universe, and represents and truly *is* the omnipresent Creator.

The saathio, on the other hand, is a powerful yet elegantly simple philosophical symbol. It is directed to the common folk like us to help us balance our life, and aspire to not forget about our Creator and moksh.

Striving to attain this balance is a must. The path towards *mukti* or *moksh* must never be misconstrued as abandoning your duty to your family, nation and God! To do that is a sin, according to Shri Krishna.

We are talking about achieving that perfect balance in life. Saadhus can achieve God, and so can Grehastis. The question is, where is your *maan*? Is it in Hari? What are *you* doing with *your* life? Are *you* living it for Hari?

Is your *maan* and your *life* for Hari? Then you will be able to live a life of balance.

As Krishna says, like a lotus in water. But never water in the lotus. You in society. Never society in you.

6.4: Parting Thoughts

Aum and Saathio are two magnificent and powerful Hindu Symbols. But they are *not* just mere symbols. For, they are symbolic of Hindu Life Itself *in totality*.

Saathio is powerful philosophy. Are you in *samaaj*? Or is *samaaj* in you?

Aum is powerful spirituality. You are in *Aum*. Is *Aum* in you?

CHAPTER 7

Divine Descensions: The Avataars

The Supreme descends, in His great mercy, to our planet for the pleasure of His devotees. It really is that simple!

7.1: Background

The Supreme works in many ways. Some of these are known to us, but most remain unknown to all but a select few.

One way to achieve a divine purpose is by descending and manifesting Himself on earth. This serves an additional inspirational purpose. Obviously, God, simply by *sunculp maatra,* or thought or wish, can achieve anything and everything. However, if He did this simply by wish, how would *we* learn anything? Where, then, would be the inspiration, the desire to achieve the truth, or the glory?

Hence God, in His supreme mercy, literally descends periodically to liberate us from our problems and show us the correct path. These divine descensions are called *avataars*.

When the Supreme descends as an avataar, His story during His stay is called a *leela*. His leelas are also called *pass-times*. A leela is like a play, and begins from the time He manifests and ends when He terminates His stay and ascends back to His *dham*, or abode. Leelas can be short or long depending on the objective of the descension. For instance, *Vaaman* avataar is a shorter leela, and *Ram* avataar is a longer leela.

All avataars descend from *Vaikunth Lok* in Param Dhaam, and all descend from Maha Vishnu, also known as Akshar Brahm. Shri Krishna is the source of Akshar Brahm or Maha Vishnu, or more accurately, Maha Vishnu is an expansion of the Lord. Therefore, Shri Krishna remains *the* source of all manifestations or avatars. Krishna, however, descends as Krishna the Supreme when He chooses to.

Shri Krishna, therefore, is *not* an avataar, but is PurnaPurshottam Bhagvan Himeself, as the *Shrimad Bhagwat* says,

Ete camas-kalah pumsah
Krsnas tu bhagavan svayam
Indrari-vyakulam lokam
Mrdayanti yuge yuge [17]

The Supreme, Bhagvan Shri Krishna, descends as Himself when He chooses to, and also as an avataar or manifestation of His energy through Maha Vishnu when He chooses to, as He does every Yug as described in the verse above.

It is important to remember that Krishna remains unaffected and untainted by *His* Maya, and our interpretation of His leela may be entirely incorrect and completely baseless if *we* only use *our* brains already and unavoidably influenced by His Maya.

The interpretations of His leelas must be learned through the correct gurus who achieved this understanding with the correct *parampara*, or discipular succession. A fool that simply relies on his own brain is arrogant and jumps to conclusions that may be completely erroneous.

Therefore, the important take-home message is that the Supreme's *leelas* achieve a divine purpose, are a divine guidance by teaching us something valuable, and are a source of beautiful inspiration and joy that would last an eternity.

7.2: Dus Avataar: The Main Descensions

Krishna descends whenever there is a decline of dharam to protect it and all that is good, to destroy evil, and to re-establish religious principles, as said so in the *Bhagwat Gita* and the *Shrimad Bhagwat*.

We will look at the purpose in just a few of these *avataars* or manifestations, and their significance. Remember Krishna descends, and is never *born* and never *dies*.

We will briefly look at the ten main Descensions, otherwise known as *Dus Avataar*.

We all know the stories of each avataar, so we will keep story telling to a very minimum. If, on the other hand, you are not familiar with the stories of each avataar, please refer to *Shrimad Bhagwat* for a brief overview of each.

The detailed stories of the avataars will need to be acquired separately, and that is highly desirable and recommended.

The Ten Main Descensions

1. Matsya Avataar

The story of Matsya avataar is well known to His devotees.

Vishnu had appeared to the King days before the great flood to warn him of the impending peril, and advised the king to gather his people, animals, plants and seeds, rishis, and so on and depart on a boat. Vishnu advised the king that Vishnu would appear as Matsya, the great fish, to guide the king to safe lands where society would start anew.

The fish-form descension of the Lord at the time of the great flood shows that Krishna will protect all that deserve His protection regardless of their predicament, and even at the time of Prahlay.

Therefore, a *true* devotee never doubts Krishna and His mercy. He performs his assigned roles and duties, *parishram and purusharth,* with honesty, integrity, and sincerity to the very best of his ability while ‘leaving’ the fruits of his activity to Krishna.

2. Koorma Avataar

The turtle descension was to allow for many *leelas* all at once, and is really a series of very important manifestations. This descension also allowed for presentations and gifts to devtas and to mankind.

It allowed for *aushadhis*, or healing materials, to be harvested from the ocean, allowed for Shiv to show His mercy by drinking the poison that emerges and thereby earning Shiv the title of *Neel-Kantth* and *Maha-Dev,* allowed for Laxmi to emerge from the ocean and be wed Vishnu, allowed for Dhanwantari Avataar, Mohini Avataar, the concept of the Planetary Orbital Polar nodes of Rahu and Ketu when Vishnu emerges from Mohini to destroy the demon, Svarbhanu that drank the *amrut* as a dev, and so on.

A lot of very valuable lessons need to be learned from these different leelas within this one avataar, and it behooves one to read about each in *vistaar*, or greater elaboration.

However, the most important summary lesson to be learned is that the churning of the *ocean of thought* within each of us will yield a great deal, not just *amrut* or pleasantries. It is a gradual progression of spirtitual pursuit, with fall-offs at every step. This is a critical lesson to be learned in life, but one can only realize this with Krishna Kripa.

Let us look at just some of the practical lessons and applications to be learned here. The first and the biggest requirement is that *you*, however, have to first *make* the decision to pursue the search for the ultimate truth, thereby becoming a *sadhak*.

The search for the truth has to first start from within, initially with the decision and commitment to seek that truth, and then engage one's self fully in first cleansing one's self. Along with seeking *vidya*, or true knowledge, introception *has* to then follow. Once a *sadhak* churns the ocean within him, the initial fruit of his efforts will be poisonous or undesirable.

Remember from our earlier discussions that our vessels, our hearts, need to be free of sansari clutter and litter that currently occupy it, and these are not pleasant. Examples include *kamnas and vaasnas*, our *asuri* materialistic desires, and the list quickly grows long from that. The sadhak needs to learn to hold the poison that is produced from his depths of thought without digesting it, just as Maha Dev. This means that once a sadhak begins to make *real* spiritual progress in life, issues rise to the surface that are clearly undesirable, and have the ability to poison all parts of his life, including relationships with loved ones, and so on. The sadhak then needs to 'hold' that poison within him and *purge* it without lashing out at society or becoming embittered in the process.

If successful, the sadhak progresses onward and is healed by the 'aushadhis' that emerge from his continued manthan or churning. If he perseveres even further, Laxmi, or wealth and success will also follow. This wealth can be any number of things in addition to just financial wealth. It could be social status, knowledge and wisdom meaning intellectual success, political status and achievement, and so on.

Laxmi only weds Vishnu, who is a *giver*, not a taker. Vishnu is all-giving and all-sustaining without being attached to His activity. Therefore, Vishnu is not arrogant about His power or His activity, magnificent though they may be.

A sadhak has to be able to similarly *digest* these successes, meaning being humble and unattached to his deeds, actions and successes, and not becoming selfish or greedy. More importantly, a *true* sadhak must *share* them for the benefit of mankind. If one is able do this, Mohini arrives to aid in luring off the rest of *asuri* desires trapped within each of us. It is not possible to even separate these, let alone extinguish them, on your own without divine help.

If finally necessary, Vishnu Himself emerges to *decisively* end our asuri desires to aid in the final progression toward His lotus feet.

So, when was the last time *you* read or heard the story of 'saagar-manthan' and the conflict between *devi* shakti and *asuri* shakti? Go through the story slowly and carefully again. It isn't just a *leela* or story people! It is a divine directive to each of us to start the incredible journey towards divinity! *That* is what makes each of us human!

3. Varah Avataar

This avataar is extremely important for current times and deserves great reflection and then action.

The avataar illustrates how the Earth fell out of orbit because Hiranyaksh, a mighty demon and brother of the mighty Hiranyakashipu who was the father of little bhagat Prahalad, plundered the *pruthvi*, or the planet Earth, for gold and depleted it, and in the process by digging so deep and so much that it ended up throwing off the planet's harmonic balance. The earth thus fell into the *Garbodhak* ocean below even the *patal loks*. This place is a terrifying and filthy place, difficult for anyone to reach.

A Pig is significant for going into places no other animal wants to, hence the *Varah Avataar*, the pig-form manifestation. In His divine mercy, Varah goes to retrieve the fallen planet. In the process, Hiranyaksh challenges the manifestation and is liberated from his body.

This descension should also comfort true devotees that Krishna's *kripa* is *aseem*, for He is willing to go to any length, even as a pig if need be, for His devotees!

The most important aspect of this descension that is relevant to current times is the simple fact that we humans need to learn that plundering the planet, such as for oil, deforestation from agriculture or timber, minerals, water, and so on may throw the planet's harmonic balance off yet again causing calamity for all life on it.

This 'calamity' initially comes as climate changes initially and then follows with 'natural' disasters such as hurricanes, earthquakes, volcanic eruptions, disease and cancer outbreaks, and so on. If we are arrogant or foolish enough to fail to heed such warnings, then… who knows?

Well, we can really only start with ourselves first. Yes, it always starts with that first step. And yes, one person can make an incredible difference, and has the capacity to positively affect a lot more people in their 'circle of influence' such as family, friends and co-workers. One just has to have the realization that we cannot continue to plunder never to replenish. What sort of legacy, headache and heartache do we leave behind for our little ones?

Have *you* done your part to help the planet today?

4. Nursimh Avataar

This descension was a leela primarily to demonstrate that one is a Brahmin by *deeds* and not by *birth.*

Prahalad was a Vishnu *bhagat* or devotee born in a *rakshas* or demonic *kul* or family lineage. His father was Hiranyakashipu, a rakshas king, who was angered when Vishnu in *Varah* form killed his brother Hiranyaksh.

This leela also in a simple way illustrates ultimately the *limitations* of human intellect, as illustrated by Hiranyakashipu in asking for a supposedly 'immortality' boon from Brahma.

Humans can learn a lot from this leela as well.

For starters, birth makes not a Brahmin, thought and deeds do. Prahalad was a *rakshas* by birth, but a *Brahmin* by deed and thought. Secondly, we humans need to realize the limitations of our physical and more importantly our mental faculties. Thirdly, Krishna is *Achyut*, for He will never fail His true devotees. Most importantly, one is a Brahmin by deed and not by birth. Similarly, one is an asur by deed regardless of birth. We will detail this very same lesson in Vaaman Avataar again. I quess we humans can be just a little slow at times and may need multiple lessons to learn even once, if at all.

Hmm. Have *you* checked on your deeds recently?

5. Vaaman Avataar

This small Brahmin-boy avataar is significant for many reasons, and we will only illustrate with a few.

First of, Maharaj Bali is of rakshas *jaati* and birth, but ends up demonstrating that he is indeed a Brahmin by thought and deed. Bali also happens to be Prahalad Maharaj's grandson, so it is not a one-time fluke that a Rakshas can become a Brahmin.

Hindus, therefore, unequivocally need to realize once and for all that *jaati* is never important. What truly matters is one's thought and deed. Therefore, you can be *born* a Brahmin and yet be an *asur* or Rakshas by your thought and deed, or the other way round.

For example, meat eating, or the trade of meat of any kind in any way whatsoever, is *never* permissible in Hinduism. A Hindu that does either eat meat or trades in it, regardless of *jaati*, is an *asur* or a *rakshas* by deed and by greed.

A Brahmin by birth and jaati that eats or trades in meat is an asur, for instance. A lower-born (by jaati) person that follows the teachings of the scriptures and is truthful and honest is a *dev* or Brahmin by deed and thought.

What *you* are by *your* deed and thought is up to *you*.

Therefore, we each need to think, *do we want to die a Rakshas or a Dev*, regardless of our birth and jaati. Look to Prahalad and Bali for inspiration. It does not matter what or where you were yesterday, for that is water under the bridge and out of your hands. Only the *vartaman*, the present, is in your hands. What will be *your* choice from now on, *sur* or *asur*?

The other significant lesson to be learned is the meaning of giving your word and keeping it. Maharaj Bali had given his word to Vaaman dev that he would give him whatever He asked for. Bali's guru, Shukracharya, advised him not to do so, for the guru could see that Vaaman was really Vishnu and would take everything from Bali.

Maharaj Bali, to his credit and character, kept his word to Vaaman nevertheless. He ended up losing everything to Vaaman dev, who, pleased that Maharaj Bali kept his word even against his guru's advise and rage, gave Bali His true darshan as Vishnu, and granted Bali *Indrapad*, among other things.

Therefore, one must learn to be careful in promising, and more importantly, in keeping such promises, for that *should* be one's character.

Without integrity and character, one has nothing and more significantly, one is nothing.

The most important lesson to be learned, perhaps, is the fact that *nothing* is ever truly yours to begin with, and you should have no compunction or hesitation in sharing it. It was never yours to begin with, and you can never take it with you, so why the *moha* and the greed?

Do what Maharaj Bali teaches us. Share, and don't fall back from your dharam.

Keep your promises, and if you are blessed with riches, be Aryan, be noble, and share your wealth and blessings. There may be a Vaaman Bhagvan in someone that you help that will put you at Vishnu's lotus feet!

6. Parashu-Ram Avataar

This avatar is significant in that it illustrates that rulers must always be in harmony with dharam.

Rulers in Hindu Shastra are deemed to be a *divine representation* entrusted by the Supreme in discharging their duties to their *praja* or nation responsibly. Rulers are supposed to be highly cognizant of their dharam, and when in doubt are entrusted to seek appropriate counsel from selfless rishis and Brahmins to help weigh in with opinions on a matter. The final decision reached is always the ruler's responsibility.

In a nutshell, it is the ruler's responsibility to safeguard the national borders, the people's interest, and those of the state with fairness, compassion and impartiality. It is a sorry ruler that allows the compromise of national borders and security, and such rulers are contemptable.

It is also the ruler's prime responsibility to ensure protection and care for the spiritually driven and enlightened rishis and Brahmins who are the keepers and teachers of Vedantic knowledge and wisdom. Hence, it is the ruler's responsibility to protect dharam and not the other way around.

If even the mighty rulers do not protect dharam and, in fact, abuse it, there shall always be divine consequences. Unfortunately, the people that *allow* an abusive or unfit ruler to come to or stay in power shall also have to suffer the ill-fated ruler's consequences to a significant degree. This is fairly apparent when one studies the history of the people under an unfit or tyrant ruler, both in ancient and not so ancient times.

Rulers and great leaders must *always* remember that *dharam* and *Brahmins* should guide them for they should never rule on their own *uneducated* whims and desires alone! Remember, Brahmins here mean those that are the wise, knowledgeable and selfless servants of the people, and dharam here means *duty* and not organized religion.

It is critical to make the distinction between *dharam* or *duty* guided by and based on *spiritual morals* rather than dogmatic or fanatical religious 'interpretations' and applications.

Hinduism and Vedantic dharam always guides rulers to be *morally* self-disciplined for the utmost well-being of their people, and never the other way around which would be based solely on greed and grossly distorted religious rules leading to oppression and destruction.

A *correctly* guided government is fair and compassionate but never weak, always non-oppressive and open to free thinking and debate but never frivolous, and never finding itself resorting to coercion, corruption, extortion, oppression and brutality to maintain law and order for its people. It is, after all, the people who allow the government to even exist in the first place.

A *fair* government is always minimalist, direct, open, shared and balanced, non-beauracratic, non-corruptible, founded on truth, honesty and self-discipline, and guided by dharam with the ultimate goal of betterment of its people and the nation.

A nation thus guided always has a mighty military arm that is never used on itself. The military might is necessary to enforce its borders or to retake what is rightfully sovereign. The military might acts as a deterrant in peace times, and moves to swiftly and definitively crush an invading enemy when provoked to safeguard the peoples' security and proseperity. The military can never be involved in the free government but must be fully under its control.

For self-discipline, a free nation needs a strong police department that is honest, fair and compassionate but never brutal to its own people. A system of incorruptible judiciary oversees their impact on the people and the nation. The judicial system should be the counter-balancing arm of the government, not its puppet!

Both the military force and the police force should be driven by a sense of patriotism, honesty, nobility and fairness, the true hallmarks of a Kshatriya.

Current rulers could easily learn some character-building virtues from true kshatriyas, and be the ultimate Kshatriya as past rulers have been.

In a free society guided by dharam, there is really no place for true 'politicians' then, is there? The very word invariably conjures up thoughts of corruption and greed, and evokes strong emotions of disgust and contempt!

What do you think the *current* rulers should learn from this avataar?

Are you listening, Hindustaan? Are you taking notes, my Hindu friends? You put the current rulers in power. Do *not* let them turn into corrupt politicians – you have the power to remove such greedy and bloodthirsty parasites if they do decide to become that. *Awake!*

7. Ram Avataar

Lord Ram is the very epitome of a Kshatriya ruler. With an unequalled sense of justice, freedom and compassion matched with unparalleled might, *He* is the ruler to emulate!

This great and wonderful avataar needs to be studied in great detail, and one needs to spend one's life learning from it and implementing the lessons learned from it. Whether you are a ruler or a citizen, Ram sets *the* benchmark to attain to in life, irrespective of your position in life or society.

Ram Avataar is a *Maryada Purshottam* avataar establishing *adarsh* (roughly meaning morals and principles) by example and self-sacrifice, for this avataar delightfully and delicately establishes the complex and intricate relationships for family and society. This avataar defines the *true meaning* and *joy* of relationships of every kind, the appropriate behaviour, the appropriate principles, and so much more.

Lord Ram carefully avoids demonstrating his Supreme or divine abilities as His goal was to establish a path that even the simplest of all in a society is able to follow. However, Lord Ram's return to Ayodhya is one of the very few places that Bhagvan Ram demonstrates His *Ishwariya* by becoming many from one.

Ram Avataar is a Maryada-Purshottam Avataar because He establishes *by example* many important principles that make each of us ultimately a decent human. Ram was not kind or compassionate, for kindness and compassion are momentary and temporary, and have unkindness and rage on the flip side. Ram had *karuna*, which means there was *never* a time when He was not merciful, kind, gentle and compassionate. Not one single moment! Not even towards Ravan. Therefore, to say Ram is kind, compassionate and so on is a gross understatement of what He really is.

Ram, Goswami Tulsidas tells us in his *Ram Charit Maanus*, is truly *Sahaj Anand* or *Sahajanand*, for he is always pleased and is always *anand-may*. In fact, on His *naam-karan sanskaar*, it was said that He was being named *Ram* for even the simple recitation of His name would bring *aaram,* or peace and bliss, to one. Ram's very name, Ram, is the simplest mantra one can chant to make great spiritual advancement. Recall the story of Valmiki, and how this simple name, Ram, changed everything.

What do you think *Sahajanand,* Ram, can do for peace in current times?

Therefore, a lifetime of study and devotion needs to be devoted to this avataar, and such a short treatise can never do it any kind of justice.

8. Balram Avataar

Balram is the *first* quad expansion of the Supreme Lord Shri Krishna and is *always* at His service.

Balram manifests in different forms via *His* expansions, such as *Shesh Narayan*, on whom *Maha Vishnu* lays in the Garbodhak or causal ocean, as Laxman, Lord Ram's younger brother, as Balram, Krishna's elder brother, and so on.

Together, Krishna and Balram are the *two greatest shaktis*. There is none other above them. Mull that over in your mind for a minute, and let it sink in.

Lord Balram, as Sankarshan or Baldev, the second greatest *shakti* in the *entire* Cosmos, is Shri Krishna's *eternal* and *humble* servant, never for a moment wishing to leave His side.

What do you think Lord Balram can teach us?

Awake, man, awake! Learn from the second mightiest personality in *all of cosmos*. Learn to serve with dignity and humility!

Look at *how* and *whom* Balram serves! Who will *you* serve?

9. Krishna Leela

Krishna Kanaiyo, bansi bajaiyo. *What* to say of Govind? *Where* do we even start?

Krishna 'Avataar' is really much more than just that. Krishna is the *one* avataar that is a *full and complete* descension of the Supreme Lord as Himself. Read and understand that again, for it is just that important.

Although it is an *apraadh* to attempt to weigh the different forms and manifestations of the Supreme, it is only prudent to point out that Krishna the Supreme descends as Krishna the Supreme. Krishna is *Advait*, for there is none other before Him or above Him. He is *Adi Purush*, the original, the Supreme, and nowhere in this avataar does He hide this fact from His true devotees. In fact, Krishna takes great delight from His devotees' ecstasies upon granting them His darshan!

His *charcha*, His discussion, His warta-lap, His thoughts, His stories, His leelas, just anything about Him *tat kshan*, at once, fills volumes without end, paradoxically that, too, without an end or even a beginning.

Kanaiyo is Anand Swaroop, whose very name is intensely attractive, captivating and magical. Kanaiyo, wrongly accused of being *makkhan chor*, for how can one steal what belongs to one? What is there in the *whole of cosmos* that is *not* His or indeed outside of Him?

Having said that, let us visit just for a moment His makkhan-chor leela, for that is what gets Him wrongly accused of stealing. As we mentioned, nothing truly exists outside of our little Kanaiyo, and there is truly nothing that isn't His. Therefore, He can't be accused of stealing what was already His to begin with. Secondly, there is much deeper significance to His makkhan-chor leela than meets the eye. That insight deals with the *nectar* of devotion, which we will address in another discussion.

Kanaiyo's kathaa is one that one could listen to life-long and yet it will always be fresh and new all over again. His kathaa and pass times are blissful and magical and magnetic in ways that are difficult to describe but oh so easy to experience. It is a process that, once started, is divinely serene, peaceful and blissful, and one would not *want* to stop listening and experiencing this over and over.

However, one never knows or fully comprehends the taste of sugar, till one actually experiences for himself. You really can't understand 'sweet' fully, irrespective of chemical write-up, pictures, chemical structure, pictures or descritions until one actually physically tastes it. Therefore, to fully understand the bliss of Krishna's leelas, one must dive into it personally and experience it with one's own ears, eyes, *raday*, *vichaar*, *manthan*, and so on. Then and only then is it even possible to start to understand the timeless and eternal attraction for it.

This 'avataar' does not need only a lifetime of study; it needs our full and complete devotion with our very aatma. The Supreme Lord's leelas and pastimes will entertain us for an eternity if we let them.

Remember, however, that the *amrut*, the *nectar* of Krishna kathaa, Krishna bhajan, Krishna vaanchan, and Krishna manthan is *only* possible after the cumulative *poonias* of many lifetimes and Krishna's kripa! Do not waste this lifetime!

We need to put ourselves completely at His mercy with full faith and devotion with the *correct knowledge* that Krishna *is* the Supreme, the Advait, the Adi Purush, and it is indeed Him that we worship with full faith and devotion, for that is the only prescribed way to salvation in KalYug.

10. Buddh Avataar

This avataar, tragically, is the most misunderstood in Hindustaan and Hinduism, and for that reason, has been ostracized in India. It is a very important avataar in many ways, and we will just point out a few.

First off, Buddhism *is* an important and integral part of Hinduism. Read the *Padma Puran* if you need convincing and authorization. Second, Buddh avataar *is* Shri Krishna's avataar, or Shri Krishna manifested, so if *you* cannot see Krishna or Akshar Brahm in Buddh, shame on *you!*

Next, Buddh did what was necessary for the times to stop *hinsa* and meat eating which was being done under the *falsified* authority of the Veds. Therefore, Buddh *had* to deny the authority of the Veds to stop the rampant hinsa of innocent creatures.

So get it straight in *your* head and your heart first!

Do not *mindlessly* and *shamelessly* shun Buddhism or Buddhists, for they are indeed true Hindus, and in many ways, much better than you and I! Whereas they *practice* what they learn, many of us so-called Hindus rarely even *know* what to practice, let alone *implementing* it in our lives! *That* makes us not just hypocrites, but the *worst* kind of hypocrites!

Turning us into *decent* humans is the first thing we learn when we turn to Lord Buddh. Humanising us, teaching us kindness and compassion, teaching us to first look within ourselves for the hidden poison within, and many other such 'human' qualities is what Lord Buddh is about. There are only a few important distinctions between humans and the other animals, and Lord Buddh teaches us about them.

The Buddh avataar teaches us many valuable lessons that will put us right before Krishna if we let it. Therefore, *learn* from what this avataar teaches us.

Remember, Buddhism *is* a significant and important part of the treasure that *is* Hinduism.

If *you* as a Hindu are not able to *comprehend* Buddh avataar as a Supreme shakti, what do you think this says about *your* ability (or *really* the lack of it!) to not just comprehend but to truly *digest* shastra?

Awake! Perhaps its time to go look within! It is never too late!

7.3: The Avataars

The avataars listed here are in the sequence they appear in the *Shrimad Bhagwat*. Note, therefore, that it is not a chronological sequence. Nor is it by importance, either, for there is no such thing as an *unimportant* avatar. The list of avataars is directly from the *Bhagwat*, and presented here for the sake of completeness.

Each avatar teaches us something valuable, and you are *urged* to look up and study each one (except Kalki avataar) further.

1. The Kumars: the four bramachari sons of Brahma the original progenitor
2. Varah, also called Saukaran
3. Narad Muni
4. Nar and Narayan, the twin sons of Rishab dev
5. Kapil Bhagavan, founder of the *Sankhya Philosophy,* or elemental physics
6. Dattatrey
7. Yajna
8. Rishab dev
9. Prithu
10. Matsya, or fish form
11. Koorma, or turtle form
12. Dhanvantari Bhagvan, who appeared with the nectar of life
13. Mohini, who served this nectar to the devtas
14. Nursimh Bhagvan, who manifested to save little bhagat Prahalad, killed Hiranyakashipu
15. Vaaman, the little Brahman who tested Maharaj Bali, grandson of Prahalad
16. Parashuram
17. Vyas Bhagvan, also known as VedaVyas for elaborating the single Ved into many
18. Ram Avataar, also known as Maryada-Purshottam avataar
19. Balram. Not an avataar, but an expansion
20. Shri Krishna. Not an avataar but a full and complete descension of the Supreme
21. Buddh.
22. Kalki. Yet to happen according to some, but description already in place in the scriptures.

7.4: Hindu Gods & Goddesses: What are they?

The initial concept that we must get right is that all Hindu Gods and Goddesses are considered a divine *shakti*, but not all divine interventions are *avataars*.

We have already reviewed avataars, but let us briefly explore the other divine shaktis that we also worship. There should not be a construed or implied importance or difference in magnitude between divine shaktis and divine avataars. To consider an avataar or a shakti to be more significant in one way or another is *apraadh*. Our mental faculties are extremely limited to begin with, what to speak of their function under *Mayic* influence! Therefore, only fools and mundane people will seek to differentiate in the importance between divine *shakti* and divine *avataar*. They are both divine, and are only different in function and execution. With this premise in mind, let's tease them apart. Remember, one is *not* more important than the other!

An avataar is a *manifestation* of the Supreme Personality. The most important function of an avatar is to illustrate or demonstrate a way or means to a divine purpose, this lasting a *finite* period of time. This *period* of time is termed His *leela* or *pass-time*.

As an avataar, the Supreme manifests from Vaikunth Lok, and returns there when His leela is over. His leela shows us many important things in many different ways. If we are able to learn and implement even a single teaching, our life changes completely. This change is called *parivartan*. We have already reviewed the avataars as told in the *Shrimad Bhagwat*, and have briefly looked at possible lessons to be learned from them. Let us now turn our attention to the Lord's *shakti*, His other divine energy.

A *shakt*i represents a potency or energy of the Supreme for a specific divine Universal *karya* or purpose and its execution. A divine *shakti* has a significant role to play, is divine in origin, but is *not* a manifestation or an avataar in the true sense, for It is an *expansion* of His energy. Unlike a manifestation or an avataar, divine shaktis have no *nimit* parents, do not teach us or educate *per se*, and have specific and universal functions to execute. They are also immensely powerful, adorned with the Supreme's abilities to varying extents as necessary for implementation of their duties.

Therefore, their presence can be finite or infinite, and their appearance can be a single time or multiple times. An example of an *eternal* and an *immensely powerful* shakti is Bhole-Naath Shiv. An emample of a *finite* shakti is the secondary creator of the Universe, Lord Brahma.

Whereas *Shiv* is timeless and eternal, *Brahma* has a finite role and function, and is concluded at the time of Maha-Prahlay or the complete dissolution of each universe. Recall from the Chapter on *Creation* that our *Brahmaand*, our Universe, is but one of an infinite number. Hence, an *infinite* number of Brahmas with *finite* time periods and functions exist, and come and go as entire Universes emanate and are then unmanifested.

Other powerful examples of His *shakti* are Akshar Brahm, Maha-Vishnu or Narayan, Vishnu, Shiv, Brahma, Aamba, Durga, Maya and so on. These shaktis are powerful examples of His potency, and these Shaktis emanate from Him obviously with no *nimit* or apparent parents. These shaktis vary in potency based on the need for achieving a specific divine purpose.

These divine shaktis are also worshipped in the same way that the Supreme is worshipped, as they are *direct expansions* of *Him* with the understanding, comprehension and realization that even though they are not *the* Supreme, they fully *represent* the divinity of that same Supreme. To do otherwise is arrogant, ignorant, foolish and naïve, and represents a gross apraadh to the Supreme.

How can it be otherwise?

Some literature classifies these *divine shaktis* as 'Demi-Gods,' which is a gross misrepresentation and is highly derogatory in its connotation. The term *denotes* a personality that is a *portion* of God, but the *connotation* read by many into the term is that this 'portion' is not worthy of our worship! Awake! Nothing is further from the truth!

To see 'God' in man, and then serve *man* as serving *God* is admirable, but if that same person can't see 'God' in any of His other divine shaktis, the so-called *demi-Gods*, than he is nothing but a sheer hypocrite! Such a person becomes worthy of contempt, for this person has learned nothing from the shastra and yet prophecies to 'serve' God through man! Show me a bigger *mithyachari* and a fool than him!

A final concept of divine representation is one of *Vibhuti*, which is a *miniscule* and *infinitesimal* portion of divine energy, and is represented *through* a human. A vibhuti is not a divine manifestation or an expansion. It is a representation of divinity through a human, and is therefore present as long as that human is present.

The term 'miniscule' is *relative* in terms of potency but *not* significance. Be clear about this. An avataar or a shakti is infinite, omnipresent, omnipotent, and infinitely capable. A *vibhuti* is of *shukshma* or infinitely small capability since it is indeed a human *aatma* that has achieved a divine status by its knowledge of the Supreme, implementation of that knowledge and finally through the *sharing* and *spreading* of that knowledge.

This vibhuti, this aatma, is now much higher on a divine scale compared to an ordinary jiv, as it is a shuddh aatma that has realized this status in its lifetime. Hence, this aatma may also be referred to as *Jivan-Mukta*, or God-realized and liberated (while alive) aatma. This aatma is *mahaan*, or great, and has some wonderful divine abilities, although they are greatly limited compared to a shakti or an avataar. Hence, the term *Vibhuti* is reserved for a God-realized person. Examples of vibhutis are God-realized rishis, acharyas, saadhus, saints, and bhagats.

In conclusion, *all three* divine energies are worthy of our utmost respect, and the two direct potencies that *we* separate as *avataars* or *shaktis* are to be worshipped *as a representation of the Supreme* without hesitation in any of His glorious forms.

7.5: Parting Thoughts

Krishna descends to our planet because He, in His great mercy, wants to strengthen the resolve of His devotees, pure and simple. The other reasons are important, but this one is the most important - He descends for the pleasure of His devotees, and it is really that simple!

While here, though, He cleans up the accumulated evil, re-establishes and strengthens dharam, and by His aseem Kripa, enables one or two lucky jiv-aatmas who have regained their shuddh-aatma status by true devotion and Shiv's mercy to have His darshan and interaction, which enables them to return home to Vaikunth.

Fools and arrogant persons, legends in their own minds, are bewildered by their own limited and mundane intelligence and fail to realize that the Supreme descends as the Supreme – Krishna. Unfortunate aatmas they are indeed! Do not allow yourself to be so arrogant and foolish, and let this opportunity and this lifetime slip away! Do not be one of the unfortunate aatmas!

The *ultimate* thing that Hindus need to appreciate is the *very fact* that Krishna chooses to descend to Hindustaan *at all*. Everywhere else, He sends messengers, *never* to reveal Himself. Ever wondered about that? How merciful is that? How wonderful is that? Only in Bhaarat and only in Hindustaan!

Awake, therefore, my Hindu friends! Realize who Krishna is, then realize His Pushti, His mercy, His aseem Kripa in descending personally for *us* rather than sending divine messengers and emissaries.

Hindus Awake! Awake to your treasure and His mercy!

CHAPTER 8

An Abbreviated Hindu Almanac of Important Yearly Events

Celebrate, hey manav, and be joyful!
Life is truly festive with Hari in it!

This is not an all-inclusive list. The ones most relevant to a Vaishnav are listed. There are other important ones not listed, and the reader is encouraged to refer to a panchaang regularly.

To correlate with the calendar date for the year, one must get a current version of the Panchaang, which may also list additional information.

Remember, there may be additional days, or even months when adhik maas occurs, as occurs in leap years.

Important Hindu/Gujarati Events

1. Kartak (October-November)

Bestu-Varas / Nutan Varsh / New Year: Kartak Sud Ekam. New Year's blessings from the deities at the Temple
Govardhan Puja: Kartak Sud Ekam, same day as Nutan Varsh. Govardhan puja along with *Annakot*, or offering of multiple dishes and feasts for offering to God.
Bhai Beej: Kartak Sud Beej
Laabh Pancham: Kartak Sud Pancham. Auspicious day to start new endeavors.
Jalaram Jayanti: Kartak Sud Satam
Tulsi Vivah: Kartak Sud Ekadashi
Dev Diwali: Kartak Sud Poonam

2. Magshar (November-December)

Kamurta, or Dhanur maas starts. Lasts one month from December 16-January 13. Auspicious activities should not be performed during this time.

3. Paus (December-January)

Makar Sankrati: January 14, the only solar-based date. Always on January 14 every year. Also called Kite day.
Auspicious activities can resume.
India's Republic Day: January 26.

4. Magh (January-February)

Maha Shivratri: Magh Vad Chaudus

5. Fagun (February-March)

Holi: Fagun Sud Poonam

6. Chaitra (March-April)

Ram Navmi: Chaitra Sud Nom

7. Vaisakh (April-May)

Ganesh Choth (Lohana): Vaisakh Sud Choth

8. Jetth (May-June)

Bhim Agyarus or Ekadashi: Jeth Sud Ekadashi

9. Asadh (June-July)

Rath Yathra, Sea puja: Asadh Sud Beej
Naag Pancham (Lohana): Asadh Sud Pancham

10. Sravan (July-August)

Shitala Satam: Sravan Sud Satam
Raksha Bandhan: Sravan Sud Poonam
Bol Choth (Worship the holy cow): Sravan Vad Choth
Randhan Cchath: Sravan Vad Chhath
Janmashtmi: Sravan Vad Aatham

11. Bhadervo (August-September)

Ganesh Choth: Bhadervo Sud Choth. Ganpati sits for 10 days
Rishi Pancham: Bhadervo Sud Paanchum
Shri Radhashtami: Bhadervo Sud Aatham
Shraadh starts: Bhadervo Vad Ekam to Vad Amas
August 15: India's Independence Day

12. Asho (September-October)

Navratri: Begins Asho Sud Ekam to Sud Nom (9 nights)
Dussera: Asho Sud Dusam
Sharad Poonam: Asho Sud Poonam
(Diwali starts)
Rama Agyarus / Ekadashi: Asho Vad Ekadashi
Vagh Barus: Asho Vad Barus
Dhan-Terus: Asho Vad Terus
Kali Chaudus: Asho Vad Chaudus (Hanuman Puja)
Diwali day: Asho Vad Amas
October 2nd: Gandhi Janyanti

CHAPTER 9

Important Hindu Festivals

The festivals are glorious. Their meanings are glorious. The people that participate in them are glorious. Wouldn't it be wonderful if the purpose served ultimately at each and every one of them was truly glorious too?

9.1: Background

There are many important Hindu festivals, and all are demographically or geographically significant. Regardless of demographics, there is almost always a deep-seated and religious philosophy behind them. Sure, they are festive. Religion and hari-bhajan is very festive. But if *Hari* is taken out, and festivities are all that remain, then the significance is lost, and there is no spiritual or beneficial cultural purpose served.

Sadly, this is indeed what is happening today. Only the social aspect remains today. People gather and have a 'great' time. There is dancing but, alas, what kind of dancing! There is no Hari in the festivities. What is even more ominous is that organizers have added a financial aspect to it thereby making it a lucrative business.

So, what used to be great religious, sentimental and glorious functions have been pared down to highly profitable and social gatherings.

We are going to use a different approach to these gorgeous festivals. Everyone seems to know 'what' to do. We are going to examine 'why' we celebrate instead of 'how' we celebrate and 'what' we do.

If we truly *understand* the meaning and purpose of our festivals, they will take on a whole new richness and significance, and we will see them in a whole new light, full of respect and divinity that are befitting them. They each serve to teach us and remind us of something critically important to us – our liberation and ultimate salvation.

9.2: The Main Festivals and their Significance

The festivals following are in chronological order. There are many beautiful and meaningful festivals, but we are only going to look at a few. These are the ones that we truly need to understand so that not just the festival but life itself assumes a new and more meaningful meaning.

The festivals are glorious. Their meanings are glorious. The people that participate in them are glorious. Wouldn't it be wonderful if the *purpose served* ultimately at each and every one of them was also *truly* glorious?

Nutan Varsh

This is Hindu New Year's day. It is also sometimes called *Bestu-Varsh* in addition to *Nutan Varsh*. It falls on *Kartak Sud 1*, (October – November). The *only* correct greeting for Hindus on this auspicious day is "Nutan Varsh Abhinandan!" Please take pride in this Hindu greeting and use a *Hindu* greeting, not a non-Hindu one!

A New Year's Day is important in many ways, but is very simply, a second chance for a fresh start. Humans are very resilient in many ways, but we are also somewhat predictably regressive.

Humans tend to have the best of intentions with the best of resolve when starting something new, but usually tend to slack a little over time in both the strength of that resolve and the adherence to its functionality.

For example, we would resolve to lose weight and initiate a diet and exercise program to help achieve our goal. In the beginning, things would probably be difficult, but our resolve would be strong, and we would usually stick to our intended regimen. However, as time progresses, we would probably start to make small 'allowances' for what we would not want to stick to. These 'allowances' would be justifiable in our mind, and small at first. Over time, our resolve would probably weaken a little, and the 'allowances' could become larger even though they would no longer be just as justifiable even to ourselves. Sound familiar?

Here is where New Year's Day comes in!

It is a time and a chance to *freshen* everything, psychologically speaking. It allows us to shed the baggage of guilt that we may have accumulated through then without feeling terribly guilty. It allows us to strengthen our resolve yet again, and set new goals with renewed hope and determination. It allows us to freshen family and social ties, renew relationships that may have gone stale, and invigorate existing ones while building new ones.

Nutan Varsh is a wonderful time to rejoice, feast and be merry. Life is short, and another year beckons. Be festive, be merry, celebrate.

But where is *Hari* in all this?

Where *does* Hari fit in with your New Year's resolutions? What about *your* relationship to Him? How important is *your* commitment to Him? What are *your* goals towards achieving Him? How are you going to achieve *your* goals, if any? What kind of discipline will *you* maintain? What kinds of 'allowances' are tolerable and justifiable in *your* mind, and which ones aren't?

This Nutan Varsh, what is *your* resolution going to be?

Govardhan Puja

This is an important festival where we worship Govardhan Hill, personified. This beautiful and highly meaningful festival falls on Kartak Sud Ekam, New Year's day (October – November) on Nutan Varsh.

We know the story of how Krishna changed the *puja* from Lord Indra's puja to Govardhan Hill's puja, how Lord Indra became furious at Krishna and the Gokul townsfolk, how Krishna, at the tender age of seven, lifted Govardhan with the tip of the thumbnail of His left pinky finger for seven days through the torrential rain and storm initiated by Indra, and then suspended Govardhan simply on the *sound* His flute for a few more days, and how Lord Indra finally came to His senses and came to beg for forgiveness at Shri Krishna's lotus feet. The lifting of Govardhan Hill gave Krishna His name of Shri Giri Govardhan-dhaari Naathji, or Shri Naathji, for short.

So now, we worship Govardhan hill instead. But why do we *really* do this? What *is* Krishna trying to teach us here? Well, many important lessons, but we will highlight just two. These are *not* the most important, mind you, as there is no such nonsense as a 'less' important lesson from Krishna! With that in mind, let us look at just a couple of very important life-changing lessons to be learned.

Lord Indra should remind us instantly of whom? Ourselves, of course! Though Krishna is the *sarva karan karanum,* we in our arrogance think that *we* are the cause or the source of something, just like Lord Indra.

Indra thought that He, Indra, was the *cause* of the peoples' wealth and happiness, and therefore 'deserved' the credit and the worship. That is arrogance; just like when we take credit for whatever good we do others. We have to realize, just like Lord Indra, that *we* are just the *nimit karan,* and it is truly *Krishna* who is the *upadaan karan* and real cause.

Govardhan Hill, on the other hand, is a *real* provider but has no such arrogance like Lord Indra or ours'. It is humble even though it supplies all, such as food, water, shelter and so on. Therefore, it is worthy of worship. Krishna, being the *true* cause, is also then the *receiver* of that worship through Govardhan Hill. Therefore, the Govardhan Hill is Krishna's manifestation and kripa, or Shri Krishna Himself, whichever way you look at it.

The other part of this magnificent festival is that a multitude of food is placed before Govardhan Hill as offering to it as a token of our appreciation for what it does so selflessly for us. This grand offering of food is called *Anakoot.* Look at this aspect for a moment. It should teach us two things immediately, this being the second lesson to be learned. First, that we should not keep everything to ourselves, that we should share our fortune as our way of saying thank you. Second, we should realize that Govardhan, or really Krishna, should be the true *bhogi*, the true enjoyer, not us.

The Govardhan puja and festival is very festive. In addition to celebrating Nutan Varsh, it celebrates a time of renewal, a time of plenty when there is a new bounty of crops. But it *really* celebrates the selflessness of Govardhan and Krishna's mercy. But learn from the Govardhan. Humility is divine. Give, forgive and forget. *That* is true giving and true service, just like Govardhan. Do not hold on to the arrogance of giving. And remember who should really be the true enjoyer. When you remember these simple things it will make *Krishna* come looking for *you*, and not the other way around. Now, how cool is *that* notion?

You can spend an eternity looking for Krishna and still never find Him. Or, you can simply learn what Krishna is trying to teach us through Govardan, and He has to come find you! Problem solved! That is very cool indeed!

Remember, Krishna manifests to strengthen the resolve of His devotees, and to select a few by His mercy.

Are *you* ready to receive Shri Naathji's kripa?

Are *you* worthy yet?

Maha Shivratri

This festival is celebrated on the fourteenth night of the second half of the lunar month of Magh (February – March), or *Magh Vad 14*. It celebrates the auspicious re-union of *Sati* in the form of *Parvati* to Shiv on the night of their marriage.

The story of Sati's desire to go to Her father's yagna *uninvited* is known to all of us. Shiv asked Bhavani not to go, but She insisted. Shiv, being anter-yaami, knew what would happen, but could not stop it. Sati, humiliated, ignited Her body refusing to be a part of a family that would dare to dishonour Maha-Dev. Daksh, Sati's earthly nimit father, ended up getting the head of a goat at the end of it, a suitable outcome for those that dishonor the human form, dishonour Maha-Dev, and continue to blab "Meh-Meh" meaning "me" all their life!

The simple and yet highly significant lessons one needs to learn just from this little leela are several. First, one should not go where one is not welcome. Nothing good ever comes of it. Second, honor and worship genuinely all divine shaktis, and especially the special and truly bhole, Shiv. Third, if there is an elder in the family, whether a husband, a father, a mother, a sister or brother, listen to them thoughtfully, don't just hear them. If Sati had indeed listened to Shiv, the leela would be much different.

The most important lesson to be learned from this is by looking at the plight of Daksh raja. Cherish the human form and everything it stands for – truth, honesty, honor, integrity, respect, and ultimately the search for the ultimate truth.

This union of Shiv and Parvati is highly meaningful, but you must look deeper. Parvati is representative of a Jiv-aatma, so the union of Jiv and Shiv is indeed highly significant. This is really what *we all* need to be striving for when we celebrate Shivratri. We should endeavor to *achieve* our true purpose in life, which is where we, the Jiv-aatma, can unite with Shiv, the almighty. *That* is our true purpose, our true goal in life. The union of jiv with Shiv should be our ultimate motive, goal and priority in our human form. It is the only chance we get. Or else, we risk ending up like Daksh, in a multi-legged *Uni* or worse.

Of course it is a challenge. We have to earn that right, since we lost it once or more times. The fact that we are here at all is testimony to the realization that we are shuddh Aatmas no more! We know that even Parvati had to perform a lot of *tapasya,* austerities and sacrifice to achieve Shiv. We should be inspired by Her and learn from Her! We should also realize that unless we start early, achieving Shiv may remain only an illusion. Therefore, waste not a *kshan* or a moment of this precious human life! Worship Shiv with every fiber of your being, for that should be the ideal and the goal for any Jiv roaming the Universe inside the human form.

Shiv is best worshipped by worshipping the Shiv *ling* or *lingam*. The word *ling* means to unite with and merge in. Therefore, as Jiv, our purpose is to ultimately *unite* with Shiv. Look at the ling or lingam carefully. Think of uniting with it, for Maha Dev's Kripa is pre-requisite for ultimately escaping Maya.

Celebrate Shivratri festively, for it is the symbolic *milan* of Jiv with Shiv, illustrated and glorified by Parvati's union with Shiv. It is not easy, but nothing significant ever is. It requires a deep and burning longing on your part to achieve Shiv, and then the discipline to achieve victory over your own desires.

So, *hae Jiv*, *hae manav*, celebrate! Rejoice! Shivratri is what we have been waiting for. It is the culmination of everything that we aspire to, long for, work for and certainly live for as human beings.

He maanav, celebrate! For you, too, should aspire to be one with Shiv!

Of note, *Janmashtami* appears exactly a hundred and eighty days after *Maha Shivrati*, so that these two festivals neatly divide our calendar into two. How significant is that?

A *Jiv* gets not *one* but *two* opportunities a year to get Krishna's Kripa. Once at Janmashtami to invite Him into your heart, and once at Maha Shivratri to finally be one with Him.

Have *you* taken advantage of *either* opportunity yet?

Holi

The festival of Holi is celebrated on Fagun Sud Poonam, or *Fagun Sud 15* (February – March). Demographically, Holi is celebrated for different reasons, but we will look at this festival from one angle with one story only.

Holika, or Holi for short, was a paternal aunt to Prahalad Maharaj. Little Prahalad was a Vishnu devotee who would not give up singing praises of Narayan or reciting His holy name. Hiranyakashipu was the asur Raj, or Rakshas King, who was Prahalad's father. Hiranyakashipu also hated Vishnu because He had killed Hiranyaksh, who was Hiranyakashipu's brother.

Hiranyaksh and Hiranyakashipu were mighty asurs that were wreaking havok on the planet. Hiranyaksh was plundering the planet for gold, and had retrieved so much of it that the planet's harmonic balance was destroyed. Earth fell out of orbit and went to the bottom of the Garbodhak Ocean.

Vishnu, as *Varah*, retrieved the planet and restored its orbit. In the process, Hiranyaksh challenged and attempted to stop Varah, and the avataar ended up liberating the demon Hiranyaksh.

Hiranyakashipu was furious at His brother's death, and performed severe austerities to please Brahma, the Creator of the Universe. He got a boon from Him for supposed 'immortality.' Hiranyakashipu now became suddenly powerful and vowed to erase all devotion to Vishnu from earth, and to kill anybody that refused to do so.

To Hiranyakashipu's dismay, Prahalad, his very own son, was a devotee of the Lord from the very beginning, reciting His name from the womb under Narad Muni's blessing. When the mighty asur King punished little Prahalad in various ways to dissuade him from chanting the Lord's name, Prahalad persevered. Infuriated and mad with jealousy, Hiranyakashipu ordered little Prahalad's death. The many attempts to take Prahalad's life failed. Hiranyakashipu turned to his sister, Holika, who had a boon from Brahma to be protected from burning fire. Holi agreed to sit on a pyre with little Prahalad in her lap, and the order to light the pyre was given. Holi burned and Prahalad was untouched. Who can harm one who is under Narayan's protection?

We have several important lessons to learn from this story. One is that Narayan's protection of His devotees never fails, for He is *Achyut*.

Second is that we must never waver in our belief in Narayan. Third, Narayan should be the *kendra*, the center of our life. Fourth, we must burn the evil within us, symbolized by Holi. If and only if we burn the Holika within us can Prahalad, our innocent and fragile child of devotion, be safe. Otherwise, the fire of evil is always burning and is ever close, ready to engulf and consume our baby of devotion.

Celebrate Holi, do so festively, but do it meaningfully. *Look within*. Do genuine introspection and seek out the 'Holi' within each of us. Burn it, and let our devotion be safe. Do not shout abusively outwardly, for that will simply render you an arrogant fool who has no concept of the true meaning and significance of Holi.

Sing, dance, and rejoice! *You* have a chance to seek and burn the Holi within you!

Have *you* started yet?

Ramnavmi

This beautiful day falls on Chaitra Sud Nom (March-April), the ninth day of the bright half of the lunar month of Chaitra, *Chaitra Sud 9*. It celebrates the appearance day of Lord Ram, who is a *Maryada-Purshottam* avataar of the Supreme. Ram is also the very heartbeat of every Hindu and indeed Hindustaan.

This avataar establishes *adarsh* by example and self-sacrifice, meaning this avataar establishes the intricate relationships for family and society. This is an avataar that is also covered in some detail in *Chapter 10.5.1* dealing with the *Essential Hindu Scriptures*.

Though Lord Ram is an avataar capable of the magnificent feats of the Supreme, He is cautious and takes great care to avoid displaying this fact.

Ramnavmi is an important and festive celebration. Ram represents everything that is great in a person, a ruler, a husband, a son, a brother, a friend, and yes, even an enemy. There is so much to learn from this avataar that a mere lifetime becomes too short.

The importance and significance of this avataar is that the ten-headed demon lives *inside* each of us. When we cut off one head of desire or vaasna, another one will surely grow back. We need the help of Vibhishan as a *nimit karan*, signifying *vidya*, and Ram, signifying the Supreme's mercy, in ultimately killing this multi-headed and rejuvenating demon. Both *vidya*, the correct knowledge, and Shri Ram's kripa are necessary in overcoming *our* own demons.

Awake, my Hindu friends. Don't just *celebrate* RamNavmi. *Live* the true meaning of RamNavmi. Allow Shri Ram to be born in *your* heart as well, for that is the whole purpose of RamNavmi. Live *your* life with *adarsh*, with principles and morals, and love and cherish your relationships, for life is extremely short. What is life without truly meaningful relationships, honesty and integrity?

Are *you* truly ready for RamNavmi in *your* life? Has Shri Ram appeared in *your* heart yet?

Does *your* heart beat just for Ram?

Janmashtami

This magnificent day falls on *Sravan Vad Aathhum* (July-August) at midnight. It is the appearance day of the Supreme Lord Shri Krishna.

Remember, Shri Krishna descends as Himself. Shri Krishna is not merely an avataar, for He is PurnaPurshottam Bhagvan, descending as Himself in His supreme mercy and love for His true devotees.

At the initiation of this leela, He appeared before Devki and Vasudev as a *Chatur-Bhuj,* or four-armed, form to award His darshan to Vasudev and Devki, and all His devotees and devtas on Earth who had assembled in the prison for His first darshan. Upon Devki's request, He transforms into Ladoo-Gopal, nand-nandan Shyam Sunder bal-gopal Shri Krishna.

Pushti Maarg followers in the Vallabh Acharya sampraday worship this beautiful and most adorable baby form of the Supreme Lord Shri Krishna.

Janmashtami is a beautiful festival where bhajan and kirtan take place through much of the day, and devotees patiently fast. An idol of the lord is bathed with *panchamrut* and decorated. A small cradle is readied for baby Krishna's arrival at midnight. After midnight and the Lord's appearance, there is a midnight aarti and puja of the Lord, after which the fast is broken. This festival is the *only* exception to the rule of Hindus not eating late at night.

This festival is significant for many reasons, and most of them are well-known to all of us. However, what we need to take home is the fact that we need to have the Lord manifest in *our* hearts to fight the demons inside each of us that we alone can successfully not.

Krishna did not kill Maharaj Kans at birth. He basically grew up in Gokul to entertain His devotees with His leelas, and kill a few other great demons while He was at it. He was performing His leelas, but He was also testing the resolve of His devotees who had been so patiently waiting thus far. And this is an extremely important lesson for *us* to learn as well.

Just as Krishna's earthly parents Vasudev and Devki waited tolerantly for freedom from their bondage so, too, must we learn to patiently bear and wait to be free from *ours*. Krishna will also test our resolve and patience if we are His devotees.

Therefore, do not expect miracles, and especially overnight ones, in the path of divine bhakti. We have to get our heart ready and purified first, then patiently wait for Him to manifest in it. Once He manifests within, expect for there to continue to be challenges, just as Putna, Tarkasur, and so on arrived. These demons are within *us*, and come from *our* attachment to Maya. They are *our* demons, *not* Maya's and certainly not Krishna's. Remember that! He basically will help us overcome our challenges *if* we let Him.

The fasting period awaiting Krishna's arrival at midnight is significant. The fasting period signifies the purification process we must each go through before we can expect Krishna in our hearts. How can we invite Him into a filthy heart?

Therefore, once the heart is purified, Krishna will manifest. He will do so at midnight, and in the dark, while the rest of the world sleeps. Remember that while Ram comes by day, Krishna comes at night. This is significant as well. We must each be awake and vigilant while the rest of the world sleeps. Krishna calls this person that is vigilant while the rest of the world sleeps a *Muni,* or 'stable' person.[18]

Therefore, *if* we are able to purify our hearts, Krishna will come, for He is *achyut*. Ladoo-Gopal granted our initial desires and allowed us to play with His Maya, and to learn for ourselves firsthand that it really isn't where we truly belong. When we realize this and genuinely call to Him, He will come to root out the final demons from *within us* that we are too weak to root out on our own. These are strong demons, the ones in our hearts, and *we* produced them from our attachment to Maya. These demons grow in strength over time, and are beyond our ability to overcome by sheer self-discipline alone. These demons again are our indriyas, kamnas, vasnas, moha, and so on. Who can win alone against such mighty forces? Even the mighty rishis and sages fall prey to their own desire.

Krishna kripa is absolutely prerequisite and necessary, but it only comes to those that deserve it. Only by Krishna's mercy can these mighty obstacles be finally overcome, allowing us to go where we *really* and *truly* belong – Shri Krishna's lotus feet.

Celebrate, sing, dance, and be festive. But do it for the right reasons. Realize the limitations of your own ability and self-discipline to overcome your own dark demons. Understand *where* the battle needs to be fought. Look deep within your heart. Is it *really* ready for Krishna, or is there a little more cleansing to do before Nanda-Nandan Bal-Gopal can be welcomed in? Shyam Sunder in His *aseem kripa* is ready and waiting to descend and manifest in *your* heart.

Are you?

Radhastami

This glorious day falls on the *ashtam*, or the eighth day of the bright half of the lunar month of Bhadervo, or Bhadervo Sud Aathum, Bhadervo Sud 8. This is when Radharaani mercifully appeared in Barsana.

Radharaani is an ideal devotee of Krishna. Her mercy is easier to obtain than Krishna's. Krishna is mann-mohan, and Radharaani is mann-mohan mohini, the one that wins the heart of the one that wins all hearts! Her bhakti and prem for Krishna is solely for Krishna. It is never self-serving. That makes her *the* ideal devotee of the Lord. Therefore, a greeting of *Radhe-Radhe* is highly meaningful and full of love and glory for Krishna.

Radharaani is Shri Krishna's internal and integral energy, and therefore not an ordinary person. Radharaani is Krishna's eternal transcendental consort, and the main participant in the *Raas Leela*. She is the ideal devotee, one that exists solely for Krishna. Radha's relationship to Krishna is a transcendental secret and mystery, just like Krishna Himself!

Why Krishna does what Krishna does is only clear to Krishna.

For His devotees, learning from Radharaani and the gopis the *meaning* of sacrifice for the love of Shri Krishna is the *real* lesson to be learned. Let the Gopis and Radharaani show us *how* to worship Krishna, cherish Krishna, cry for Krishna, and bathe in the *shravan* and *kirtan* of Krishna's name for the sole purpose of *pleasing* Krishna, for that alone shall save us in Kal-yug.

We, with our limited faculties and tarnished hearts, can never understand Krishna and His mysteries. We can only *learn* what Krishna attempts to show us from His leelas, not *understand* them with our feeble and tainted minds. Only fools and arrogant thinkers attempt foolish and blasphemous attempts at 'understanding' Krishna and His relationships, for they fail to account for the simple fact that Krishna is simply interacting with His own internal transcendental energy! For such arrogant thinkers and fools, *eternal* misery awaits in the deepest fires of the darkest hells.

Learn from Radharaani and the gopis. Worship Krishna *solely* to please Krishna. Keep Krishna at the very core of your life. Love Him to please Him, not to extract anything out of Him. Live for Krishna, sing for Krishna, dance for Krishna, cook for Krishna, work for Krishna, eat for Krishna; in other words, your very life should revolve around Krishna.

Do *you* live just for Krishna? Is your *bhav* truly *Gopi bhav*, like Radharaani's?

Ganpati Visarjan

This is a beautiful and highly meaningful festival that has originated from southern India whose observation has been grossly distorted.

The festival starts from *Bhadervo Sud Chhutth*, or Bhadervo Sud 6, and lasts through Bhadervo Sud Chaudus. It is a ten day long festival in which Lord Ganesh is decorated and ceremoniously worshipped for this period, and at the conclusion of the festivities, is cast into the ocean.

The *meaning* behind this important festival is highly significant, but the *way* it is carried out is apraadh!

Awake, my Hindu friends! First realize *why* it is that we devote these ten wonderful days to worshipping Ganesh, and *why* it is that He is cast into the ocean. The way it is observed is incorrect, so the meaning and performance has become hugely altered.

Do not participate in apraadh! *Dev Apraadh!* We need to change one critical detail to give the correct meaning and significance to this beautiful festival.

Follow the logic in *Chapter 11.7*, and decide for yourself if *you* wish to participate in Dev Apraadh or change the one critical detail that tansforms it to DevPuja.

Navratri

Navratri is celebrated for nine nights beginning on the first night of the bright half of the lunar month of Asho (September-October), *Asho Sud 1*.

This is a glorious festival to celebrate and thank Krishna's feminine motherly divine shakti, *Maha-Devi* or *Mataji* who is known by many names such as Amba, Ambika, Durga, and so on. Mataji is *the* energy, the intelligence and the driving force, of us all.

We celebrate this festival to celebrate Her glories and properly thank Her for everything that she has bestowed upon us. This festival truly celebrates the 'motherly' aspect of the Supreme for there are several festivals that celebrate the 'fatherly' aspect of the Supreme.

This festival was also properly celebrated by Lord Ram and Lakshman, which should be of little surprise to anyone since Ram is maryada-purshottam Himself. Maa Durga is also celebrated for killing the demon Maisasur. Dashera, the tenth day of Navratri also known as Vijyadusmi, celebrates Maa Durga's victory over Maisasur.

We festively dance around a beautiful arrangement in the center consisting of a *garbo*, a clay pot with multiple holes in it, and a divo ghee lamp in it along with a picture of Mataji adorned with a beautiful garland of fresh flowers next to it. The philosophy in this set-up is astoundingly deep, simple and beautiful.

The garbo or clay pot with holes in it represents our material body, for our body is *sthool*, just like the *clay* of the pot, and has multiple holes in it such as ears, nostrils and so on, just like the clay pot does.

The divo inside the garbo signifies two things – our *chetna* or energy, which is really and truly a separated portion of the *divine* energy represented by Mataji. Therefore, this beautiful arrangement in the center is richly meaningful, and proper respect must be observed at all times.

There is also deep meaning in the purpose and the way that we celebrate. We festively dance around Mataji, reminding ourselves that as we do the dance of life, we will keep *Her* in the center of *everything* we do, think or say. With the goddess in the *kendra* or centre and focus of our life, we strive toward divinity. This is a promise we each silently make to Mataji as we dance festively around Her.

The purpose then is not simply to have a good time (which you assuredly will), but to also refresh yearly our vision, our purpose in life, and our promise to the merciful Mataji. Remember, she gives the vitality, the intelligence and so on, and therefore is responsible for our complete well-being, just like a mother. Therefore, with Mataji at the kendra, due respect must be observed at all times, and the dance festivals should be organized accordingly.

There is no hesitation in adding that those that do not believe in this philosophy and *observe* this respect need not put Mataji at the center simply as a show when they dance either obscenely or without faith. They belong in a dance hall, and not on a raas or garba floor!

Our raas and garbas are to be revered, and hark back to Vishnu's reverence of women in society, the respect they must command, and to the parampara that women pay homage to Maha Laxmi or her other energies as Durga, Aamba, etc., which are the 'motherly' aspect of the Supreme.

In Hinduism, mothers are truly revered, and this festival is the ultimate celebration of that motherly aspect of the Supreme. Please do not allow the soiling of this glorious festival and its celebration in any way all, for it will shame us all!

Finally, remember that the demon of Maisasur is alive in our *own* hearts.

Will you ask Durga to come to your aid in overcoming and killing that demon?

Are *you* ready for Maa Durga?

Diwali

This is a magnificent festival celebrated by lighting a multitude of rows of *divo* lamps, so it is also known as the *festival of lights*. It falls on the dark half (*Vad* or *Krishna Paksh)* of the lunar month of Asho, and is usually celebrated over three or five days. It starts on the thirteenth teethi with *Dhanteras*, and Diwali is on the fifteenth day, or *Amaas*, the darkest night of the month.

The first day of the festival is called Dhanteras. *Dhan* means wealth, and *terus* is the thirteenth day, which is why it is called dhanteras. Dhan is wealth, and is signified and personified by the Goddess *Laxmi*. Typically, this day is for Laxmi-Puja, and colorful divo lamps and rangoli patterns await her visit to the homes.

Remember, Goddess Laxmi is Vishnu-Pattni, and she is most delighted when one welcomes Her by welcoming Vishnu into their hearts and homes. Laxmi is agitated when invited by Herself, becomes *chanchal*, and leaves in a fit of anger if Vishnu is not adequately welcomed, leaving behind sadness and destruction in place of happiness and *pragrati*.

Therefore, earn *your laxmi* correctly, with honesty and integrity. Typically, traders worship their accounting books on this day, so it is also called *chopra*, or book, *poojan* or worship. The idea is still the same, which is to signify Laxmi puja, and chopra, or business books, are only existent if there is any wealth to speak of, or rather, write of.

Dhanteras also signifies and celebrates the appearance of Dhanwantari Bhagvan, the divine physician, who appeared with medicine. Thus was the start of ayurvedic medicine.

The second night, which is the fourteenth night of thc dark fortnight, is *Kali Chaudus*, or 'dark' chaudus. Typically, Hanuman puja is done on this dark night to ward 'evil spirits' away that may take advantage of the dark night. Hanuman Chaalisa is faithfully recited, for Goswami Tulsidas tells us in it that by doing so, *bhutt pisach nikat nahi aawe,* meaning horrible ghosts and goblins are kept at bay by Lord Hanuman's protection.

The next day is Diwali, also known as Deepavali, which celebrates two wonderful victories and occasions. The first is the glorious return of Lord Ram to Ayodhya after 14 years of exile. The Ram Avatar is a *Maryada Purshottam* avatar establishing *adarsh* by example and self-sacrifice, meaning this avatar establishes the intricate relationships for family and society.

Lord Ram carefully avoids demonstrating his Supreme or divine abilities in Krishna's descension as Ram as His goal was to establish a path that even the simplest of all in a society is able to follow. However, Lord Ram's return to Ayodhya is one of the very few places that Bhagvan Ram demonstrates is *Ishwariya* by becoming many from one. He does this to satisfy the *Ayodhyavaasis*' unspoken desire to *individually* and *simultaneously* greet Lord Ram *immediately* upon His return.

This is also significant in that the return of Ram to everyone's hearts individually and personally is what banishes darkness, even if it is as dark as the darkest fortnight in Krishna Paksh, *amaas*. Therefore, deepavali must entail the personal and individual entrance of Lord Ram, after what may seem or even be an eternity, into even the darkest of hearts, *ours*.

The second victory celebrated on this day is Krishna's liberation of the demon Narakasur, who would kidnap young and defenseless maidens. This was a demon too powerful to be killed without divine help, and Krishna, in His mercy, obliges. These defenseless maidens signify our fragile and defenseless devotion and spirituality, which are routinely kidnapped by our demons signified by our maan and our indriya.

In some places, to celebrate Diwali, a ten-headed Ravan-figure is set alight with great festivities. However, this is an *apraadh* and a display of avidya and ignorance.

There are several reasons for saying exactly this. Firstly, because Ravan is also an avataar, a divine shakti. Do not forget that Ravan was a Pundit, A great Shiv bhagat, an avataar of Lord Vishnu's *dwarpal*, the door sentry, and someone who treated Sita with the greatest of respect by keeping Her *separately* in Ashok Vatika! Would a barbarian act in such a divine and respectful way? Of course not! Only misguided fools think of Ravan as a barbarian. Ravan had a role to play in Ram's leela, one that he played sincerely and yet very respectfully. In fact, when the *yudh*, the war, was on with Ram the rule was that all fighting was stopped at sunset. Once the fighting stopped, there was no 'friend' or 'foe,' and everyone was free to mingle without fear. Ravan was such a pundit that Ram actually sent Laxman every evening to Ravan to learn the scriptures from Ravan! Therefore, Ravan's *punditai*, his knowledge and bhakti, were immense and unquestionable!

Hence, though Ravan was an asur for sure, he was also a bhagat and a pundit as well. If you look closely within yourself, do you not see that, to a varying extent, we each posses these same diametrically opposed qualities as well?

Look within, then, and you will quickly realize the significance of this statement. Who, then, are *we* to judge Ravan? Only Ram can judge! And even then, and especially then, Ravan's fallen body was treated with respect befitting a fallen hero by Ram! So why should we do something that even Ram would disapprove of? We should not be performing such barbaric acts, for *we* are not judges! Furthermore, the ten-headed demon resides in each of our hearts, and *that* is where the battle must be fought! Even Mahatma Gandhi said as much!

So learn from Ram and Gandhiji!

Enough of these barbaric and outward shows of bravery! Let us see how *we* really each fight the *true* battle for Hinduism, our samaaj, our culture, and our dharam!

Diwali, ultimately and truly, is a festival where we light rows of *divo* lamps to banish darkness, or *avidya*, and celebrate the return or entrance of Lord Ram and Lord Krishna, or *vidya* and light, back into *our* hearts and lives, pure and simple. This is the whole meaning and purpose of this beautiful festival. If all you do is light rows of divo lamps, burn Ravan-figures, or have a great time, you will have missed the boat! The one boat that will enable you to cross bhav-sagar. That *would* be a genuine tragedy indeed!

So, let us summarize the *significance* and true purpose of Diwali.

Ravan and Narkasur are symbolic of the demons in our own hearts, and the dark half of the lunar month of Asho signifies the avidya, the lack of knowledge of Ram and Krishna, in our hearts. The lighting of the rows of divo lamps should signify the return of vidya, personified by Lord Ram and Lord Krishna, within our hearts with the true knowledge and wisdom.

What makes us human above other creatures in creation is our *ability* to discriminate between Ram or Krishna, the Supreme, from His Maya.

Is there illumination from the divo lamps simply in your external house, or is there really illumination within the house that your aatma resides in? What demons do we harbor within our hearts that need Ram and Krishna's help?

Ponder, man, ponder. But don't wait too long. Life is very short, and will be over before you know it. Be festive. Rejoice. But only if you are willing to let the *prakash,* the light, of vidya into your own hearts, and let Ram and Krishna help kill your demons.

Therefore, first look within. That is the first step. Identifying these allows us to realize our own shortcomings. Is there festivity in your heart illuminated by little divo lamps of vidya, or is your heart dark and unilluminated from avidya and ignorance?

Hence, first look within, and identify the demons *Ravan* and *Narakasur* within yourselves. Having identified these, seek divine help. Ram and Krishna are *achyut*, and they will always respond to a true devotee's call for help.

Have *you* identified *your* multi-headed demons?

Are you ready to ask for Ram and Krishna's help?

9.3: Parting Thoughts

There are many important Hindu festivals, and they are demographically or geographically significant. Regardless of demographics, there is almost always a deep-seated philosophy behind them. Sure, they are festive. Religion and Hari-bhajan is very festive. But if *Hari* is taken out, and mere festivities are all that remain, then the significance is lost, and there is no spiritual or cultural purpose served. The gathering becomes a façade, a social and bogus pretext, and ultimately a place that broods idle gossip, malice, and mischief.

Sadly, this is indeed what is happening today. Only the social aspect remains today. People gather and have a 'great' time. There is dancing but, alas, what kind of dancing! There is no Hari in the festivities. What is even more ominous is that organizers have added a financial aspect to it thereby making it a lucrative business. So, what used to be great religious, sentimental and glorious functions have been pared down to highly profitable and social gatherings.

Without Hari at the center of your festivities, the festivities that should be highly spiritual, beautiful, meaningful and reconciliatory become social miscarriages that are mindless, meaningless, derogatory, blasphemous, arrogant, pretentious, and divisive.

Awake, my Hindu friends! Shun such activities that ridicule our beautiful and deeply meaningful festivities. Let brokers of fraud and religious malice flock alone and propagate their own karam and subsequent misery. *Vote with your absence in such activities!* Find ways to re-vitalize the *true* religious and cultural festivals and festivities that used to be the envy of even the devtas.

To glorify Krishna by singing and dancing is the most joyous expression of our *bhakti*, our devotion. He should be at the very core, the very center, of *everything* we do in life. *That* is the real meaning of festivities.

Awake, my Hindu friends, and understand *why*, for it will forever change your life! Your festivities will take on a beautiful and blissful new meaning. *Festive* will be inside every atom in your body *if* you can understand the significance of the festivities. You will be bursting with joy and happiness that is otherwise difficult to experience and realize. Therefore, knowing for whom you sing and dance, and why you sing and dance will transform that festivity into a divine and spiritual experience that will stay with you for an eternity.

If we only let the festivals teach us their *true* purpose, we will *bloom* with *true* joy and burst with happiness. Then, with joy in our hearts, we can truly rejoice, truly sing and truly dance!

Let the festivities *truly* begin!

CHAPTER 10

Hindu Spiritual Philosophy I: The Essential Hindu Scriptures

The Veds, the Ramayan, the Shrimad Bhagwat, and the Shrimad Bhagwat Gita are the spiritual treasure, the true guide and, indeed, the very life of all Hindus.

10.1: Background

Before there were computers and e-mails, there was paper and written text for the storage of knowledge. Prior to that, it was the papyrus. Before that was stone etchings, wall paintings and carvings. And prior to even that?

There were really two ways that knowledge was imparted in ancient India among the great *rishis*. It was either heard (*shravan*) or remembered or meditated on (*smaran*). Vedic knowledge then, in its earliest form, was passed down in a discipular succession, or *parampara*, by either of these two methods. It was not until much later that knowledge was actually recorded in a written form. When it was finally written down, it was done so in *the language of the gods*, Sanskrit.

Shruti: Knowledge acquired by *shravan*, or hearing. This knowledge is considered more perfect because it is *revealed* knowledge. Therefore, scriptures are sometimes referred to as *shrutis*.

Smruti: Knowledge acquired by *smaran*, that is, by remembering or meditating. However, realize that knowledge acquisition by meditation can only be accomplished by yogis.

Sanskrit; *The* language of the Gods

Sanskrit is the original and most complete language, one so rich and full that it is not subject to interpretation in pronunciation. Yet, Sanskrit is highly flexible. Simply put, it is *the language of the gods*.

The most important scriptures are recorded in this language that has no equal. It can be challenging to learn Sanskrit at any age, but the rewards are immense to a Hindu. When one is not able to read, write or understand it, several problems arise. The most important one is that since Sanskrit has no equal, translating *from* it may cause a loss of meaning, value or diminished significance or impact. You are then at the mercy of the mental faculties, attitudes, training and the school of thought *tampering* the deliberation process of the translator. Even more ominous and derogatory to entire generations of scholars is the deliberate misinterpretation for the masses by some non-Hindus or their paid Hindu representatives with a purpose to misinform and mislead or misguide as is thought to have happened with Vedic translations in colonial and pre-colonial times.

Therefore, interpretations by non-acharyas should be treated with a grain (or should I say a tonne?) of salt! Hence, when reading translations of scriptures, one must only follow paths that are "personalist" rather than "impersonalist" and have the correct discipular succession. A translation of a scripture without the correct such *parampara* may result in a confused, altered, distorted, or even incorrect message to a *sadhak*, resulting in loss of your ultimate spiritual goal, Shri Krishna.

10.2: Overview of the Classification of Hindu Scriptures

It is very helpful to have a brief *overview* of the classification scheme that is used to generally organize the main Hindu scriptures. The basis of this system is whether the scripture is a *shruti* or a *smruti.*

As we proceed through this section, it is important to note that although traditionally a *shruti* scripture has had more weight as a revealed scripture, *smrutis* are not to be considered less significant in any way, especially when a *smruti* scripture has been authored by a known or revealed avataar.

For example, the *Veds* are considered to be a *shruti* scripture, and were traditionally considered *the* most important for they are a revealed scripture. However, the same author and avataar also wrote the scriptures that became classified as *smrutis*, such as the *Brahma Sutras*, the *Shrimad Bhagwat,* and so on.

Consequently, one must not be judgmental in this organizational method. It is merely a broad system to *classify* the scriptures based on their origination, plain and simple. Therefore, classification of the Hindu scriptures is simply based on whether the scripture is a *shruti* or a *smruti* in its origin.

It may be helpful to refer to *Illustration 5: The Broad Classification System of Hindu Scriptures* on the following page as needed a we proceed through this section.

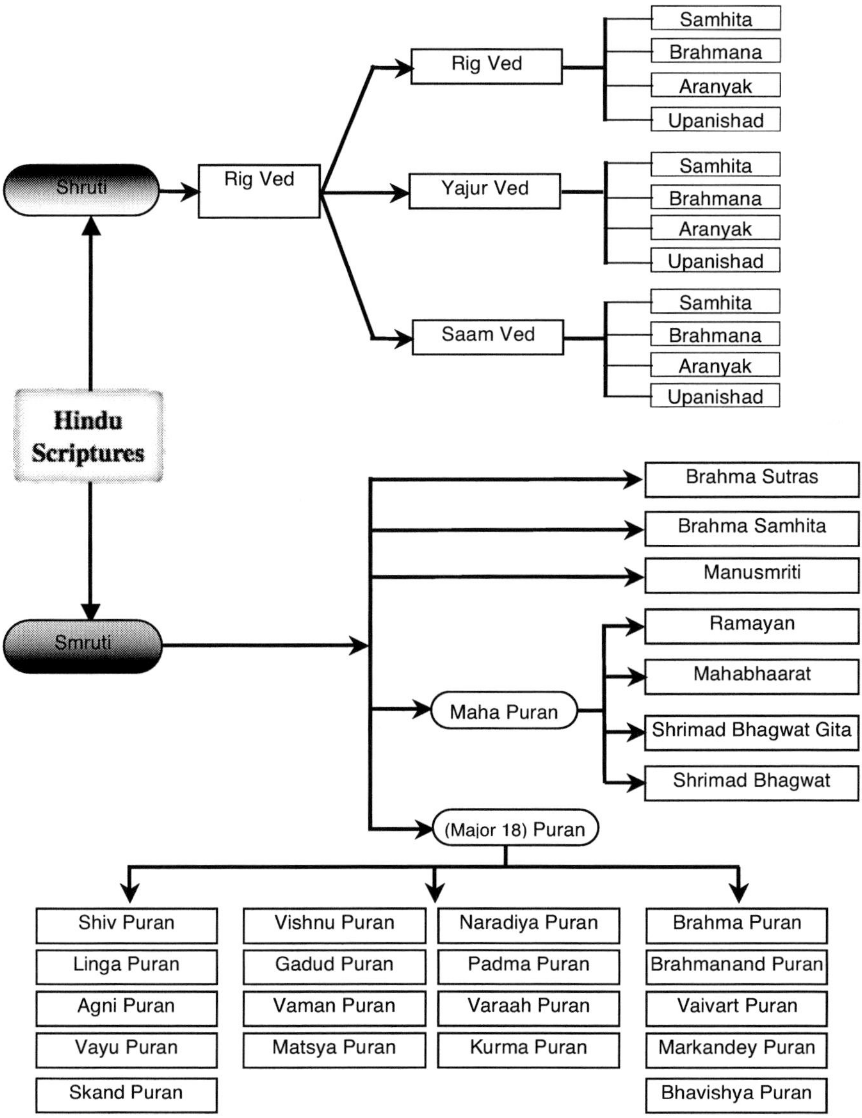

Illustration 5: The Broad Classification System of Hindu Scriptures

10.3: The Veds

Background.

The term *Ved* is derived from *Vid*, or to know. This implies that the Veds contain *vidya*, or the correct knowledge.

The Veds are technically classified as a *shruti*, or revealed scripture, but really and truly are neither a shruti nor a smruti. They are formed from Krishna's breath and are, therefore, truly eternal. Hence, they always exist, and are never lost or attained.

The *parampara*, or discipular lineage is by *shruti*, so they are classified as a *shruti* in that regard. Realize, though, that the Veds are eternal, and they *always* exist. Technically and correctly, then, the Veds are neither a shruti nor smruti.

The Veds are the original recorded scriptures. The *Veds* are the *original* and ancient scriptures of not just the Hindus, but indeed of the entire world!

From the Veds were derived the *Upanishads*. After the Upanishads came the *Purans*, three of which are the most familiar to most of us as *Shrimad Bhagwat Gita, Shrimad Bhagwat,* and the *Ramayan*, all three of which are categorized as *Maha*Purans.

There are many other important works and treasures such as the *Brahma Sutra*, *Shri Brahma Samhita*, and so forth, but which are outside the scope of this outline to detail.

The Origin of Veds

The correct derivation of the original Ved, *Rig Ved* is as follows. Shri Krishna gave the knowledge of the Veds in an abbreviated form via His flute to Lord Brahma, the secondary creator. Brahma then granted this knowledge to His son, Naarad Muni, who then gave this knowledge to Veda Vyas.

The 'origin' of the Veds is sometimes sticky but it should really not be, for the scriptures themselves describe the beginning of the Veds. For our purposes, understand again the simple fact that they are eternal and always exist. Okay, let us continue with their origin.

Veds were initially contained in one Ved and spread by the *oral* tradition, by *parampara* and discipular lineage, and so existed as a *shruti*. VedaVyas, as He came to be known, took the one Ved as it existed, the *Rig Ved*, and recorded them as the three Veds, *Rig*, *Yajur* and *Saam*.

VedaVyas is the Supreme's seventeenth avataar, in the form of *Krishna-Dvaipayan*, who came to be known as *Bhagvan VedaVyas* after expounding the Veds, according to the *Shrimad Bhagwat*. VedaVyas also wrote the definitive commentary on the Veds that came to be known as the *Brahma-Sutras* or the *Vedanta-Sutras*.

So originally, there was only one Ved. The other two are derivatives of the first. The fourth, *Atharva* Ved, may really be an 'adopted' Ved, and is not always readily or widely accepted as part of *the* Veds. To highlight this fact, Krishna mentions the three Veds in the Gita but not the fourth, Atharva.[19] Therefore, the *strong* inclination here is to abide by Krishna's notation of the three Veds mentioned, and hence to classify the fourth as an 'adopted' *granth* and not necessarily a Ved.

The original Ved was initially handed down verbally from one generation of great sages to another, and was eventually expounded upon and compiled and recorded in the written form. This monumental task was done by VedaVyas, who took the one existing Ved and expounded it into three or four Veds. These 'new' volumes of Veds were then painstakingly recorded into the written form. But recorded and written by whom? Who *actually* wrote them down on paper? Not Bhagvan VedaVyas! He undertook the monumental task of expanding the one Ved into the multiple volumes, and dictated them to be written down. And His scribe? Well, the answer may even surprise you. It was none other than Lord Ganesh!

Wow! *Aum Shri Ganeshai Namahah!*

The Veds generally each have four sections to them. The first part is the *samhita*, or the section on Hymns or *Mantras*. The *karma-kaand* or *rituals* are the second part, known as the *Brahmana*, the third are *theology*, known as the *Aranyak*, and the fourth are the philosophical interpretations and intellectual *manthan* of it all, and are termed *Ved-ant*, or *Upanishads*. The Upanishads are regarded as part of the Veds and are also known as Vedantic knowledge.

Another view of the Veds is presented by commentaries, or *bhashyas*, on the Veds by great people. Collectively the Upanishads and the bhashyas, then, comprise the teachings of the Ved – the knowledge of God – as interpreted and intellectualized by the various great rishis and also great acharyas of the past – Ram Anuj Acharya, Shankar Acharya, Nimbark Acharya, and so on. Therefore, depending on the treatise, there will evolve a school of thought from it, and its discipular succession and following. There are reportedly six great such acharyas, and over a hundred Upanishads.

The Veds

The three, or four, Veds, then, are as follows:

Rig Ved.

It is reputed to be the oldest work in the world. Its' date is difficult to ascertain, and was written in the original version of Sanskrit. It is the book of *Mantras* or Hymns, and deals with science and knowledge of the Universe and truth, or God. It is regarded as *the* most important Ved. The *Gayatri Mantra* originates from this Ved.

Saam Ved.

A beautiful musical or 'chant' version, derived from the Rig Ved. It represents the devotional aspect of the Veds. Beautiful *stutis* by devtas are contained in here.

Yajur Ved.

This Ved deals with the rituals and performances that aim to purify the mind and consciousness.

Atharva Ved.

The "adopted" Ved, and most likely not a Ved as Krishna fails to mention this 'Ved' while clearly specifying the other three in the *Gita*. This book deals with medicine, potions, charms and the occult. It is not accepted by all as part of the Veds, and hence the concept of three Veds, rather than four. It is only presented here for the sake of completenes and to highlight the controversy over it. Although it does have some of the hymns 'borrowed' from the Rig Vd, it has more in common with other priestly handbooks which deal more with sorcey, sacrifice, and spells.

Closing Thoughts

Shri Krishna in *Shrimad Bhagwat Gita* states that *He* is *Rig Ved*, *Yajur Ved* and *Saam Ved*,

Pita hum asya jagato
Mata dhata pitamaha
Vedayam pavitram omkara
Rig Saam Yajur eva ca[20]

The *Bhagwat Gita's* message is that *Krishna* is the *Brahman*, the Supreme, which the three Veds describe and attain to. Therefore, the Supreme Knowledge of the Veds and their ultimate goal is to realize Shri Krishna.

Jai Shri Krishna!

10.4: The Brahma Sutras

The *Brahma Sutras* represent the definitive *commentary*, or *bhashya*, on the *Veds* written by Bhagvan Veda Vyas Himself.

It is so called because it is written in little *threads* or *aphorisms* called *sutras* that represent complete lines. Each sutra begins and ends with an *Aum*. The Brahma Sutra begins *Athatho Brahma Jignasa* which loosely translated means *let us begin the discovery of the Supreme* personality.

The *Brahma Sutras* broadly consist of four sections. The first two are a discussion on the relationship of Jiv and the Supreme, the third is a discussion on how a Jiv should act, and the last describes what the outcome of such action might be, with the goal being to return Home to the Supreme.

The *Brahma Sutras* represent a prized treasure in Hinduism. For those serious about the Vedantic knowledge, reading and attempting to comprehend the priceless knowledge contained in the *Brahma Sutras* is essential.

Closing Thoughts

Although the Brahma Sutra represents a *bhashya,* or commentary, on the Veds, it is written by the same author that authored the Veds and, therefore, must be treated as a scripture, not merely a *bhashya.*

Regardless of what else the Brahma Sutras may say after *Athatho Brahma Jignasa,* we as humans need to look only at this first sutra, for it will literally change your life if you *live* this sutra.

Examine this beginning comment, *Athatho Brahma Jignasa,* very carefully.

Does it not dawn on you that this sutra is not just a mere comment but rather a directive, a purpose, a message, a signboard, if you will, about what to do, and your true and real purpose in life? Wake up, *jaago*, awake, my Hindu friends!

If you can simply follow this little *sutra* all your life, you will be a giant step closer to Krishna. For this*, the inquiry into the Supreme,* should truly be the focus and goal of your life and your very existence! You should live to inquire into the Supreme all your life, every moment of your life, with every breath of your life!

If you can genuinely put into life-long practice this little sutra, *Athatho Brahma Jignasa*, then Krishna Himself will pave the way to Him for you.

10.5: The Brahma Samhita

This is an interesting scripture. Some do not see it as one, but it really is.

The *Brahma Samhita* was 'spoken' by Brahma, the 'creator' of the universe when He received His wisdom from the Supreme.

Let us visit just a portion of *Creation* as it relates to Brahma. We are going to skip a few steps as we are interested only in how the *Brahma Samhita* originated here.

When Brahma first came into being from Vishnu's navel, there was nothing but absolute darkness everywhere. Brahma, the first created being, is endowed with extreme intelligence to begin with. So Brahma initially sets out to explore His surrounding on His own using His own intelligence. This 'exploration' presumably lasted about a hundred human years and got Brahma nowhere. He returned to His lotus, and heard *'tap'* or 'meditate' within His heart. Therefore, Brahma started meditation.

Krishna, pleased with Brahma's meditation, played His flute. The sound of this flute entered Brahma's ears, and from there entered His heart. Upon this occurrence, Brahma was granted *darshan* of Vaikunth Lok. Saraswati then blessed Brahma's *vaani*, or His speech, and from Brahma's divine mouth poured the Brahma Samhita, the first verse of which is the *Brahma Gayatri Mantra*, and the knowledge of the Veds was thus granted to Brahma by Krishna's flute.

The origination of the *Brahma Gayatri Mantra*, therefore, or the *Gayatri mantra* for short, is Krishna's flute and Brahma's *vaani*. This mantra is the crown jewel of all mantras, but is a treasure that must be received in discipular succession.

Recitation and meditation of the *Gayatri mantra* must be received from the Guru, and must only be recited by males but never by females. Even the males must go through processes that a guru prescribes before being able to recite it.

The Brahma Samhita is not fully understood by many. Chapter five, the one known, was 'discovered' in a temple by Lord Chaitanya in His travels through India.

The *Brahma Samhita* is of paramount importance in that it is uttered by the secondary Creator Brahma Himself upon the receipt of Krishna's wisdom and mercy by Krishna's flute.

10.6: The Purans & the Maha Purans

Background

These are books of events that Hindus believe actually occurred in the past. They are regarded as historical books or epics, rather than simple mythology. There are eighteen main Purans in all.

The three most important Purans are the *Ramayan*, the *Shrimad Bhagwat*, and the *Shrimad Bhagwat Gita*, the last derived from, or actually a part of, the *Mahabharat*. These three, the *Ramayan*, the *Bhagwat*, and the *Gita* are categorized as *Maha* Purans, or *great* Purans, within the broad category of Purans.

The term 'Bhagwat Gita' translated means the *Geet* or *song* sung by *Bhagvan Himself*, or the Supreme Lord Himself, Shri Krishna. For one who is fortunate enough to read and understand this last scripture, this is *the* very *essence,* the very cream of the knowledge hidden in the Veds and spoken by Shri Krishna Himself.

Shrimad Bhagwat and *Shrimad Bhagwat Gita* are regarded as *Maha*Purans, because the actual speaker is Lord Krishna Himself. These are the only two instances, then, where the term 'Shrimad' is applicable. Along with *Ramayan*, these are *the* most important scriptures for a Vaishnav. Therefore, a very short introductory description of each will be given here along with a prayer to the reader to explore these divine treasures individually, as fully as possible, and then repeat, over and over and over again for eternity. Sounds like a prescription, doesn't it? It is – one prescribed by the great sages of Bhaarat to attain the ultimate truth.

Most Hindus also know the story of Gopeshwar. Lord Shiv attained without hesitation a Gopi form in order to enter *Maha Raas* with Shri Krishna and the rest of the gopis. This beautiful form of Lord Shiv is called *Gopeshwar*. This demonstrates the divine love that Lord Shiv has for Shri Krishna, and His message to us then is also the same: Shri Krishna's *bhakti* is the ultimate goal of human life. On a side note, it is very important to have complete faith in Shri Krishna, for without complete faith, one is not granted access. The story goes that the Goddess Laxmi was not able to participate in the *Maha Raas* simply because She had the aham, or ego, of being the great Goddess Laxmi and not that of a gopi, a devotee.

10.6.1: Ramayan

The *Ramayan* is the single most important teacher of the principles and relationships in and of life. It teaches a society, nay, a nation, how relations and relationships are to be treasured and cherished. It demonstrates how various interpersonal relationships should be such as father-son, mother-son, husband-wife, brother-brother, guru-disciple, King or ruler and its people, and so on. Ramayan teaches us the value of the spoken word and here is where the adage *Praan jaaye per vachan na jaaye* is derived from. Lord Ram is the *Maryada Purshottam Avataar* that leads by example, and Sita, His earthly wife, represents the embodiment of *bhakti*.

This scripture is most enjoyable in the *rus-filled* version written by Goswami Tulsidas, but the original and historically correct version is the one written by the great sage Valmiki who achieved perfection only after *sansari disillusionment* and sixty thousand years of *tap*. Valmiki rushi derived this great scripture from Naarad Muni. Therefore, the authoritative and discipular succession and rendition of Valmiki Ramayan is undeniable.

The style of the Valmiki Ramayan is more of a historical narrative or documentary, and therefore, more "dry" and less appealing for a sadhak seeking bhakti rus. *Tulsi Ramayan,* or *Ram Charit Maanus*, is more of a story-telling approach with more emotion and feeling, and thus more able to satisfy a *rasik-jan's* desire for bhakti. *Tulsi Ramayan*, then, is immensely more popular and therefore, more frequently quoted from.

This 'epic' is comprised of several books, known as *kaands*, with each kaand having several chapters. These represent the original books, and most experts ascertain that *Uttar Kaand* was added later, but it remains unclear whether it was added by Valmiki or not.

The value of Ramayan recited over and over in a Vaishnav family cannot be over-emphasized. Goswami Tulsidas says in his *Ram Charit Maanus* the phrase *ek ghari adhi ghari, adhi me puniyad,* stressing the importance of daily and regular recital from the *Ramayan*. Loosely translated, if not 24 minutes a day *(ek ghadhi)* then at least half of that *(aadhi ghadhi),* and if still more pressed for time, than a quarter of that or 6 minutes a day, one must with family chant or recite daily His holy name to cut innumerable sins *(kate koti apraadh)*. Therefore, sins accumulated from over several lifetimes start to get washed away if one follows this simple practice.

The additional benefits from a family doing this, or any such activity stressing the importance of regular bhakti, bhajan or kirtan, has immeasurable benefits that are not simply religious, but social as well, infusing peace and harmony within the family through a multitude of generations. A family that encourages and practices such 'ghar sabhaa' becomes sublimely transformed. Such a family becomes a *prem-parivaar*, where the only quarrel would be who would do more for the other. Such a family becomes well positioned not just in spiritual advancement, but also financial, communal and social advancement as well. A prem-parivaar survives trials and tribulations of life much better.

Also in *Tulsi Ramayan* is the beautiful *Hanuman Chaalisa*, a glowing tribute to Hanuman, Ram's eternal and humble servant. Hanuman is the very embodiment of selfless service to the Lord in *dasya bhav*, which is *exactly* what all true Vaishnavs should aspire to.

A Vaishnav family should have a special altar to Lord Hanuman to derive strength and inspiration from Him, as well as guidance on how a Vaishnav should serve the Lord simply for the Lord's satisfaction, and want or expect nothing in return.

10.6.2: Shrimad Bhagwat

Shrimad Bhagwat is cherished as the *dhan* or treasure of the Vaishnavs, and as thc *Samhita* of the *Paramhansos*, the great renounced sages and rishis of Bhaarat.

It is said that it takes the cumulative *poonias* (good deeds) of many, many births to finally be privileged enough to be able to listen to this priceless scripture. It was originally recited in only four *shloks* (thereby known as *Chatur-Shloki* Bhagwat) by Bhagvan Narayan Himself to Brahma, the secondary creator in the holy Trinity.

Brahma recited it to His son, Naarad Muni who then recited it to Veda Vyas. Veda Vyas then expounded and detailed it *(vistaar)* and passed it to His son, Shri Shukdevji maharaj, a great renounced sage from a very young age. Shukdevji then recited it to Abhimanyu's son, the great Emperor and King, Parikshith, at the banks of the holy Ganges River at King Parikshith's request. This *samwaad,* their divine interaction, was witnessed by many great rishis.

King Parikshith, a mighty King, had made a gross error by looping a dead snake around the neck of a rishi submerged in Samadhi, or deep meditation. He had been out whole day and was hungry and thirsty when he happened upon the rishi's ashram. However, the rishi was completely oblivious to the King in his state, and the King became frustrated. Angry, his eyes fell upon a dead snake lying off to the side, and he picked it up thoughtlessly, aware only of his unmet need for nourishment or welcome as a King by the rishi. The rishi's son was enraged when he returned and saw this and cursed the King to die in seven days from a lethal snakebite. The King, having realized what he had done, sought penance, and was pleased when he heard that he was to die in seven days as this was punishment that fitted the heinous crime he had committed.

However, having thus been put on notice about the remainder of his life, the great king lost interest in all things earthly and material, and sought only spiritual enlightenment and eventual salvation. He gave up his throne, renounced everything and left. At the banks of the Holy Ganges River he sat fasting without food and water seeking this amongst the rishis there, seeking the answer to his question of what a man who only has seven days to live should do. However, when none of the present rishis could satisfy his inquiry, Shukdevji appeared (manifested) and granted him the knowledge that is the *Shrimad Bhagwat*.

Note here a simple but enormously important lesson. That is, if you genuinely and *truly* have a *burning* desire for the ultimate truth, just as the great Emperor Parikshith did, then Krishna Himself will manifest through a guide and teacher as a Shukdevji to fulfill your *just* longing and yearning for the ultimate truth and for *your* ultimate benefit.

This treasure, then, the *Shrimad Bhagwat*, represents a dying man's desire for freedom from all bondage, spiritual enlightenment and subsequent salvation. Shrimad Bhagwat banishes *avidya*, or ignorance, and induces the *rus*, the *bhakti* and *prem*, the nectar for Krishna bhakti as well as to free the aatma from bondage for eternity. The seven days are highly meaningful, for we all really have only seven days, Monday through Sunday. We, too, should be urgently seeking freedom from the fear of death and freedom from bondage. King Parikshak was fortunate enough to know he was going to live for seven days. *We* can't even be sure of seven breaths!

Shrimad Bhagwat to a Hindu represents God, simply put. It *is* God. It is Shri Krishna. This is why this Holy Scripture is adorned with flowers, Puja, and aarti. The different parts of the scripture denote different parts of Shri Krishna. As we progress through the scriptures, we are treated to different *darshans* of Shri Krishna.

The plunge into *Shrimad Bhagwat* can be intoxicating – an intoxication that lasts a lifetime or an eternity if one is fortunate enough. It is ever present and available to a *sadhak*, whereas Shri Krishna as *Bhagvan* may not be. Therefore, it represents an immediately accessible and more merciful form of God – one that does not take yugs or many lifetimes to acquire. Therefore, this form of Shri Krishna is absolutely priceless.

Shri Krishna in the *Shrimad Bhagwat* states over and over that one who recites or reads regularly even a word from this treasure shall never be forgotten by Him. Realize, then, the importance of regular recitals from the scriptures, and remember that not even a drop of devotion to Krishna, not a single step towards Him, is ever wasted.

This *granth* fulfills a Hindu's desire of liberation. The one who seeks knowledge, or *gnani*, is liberated from material bondage and thus achieves *Mukti,* and a *bhagat* or devotee by faith and surrender achieves the lotus feet of God Himself, or *Moksh.*

Closing Thoughts

Shrimad Bhagwat is for *true* Krishna devotees only. It contains the confidential pass times of the Supreme Lord Shri Krishna. It is not for the *jaddh*, *mooddh*, *abhimaani, ghamandi*, *asuri*, *nasthik*, *vidyavaan*, and egotistical or arrogant people.

Approach it only if you are truly and genuinely seeking Shri Krishna and Krishna's *bhakti*. If you approach it for any other reason, such as with arrogance and *false* wisdom, be warned that on one of the ten *shules*, or tridents, as described in the *Brahma Samhita*, is where *you* will meet your fate.

It is said that it takes the cumulative poonias of many lifetimes to be able to hear or read the treasure that is the Shrimad Bhagwat. However, it takes only a *kshan*, or a moment, to dawn on you that Krishna *is*, indeed, the real and *true* goal of human life.

And realize that *this realization* can *only* come with Krishna's *kripa*, Krishna's mercy.

10.6.3: Shrimad Bhagwat Gita

The *Shrimad Bhagwat Gita* literally means the *Song of The Lord*, *geet* meaning *song*, and *Bhagwat* meaning of *Bhagvan,* or the Lord Shri Krishna. As a text, it is an integral and yet an extremely significant part of the great Puran *Mahabharat*.

Oddly enough, there is an old wife's tale that one must never have a copy of the *Mahabharat* in the house, as it will most certainly start a feud or a family *yudh!* Nothing could be further from the truth. Man does and *should* get into trouble listening to old wive's tales! Mahabharat itself is an *adhbhut granth*, a wonderful historical epic, which also deserves your sincere and unalloyed attention.

The *Gita* originates on the sacred battlefield of *Kurukshetra*.

The mighty armies of the *Kauravs* and the *Pandavs* are poised in military formation against each other. The conch-shells of the mighty Kaurav army are blown by the various commanders, and then the conch-shells of the mighty Pandav army are blown. The sounds of the conch-shells of the Pandav army are described in the *Gita* as transcendental or divine, and are described as causing fear or despair in the hearts of the mighty Kaurav army and its Generals, including Duryodhan[21]. The significance of this is important in that where truth stands, Shri Krishna stands, and where He stands, the *vatavaran* or ambience is divine.

Before the Battle cry is sounded, Arjun, seeing family and elders and spiritual masters poised against him, is overwhelmed with compassion and sorrow at the thought of annihilating them. He 'orders' Shri Krishna to take his chariot to the middle of the two armies so that he may view both armies from an equal distance. Note here that Arjun orders, and Shri Krishna, the Supreme, executes the order. Isn't that amazing? The Supreme is actually being ordered to do something! Wow! *That* is the power of a truly realized soul, an *uttam-koti* aatma, such as an Arjun! Shri Krishna, in His supreme mercy, puts Himself at the disposal and bidding of a true bhagat, a pure soul, such as an Arjun or Nursey. Now *that* is humility for the one that needs absoulutely none!

What *is* important here is that Arjun's charioteer is Shri Krishna Himself, that his horses drawing the chariot are white, and that the reigns of the horses are in Krishna's hands. The symbolism here is powerful. Horses here represent Arjun's indriya. Arjun's *ashwa*, or horses, are white, meaning Arjun's indriya or senses are pure and untainted. Even then, and especially only then, Arjun without any hesitation hands over full control over them to Shri Krishna. This is of utmost significance. Even if you think your indriyas are pure and under your control, they still need a firmer hand than yours – that of Shri Krishna's. Therefore, if you are an elevated soul or devotee, you must trust Shri Krishna fully and completely. If, however, you are an elevated soul or devotee, and you do not hand over the control of your indriyas to Shri Krishna, then you are an unfortunate soul for it will not be long before a slip happens to start you on your way to your downfall!

Arjun represents the perfect pupil, and Krishna the perfect teacher. Shri Krishna here is referred to as *Hrishikesh*, or the Supreme Master of *all* indriya. The ultimate lesson is that we, too, must strive to follow Arjun's footsteps and hand over *our* reigns to *our indriyas* to Hrishikesh, Shri Krishna, with full faith and trust in Him.

Once the chariot reaches the middle, Krishna stops the chariot and asks Arjun what to do next. Arjun, overwhelmed with compassion, feels his mighty *Gandiv* or bow slipping from his hands and he slowly sinks back into the chariot having lost his stomach and desire to fight.

What follows next is the conversation between the perfect pupil and the perfect teacher for the benefit of mankind. This conversation is the *geet* or song of Bhagvan – *Shrimad Bhagwat Gita.*

This *geet*, this treasure-house of knowledge, answers even your unvoiced questions. Reading this treasure remains the one goal that one must achieve in the *prime* of one's life. If we wait till we are old or older, it will be too late. We will have missed the boat.

Awake, my Hindu friends, for the process of self-discovery must be initiated *early* to produce any true and useful change within us in this short and extremely busy lifetime of ours!

Aspire to Arjun, and hand over your reigns to Hrishikesh, for He is the only one that you can trust to get you to your ultimate destination without fail.

Closing Thoughts

The *Bhagwat Gita* represents a technical manual, if you will, on how one must live his life, what his purpose in life should be, and how to finally die.

What is in this treasure cannot be simply *read.* One must not only read this, but also understand it as well with a lot of help, guidance and *satsang*, and then one must start to truly digest and implement it in one's daily life.

Simply reading it for knowledge leads again to the rearing of arrogances' ugly head, and one must be most careful to side-step these sort of mines.

Therefore, seek *true satsang*, the company of devotees that *live* the Gita, that truly live only to serve Krishna, to guide you on your path and in your life. Be sure to never abuse them, and to truly serve them as well. Remember, you please Krishna when you serve His servants. Count your blessings if you can be the *das* of a *Krishna's das*.

If you are fortunate enough to run into such devotees, recognize them for what they really are – *Krishna's kripa* to you, and cherish them as such, for Shri Krishna is truly smiling on you!

10.7: The stories behind the epics: Tying it all in

We are all aware of the old adage of the *story behind the story*. The same can bc said of our great and wonderful epic masterpieces as well.

There is an underlying fundamental story behind each of our great epics. We will shed light on just a few to get you started in the right direction of thought. Where do we start? How about the most popular avataars, Ram Avataar, Krishna Avataar, and Nursimh Avataar? And Varah Avataar, too.

As the story goes in *Vishnu Puran*, Lord Narayan has two *dwarpal* or guards posted to the entry to Narayan's Lok. One day the 'tiny' but eternal *Sanat Kumars* show up to visit Lord Narayan. The two sentries, named Jay and Vijay stop them. That was not their crime. Their true crime was the arrogance of assuming that *they* were better qualified to serve Vishnu, and even the *little Sanat Kumars* could be stopped from meeting with Vishnu by them, such was their power.

Obviously the Sanat Kumars saw the *ahankar* in Jay and Vijay, and cursed them, not in anger but in divine mercy to bring them back to humility. Jay and Vijay, upon hearing the curse begged the Sanat Kumars and Shri Vishnu for mercy. They were given two choices, and they opted to be manifested as three *asurs* (over three lifetimes) that would die at Vishnu's hands and thus regain their former place and glory at Vishnu's feet.

Therefore, the mighty asurs that Jay and Vijay manifested as are truly *avataars* of a divine shakti, and should not be belittled, ridiculed or misjudged. *They,* unlike you and I, played their designated *asur* roles very sincerely for the pleasure of their Lord, and are back at their cherished home at Shri Vishnu's Lotus feet. You and I, on the other hand, are facing and living Kal-Yug!

The three *asuri* teams of Jay and Vijay that thus manifested to take part in Vishnu's leelas are the teams of *Hiranyaksh* and *Hiranyakashipu* in Varah and Nursimh avataars, *Ravan* and *Kumbhakaran* in Ram avataar, and *Shishupal* and *Dantavakra* in Shri Krishna's descension.

The scriptures tell us that these are only some of the Supreme's leelas that we know about, and for every one leela that we know about, there are a multitude of others that we will never know of!

Awake, my Hindu friends! Please think carefully before ridiculing any of Krishna's *avataars* or *leelas*. They all attempt to teach us something very valuable. We are each better off paying attention and learning, rather then merely festively ridiculing and destroying *asuri* mock-ups, and feeling thus falsely catharsacised! Jay and Vijay found their place again in Vishnu's Lotus feet.

What can you say about *your* aspirations?

Learn from the 'mistakes' of Jay and Vijay. The *asurs* are really *inside* of each of *us*, deep within our own hearts, and *that* is where we must fight.

Let Ram, Varah, Nursimh and Shri Krishna help us each overcome *our own* demons.

10.8: Hindu Dharam
Laying a Rock-Solid Spiritual Foundation

Background

The scriptures were never meant to be abstracted or summarized, and I humbly offer a thousand apologies for doing just a little bit of just that in a very small way throughout our discussion. No summary or abstract can do any kind of justice to them. Not only that, the message one gets out of it depends on a multitude of things, the most fundamental of which is the qualification and the life stage of the writer or interpreter.

The reason for doing this to a small extent despite this fact is simple and twofold. First, my initial target audience is my children, not a group of theologians. Second is the very nature of the task. Looking at the Shrimad Bhagwat, for instance, one is stunned by the immense work; volume upon volume of beautiful and blissful knowledge. I know I was. I would always think I would set aside time *one day* to start reading this immense work. That proverbial *one day* never usually comes. There is always a semi-justifiable excuse (or reason, as we would like to fallaciously think) to it some other time as we would not be able to devote it the time and attention it deserves. And so it was for me. Well, thanks to my son, that one day finally arrived, although when it finally did, my hair had already turned grey.

Therefore, a summary or an abstract is helpful initially in artificially and conceptually shrinking this down to a mentally manageable task. Then, having read the summary or the significance, starting with the real thing will be that simpler and more likely to happen *at all*. And *that*, my friends, is the key. To making it actually *happen*. Simply take that first volume, sit back, and *just start reading it!*

Remember, it takes the cumulative *poonias* of many lifetimes to be able to do *even* that.

Laying the Spiritual Foundation

Let us begin by establishing some basic parameters for our spiritual foundation and salvation.

The most important spiritual texts that *every* Hindu needs to read and understand are the *Ramayan*, *Shrimad Bhagwat* and the *Shrimad Bhagwat Gita,* and in exactly *this* order. These three form the very essence and core of a *Vaishnav.*

The order in which these texts are introduced to a child or person is of paramount importance. Just as one must learn to crawl before one can walk, the order of introduction should be as stated.

Simplistically put, *Ramayan* shows one how to live, *Shrimad Bhagwat* induces the *rus* or nectar for Krishna Bhakti, and the *Shrimad Bhagwat Gita* prepares one for the knowledge of life, the universe, and eventual death. Remember, these form the core and lay the foundation. They are exactly *that* important. If one never read any other scripture in addition, nothing would be lost. If anything, reading *beyond* these three *without* their implementation and integration into daily life is meaningless and counter-productive, usually leading to arrogance and dogmatic narrow-mindedness.

The *Ramayan* lays the great complex and intricate foundation upon which shall rest a person, a family unit, a society and a nation. It will teach a person to form correct inter-personal relationships both as a microcosmal family unit, and macrocosmal unit relating to the society and the world in general. Every stage of every important relationship is demonstrated, from father-son, *guru* and *shisya*, *Raja* or ruler and its *praja*, husband-wife, brother-brother, etc.

One must partake of the richness that is offered by the *Ramayan* and then *implement* its teachings into daily life so as to become a decent and noble human being. Bhagvan Ram, demonstrating and leading by example, sets the tone for all great relationships. Forming the correct relationships and observing and living the simple priciples of truth, justice and peace then ensures harmony, prosperity and stability for the entire nation. This then comes back full circle to every individual in that nation with peace as true progress in whatever it is that they choose to undertake.

The second important scripture, the *Shrimad Bhagwat*, induces Krishna bhakti and devotion, known as *bhakti-rus*. Allowing this rus to percolate through our mind and soul's entire fabric will have untold effects on our actions and our eventual death. However, this rus must first be amassed or collected in us. Let's make an analogy. Say one wants to fill their heart (a vessel of sorts in this analogy) with bhakti-rus, or divine fluid nectar. To fill a tumbler or a vessel, the first requirement is that the vessel should be void or empty to begin with. If the vessel contains material already, there would be little or insufficient room for more, right? And if the vessel is filled with rubbish, logic follows that the vessel cannot receive further meaningful additions of any kind.

The *Ramayan*, having implemented its teachings, helps make our heart pure and devoid of *sansari* litter, ready to receive the nectar of Krishna-bhakti. The second requirement would be to point the mouth of the tumbler or vessel up holding the vessel upright, ready to receive the nectar. This is also accomplished by the *Ramayan's* implementation. With the vessel thus upright and devoid of litter, Krishna-rus or nectar can be thus readily collected, which is what the *Shrimad Bhagwat* is. This powerful nectar thus collected and drunk (through one's ears, obviously) induces a powerful and loving devotion to the Supreme Personality, Shri Krishna. It is possible to drown in Krishna-bhakti never to re-surface; such is the attractive and captivating power of His mesmerizing pass-times.

The third and final step is to internalize and digest or analyze this nectar and implement this within you and your life. In other words, the ultimate search for the ultimate truth, and the initiation of its practical application within this lifetime. This is the most difficult step of the three. This is supremely difficult without the correct or proper knowledge. This *proper* knowledge is found in the *Shrimad Bhagwat Gita.*

The *Shrimad Bhagwat Gita* really is the *complete* source of knowledge, if one can understand it. Arjun asks the questions on behalf of mankind, and the all-merciful Shri Krishna answers them. And then details all there is to know. Appreciate here, however, that without *adequate preparation* as simplistically illustrated above, one only gains *dry* and empty knowledge without *bhakti*, and such knowledge without bhakti is dangerous as it will certainly lead to arrogance, stubbornness, and *mooddhta*, opening the door to that person's *patan*.

Although it may take many lifetimes to understand all there is to know in the Gita, the simplistic but meaningful understanding is this – everything there is to know, everything there is to want or desire, everything there is to cherish, and everything there is to worship *is* Shri Krishna. Therefore, *our* ultimate goal of life in this infinitely rare and priceless human form *is* the attainment of the lotus feet of Shri Krishna by devotional service to Him.

10.9: Parting Thoughts

The *Veds*, the *Ramayan*, the *Shrimad Bhagwat*, and the *Shrimad Bhagwat Gita* are the spiritual treasure, the true guide and, indeed, the *very life* of all Hindus.

Krishna says that of the Veds, *He* is *Rig*, *Saam* and *Yajur*.[22] Shri Krishna also says that *He* is the compiler of *Vedant*, and that it is indeed *Him* who is the One to be known by the *Veds*.[23] . Kanaiyo dispels any doubts about Him being the Supreme when He proclaims in the *Gita* that *He* is transcendental, the Greatest, and celebrated as the *Brahman*, *the Supreme,* by the *Veds*.[24] This, He asserts, is *the most confidential knowledge* of the *Veds*.[25]

One must know of the Veds and their principles, Krishna adds, but Vedanitc knowledge alone, however, is not enough. Krishna says that those who simply live by *Vedic principles alone* will achieve only *kshanic*, or temporary pleasure and *must* descend to earth again[26].

Therefore, living purely by Vedic priciples alone is *incomplete* and *insufficient* in attaining the *ultimate* truth.

The *saar*, the very *cream* of the *Vedantic knowledge* and its *proper application*, is contained in the *Shrimad Bhagwat Gita*.

Shri Krishna says repeatedly in the *Gita* that for one to ultimately *attain The* Supreme – Shri Krishna, one must rely completely on Krishna and *Gita* fully and *without a doubt.*

Hence, the *complete* answer, then, is found only in the *Gita*.

CHAPTER 11

The Final Analysis: A Thought-Provoking Paradigm Shift or Two

Knowledge is Power is more correct as
Applied Knowledge is True Power.
Knowledge alone is simply not enough, and can never be power

11.1: Setting the Stage for the Final Analyses

The topics raised here for discussion are understandably contentious.

As you read *The Final Analyses*, it is understood and welcomed that your opinion may differ. Nevertheless, I urge you to reflect on my thoughts yet once again.

Remember, the final choice is always *yours*.

The Final Analyses are meant to provoke thought not just superficially in your mind, but deep within your heart as well. Examine your heart and your *aatma* deliberately and carefully. I am undoubtedly counting on you using your *cerebrum*, but urge you to go further and use your conscience, your *raday*, your heart, and your *aatma* as well.

It is very true, life is truly worth living and life is certainly worth enjoying. But unbridled enjoyment by Hindus at our samaaj's expense and a total lack of initiative toward protecting *our* dharam and *our* future by Hindus are severely detrimental to Hindus, Hindustaan and indeed the world today.

What Hindus and Hindustaan have given to the world is truly amazing, from the *shunya* or zero to mathematics, astronomy, agriculture, surgery, medicine, religion and science, not to mention culture, philosophy and the concept of Ahinsa or non-violence. Regardless of the claims made by the West of who actually contributed what, the facts are facts and cannot be denied.

A slight but highly significant change in an old adage is necessary: *Knowledge is Power* is more correct as *Applied* Knowledge is *True* Power.

Knowledge alone is simply not enough and can *never* be power. Static or potential energy can't achieve anything unless converted to useable kinetic energy. Therefore, there must be the *correct* implementation of that knowledge to achieve a desired outcome.

There are a remaining few points that need to be made boldly, loudly and clearly. Each one is extremely important and highly relevant especially now, the present day and time. Let's deal with the issues briefly and one at a time.

A radical change individually and at the grassroots level is *desperately* and *urgently* needed.

See if *you* agree.

11.2: Deliberate Mis-Interpretation & Malicious Mischief

There is great concern that non-Hindus have deliberately and methodically with great malice altered completely or grossly distorted our sacred scriptures over time, with the intention to evoke contempt and disgust from Hindus regarding their own sacred scriptures.

It is sad, distasteful and sickening, then, to keep reading Hindu literature and commentary that quotes non-Hindu sources and translators including Max Muller and the like!

Are my fellow learned Hindus *so insecure* and *in-confident* as to feel the need to quote non-Hindus in their work, or to rely on translations made by non-Hindus from Sanskrit? Are there no learned Hindus that can correctly translate Sanskrit rather than relying on translations made by non-Hindus that contain deliberate malice?

Our scriptures in Sanskrit have been translated by non-Hindus, and this includes Sanskrit dictionaries as well. The folly and the ultimate cost of using such Sanskrit dictionaries to translate our sacred scriptures are immeasurable. The totally altered or grossly distorted translation leads even the best-intentioned interpreter, the writer and their intended lay-person readers completely astray by altering the basic premise and foundation!

It is high time this was brought to light by learned Hindus that rely on non-corrupted Hindu translations by non-corrupt Hindu pundits.

A new Sanskrit dictionary database and standard should be established by a meeting of blameless and selfless Hindu *pundits*, *acharyas*, *Saadhus* and *Santos*, and everything non-Hindu based should be discarded *in toto*.

We must start from the beginning. Establish a new Sanskrit dictionary and throw away the existing contaminated ones, for if innocent Hindu scholars rely on non-Hindu translations, even they shall be lost!

Another interesting and malicious mis-fact is the fabled 'Aryan Invasion' from the north conquering the 'pagan' tribes settled along the Indus. This is indeed a fable! So-called 'Aryans' have always existed in India in the northern territories and migrated south from northern India and not Europe! But even this statement needs to be elaborated on.

The term *Aryan* means 'noble,' pure and simple. It has *never* truly applied to a race, any race, in particular. It simply means a *noble* people.

In olden days, and for example in the Ramayan, wives have referred to their husbands as 'arya' or 'aryan' meaning of *noble* nature. Noble here should not be misconstrued to mean royalty either. Noble, or Aryan, is meant to imply of noble mind and deed. Hindus have *always* been noble. Therefore, if noble is applicable to a race, it is *certainly* applicable to Hindus, for Hindus have never been the initial aggressors in the history of the world. That the Hindus are a gentle and noble people is an indisputable fact. Mahatma Gandhi and Swami Vivekanand are two great modern-day shining examples of peace emissaries of Hindus to the world.

Conversely, recognize *definitively* that nobility and gentleness have *nothing* in common with meekness and cowardice. This is a most important and noteworthy distinction, and one worth *remembering* well. Hindus are noted worldwide to be a peace loving and indeed a peaceful people. Hindus are also at the same time *respected* highly for bravery, loyalty, patriotism, determination, valor and so on. The qualities just described are all highly desirable and noble, and are truly *Aryan*. Hindus, then, are indeed Aryan. Thus, foolish and arrogant are those who interpret humble, gentle and peaceful Hindus as meek or cowardly.

Hindus are indeed *Aryan* by deed and thought, and history has proven that time and again. But the notion of an 'Aryan invasion from Europe' is a deliberate and malicious attempt to introduce fiction into history. Now *that's* cowardice!

My fellow learned Hindus, these deliberate and malicious mis-facts need to be challenged by literary Hindus who are far more learned than I.

What do Hindus need to do?

We need selfless Hindu rishis, pundits, Saadhus and professors to unite to correctly translate Sanskrit, create a new dictionary and interpret our scriptures correctly for the first time in. Do away completely with the old, contaminated and corrupted translations.

Then we need equally selfless Hindu scholars, educators and archeologists to go about disproving the rubbish or the 'Aryan' invasion, and publish their findings in the world press thereby not only correcting history but *making* history as well!

Awake, my fellow learned Hindus! *Heed the call!*

Set Hindustaan's history *and* its future right!

11.3: Global Warming: A Dangerous Understatement

There is one last major issue with respect to vegetarianism that is, for the current times, the most crucial, for it has *global* rather than personal and *local* implications.

We have touched on how the implementation of vegetarianism and ahinsa is not just a mere *personal* moral and ethical issue, but is one that actually affects the morality, ethics and behavior of an entire people and, indeed, entire nations. That is extremely important, for a morally and physically healthy person leads to a morally healthy and fit community, which ultimately speaks for the nation itself. However, this is still not global. If one nation is more 'ethical' or 'moral' or 'healthy' it is still hard to see how that would affect another nation half-way around the globe right? Wrong! One *always* affects another eventually. We just may not be able to connect the dots right away, if ever. Be that as it may, let us look at a more alarming issue that is a *consequence* of non-implementation of this philosophy.

The biggest crisis facing the planet today without a question is the so-called 'Global Warming.' We are all starting to hear about it, read about it, see it on the silver screen, or in unfortunate circumstances, actually be the victims of it.

The wording, 'global warming' is actually a misnomer, a grand understatement, designed to calm the masses for now. If something gradually 'warms' up, well it implies it is *gradual*, right? Global Warming. A gradual warm-up of the planet. Hmm. It's probably going to take quite a while before it impacts *you* seriously right? Wrong! Again!

The phenomenon of 'Global Warming' has already affected us, and continues to do so! Look at the major climate changes, the hurricanes and earthquakes, the floodings and the droughts, the temperature changes on land and more significantly in the oceans, the changes and shifts in tides, the earthquakes, the tsunamis, and the list continues to grow! What are we waiting for? Are we waiting for the sky to literally fall on us before we wake up? Well, people, WAKE UP! What we are witnessing *is* the sky falling! Or as close to it as it can get, for the sky truly does not ever fall!

Therefore, people, Awake! The climates on our beautiful and fragile planet have *already* changed. Or dare I say, they have *collapsed*? Consequently, the phenomenon of what we are witnessing should truly be called 'Global Heating' with 'Global Climate Collapse' and not just 'Global

Warming!' We are already in the 'victim' mode, not the 'potential victim' mode. It is already happening.

Hence, saying 'Global Warming' will *lull* you into a false sense of security by *veiling* the urgency of the issue, whereas 'Global Heating' or 'Global Climate Collapse' gives you the truer picture of what you already *know* and see to be true and correct. Therefore, do not be fooled and lulled into a false sense of security and lack of urgency. Our climates have already changed, and the need *is* most certainly urgent.

We need change *NOW!*

It is not too late, and we are not past the point of 'no-return' just yet. Therefore, forget 'Global Warming' and call it what it truly is – 'Global Heating' with 'Global Climate Collapse' or simply 'Climate Collapse' for short. It is truly that urgent, for it *has* occurred, continues to occur, and will only get much worse if we let it. And who has not heard the phrase 'when hell freezes over?' Well, people, when the climate collapse is complete, and our planet goes through *intense* changes before finally achieving equilibrium, most of the planet *will* freeze, at least in the Northern Hemisphere. And the Southern Hemisphere will be thrown back in the stone ages. Our beautiful and fragile planet will freeze violently, and yes, the statement will have come to pass. Only, *we* humans made that happen. *We* turned our planet into a frozen hell!

If you think even for a moment that the rendering above is an overstatement, mis-statement, an exaggeration, or an entertaining prediction that will *not* affect *you* or *your* children, stick your head (with the air in it) back into hole in the sand, crawl back under the rock that you crawled out from under, and continue to pretend that fairies and cartoons exist for real, and that earthquakes, tsunamis, flooding and droughts only happen to someone else but never to you or your loved ones!

For the rest of us that are truly serious about this, how about a review of some causative observations that you may have already made?

Let us start by looking at an interesting pyramid that scientists have known about all along. It is called the food pyramid. Yes, most of you are also aware of it. I know that. But we need to revisit its principles, for we have forgotten them or are ignoring them. We have already touched on this briefly in *Chapter 3*, but follow along as we expand this concept a little more.

It really is a very simple concept, the food pyramid is. It is also called a 'food chain' but this is mis-leading terminology, so we will stick with the *correct* version, the concept of the pyramid.

We have herbivores towards that base of the triangle or pyramid, and we have different predatory animals above them. Man, as we have already seen, belongs towards the *base* of the pyramid *by design*. At the very bottom of the pyramid are the plants.

The numbers of all living creatures within the pyramid are the greatest towards the bottom, and number the fewest as we get toward the top. This idea, represented prictorally, resembles a pyramid. The concept is deceptively simple. We need more prey than predators, for if the pyramid reversed, the predators would quickly become extinct themselves. Simple enough, right?

Next principle.

We need fewer predators also because of what we call the universal and natural *law of diminishing returns.* Grass is at the bottom of the pyramid. When herbivores eat the grass, and that is all they consume, there is balance and harmony because nature produces more grass than herbivores. The energy it takes Mother Nature to sustain grass is far less than what it takes to sustain a herbivore.

When predatory animals consume a herbivore, they have consumed more resources and are therefore less efficient in their energy consumption, meaning it takes more energy to sustain a predatory animal than a herbivore or grass. Thus, consumers towards the top of the pyramid are less efficient 'transfers' or 'yields' of energy than those towards the bottom. According to the law of diminishing returns, pure carnivores at the top of the pyramid are the most 'wasteful' of consumable resources. The pure carnivores, then, are the biggest and least efficient consumers of energy and must *always* number the fewest.

The food pyramid is in perfect harmony as long as the creatures within it *conform* to the laws of nature. That is, a deer should not eat meat, and big cats or pure carnivores should not graze. Man, a pure herbivore by design, steps in yet again to upset the perfection that is nature! In his supreme arrogance, man decides to be carnivorous even though he lacks the proper tools to acquire and digest meat. The sheer numbers of 'man' turning carnivorous and artificially moving upward in the food pyramid is a foolish and dangerous shift that completely upsets the harmony and balance of the food pyramid ultimately with gobal consequences.

Let us scrutinize this just a bit more. The *actual* estimates may vary somewhat but it is safe and logical to guesstimate about a 1:5 to 1:10 ratio of yield of meat from feed. For example, you may yield about 1kg of meat for every 5 – 10 kg of feed used to produce that meat. This feed can be simple hay, or be corn or even soy. That means you need to produce between 5 to 10 kg of such feed to expect about a kilogram of meat.

In achieving that kilogram of meat, your first *yield* of 5 to 10 kg of edible product has now been reduced to just one! Where is the sense in that? Not to mention that the 5 to 10 kg of soy or corn is naturally usually *free of toxins* and hormones, but your one kg of meat is *laced* with toxins, hormones, antibiotics, hidden pathogens, stress hormones produced by the animal killed that you will also certainly ingest, and other such products unhealthy and *unfit* for *human* consumption. It almost seems that you traded in dinner for poison, doesn't it? Rather, at a 1 in 5 – 10 ratio, you traded in a *feast* for a small *cup* of horrible and disgusting poison. Brains, Hindu man, brains! Where are *yours*?

Anyway, to return to diminishing yields, you still need to feed the masses with the 'meat' they desire. That is now the new challenge. The solution? Enter high-density and extremely cruel and brutal animal 'farming.'

These animal farms, be they poultry, dairy, beef, or so on, suck up *enormous* resources in terms of *cleared* forests, useable agricultural land, feed, chemicals and antibiotics, and other such assets. You have to realize and then visualize the tremendous *scale* of these horrendous entities to get a feel for just what is and how much is required or destroyed in this entire process.

To gain a better perspective, here is a thought. Just the feed resources alone diverted for animal farming are *sufficient* to meet the needs of the entire starving and hungry world and enough to alleviate and eliminate world hunger. Did anyone ever stop to think about that? If we simply stopped the intense animal farming, world hunger and diseases from malnutrition such as Kwashiorkor would *instantly* be a thing of the past! How shocking is that?

However, let us dig into this a step farther and gain yet another perspective on this human greed train to a dead-end. As in *dead.*

In addition to sucking up feed and land resources, the sheer number of 'feed' animals required to meet the insatiable demand for meat products requires an enormously large number of animals. Again, absolute numbers are meaningless, but let us guesstimate that the number of animals consumed is on the order of 6 to 8 cattle per year per person, and note that this doesn't account for the fact that some of us are vegetarian!

The number of chickens, turkey and so forth is also similar. These are very conservative estimates, and it is reasonably safe to argue that the actual numbers are probably much higher.

The point is, *more animals* than *humans* are required to meet the 'meat' requirements of the corpse-eating humans. Let that sink in for a second, and put it into another perspective. We all talk about 'crowding' and global over-population, especially in the third world countries. If you think that the global human population is ballooning, then can you not see the absolute madness in the 'feed' animal population just *burgeoning?*

If you do the simple maths, at 5 to 1 or higher ratios, it is really the alarmingly *burgeoning* animal population that we *really* need to worry about *urgently*, not the rapidly growing *human* over-population! *This fact alone* is simply mind-boggling! Why is it that no-one wants to talk about this? This man-made 'over-population' of 'feed' animals has *severe* and *multiple global repercussions!* It really is high time that someone somewhere sounded the *global alarm* on the mushrooming 'feed' animal population at the expense of everything else on our planet, including ultimately, the naïve, foolish and greedy humans causing it!

Consider yet another issue with animal agriculture. The large numbers of such feed animals also means that the levels of methane and carbon-dioxide gases, both by-products of these animals (and humans), go up significantly. These gases are both hothouse gases, and contribute significantly to global heating, all because of the *colossal* numbers of animals required to sustain the demand!

The flip side of the coin on global warming is another alarming issue. Plants and trees, or forests of them, remove carbon dioxide from the atmosphere to help cool the planet. These forests, responsible for 'cooling' down the planet and replenishing our oxygen and water supplies, are disappearing at an alarming rate to make room for more animal agriculture 'farms,' cash-crop farms, or farms to grow the additional corn and soy necessary to sustain the animals that feed the flesh-eating humans.

This is absolute madness! What helps us, the forests, we eliminate to make room for what hurts us! If this is not absolute and total stupidity and madness, I don't know what is! *Do you?*

And we haven't even touched on entire fish and other animal populations dwindling in or even entirely disappearing from the world oceans! That is another catastrophe in the making.

Wonderful as eliminating horrible and abominable animal cruelty and world hunger might be, then, that is not the whole story or even its biggest piece. The most shocking thing is that no-one is saying much about how much the intense animal agriculture contributes to 'Global Heating!' In fact, those that know about it are too busy counting their money when they really should be counting the loss of animal life on land and in the oceans that is heralding the destruction and chaos caused by massive climatic changes and indeed climate collapse in some cases!

Pollution, hothouse gases from industries, and so on are *significant* factors. Do not underestimate that. But what is shocking is that if someone runs the numbers, I bet the effect of methane and carbon-dioxide gases and so on from the animal agriculture is just as big if not a *bigger* contributor! Even if I am wrong on this guesstimate, which I do not think I am, I am darn sure that I am close!

The bottom-line?

We have said before, and repeat here again. We only create misery when we go against nature. Whether we are naïve, foolish, arrogant or simply just plain greedy, we need to stop and think!

In the end, man just might turn out to be his own worst enemy. It may not be nuclear war or even a meteoir strike that ends us. It may be our cruel and insatiable appetite for what we were never designed for – meat!

Awake, people!

Next time you eat meat, think gruesome and abominable animal cruelty, think stomach not a graveyard, think and appreciate that the human is a herbivore by design, think diminishing returns, think poison, and perhaps more importantly, think 'Global Heating' with climate collapse.

It is cruel, foolish, suicidal and globally irresponsible and dangerous to eat meat! Remember, these thoughts are observations and deductions, *not* judgments or opinions.

Any way you look at, we create misery when we go against nature. Climate collapse from Global Heating is here; it is not a gradual thing that might affect you tomorrow. It is here *now*. Wake up and see the handwriting on the wall, or the desalinization of the oceans and their rising levels, or the disappearing Polar ice-packs, or the tsunamis and earthquakes in eastern Asia and Sri Lanka, the increased flooding in China, India and Africa, and indeed other parts of the world, the increased drought conditions in Africa and Australia, the increased ultraviolet light radiation from increasing number of ozone holes, and the list gets sickeningly long. Or, conversely, stick your head back in the sand where it belongs, and let some hurricane, flood, drought, earthquake or tsunami rip your life (or that of your future progeny) and delusions apart at some point in the near future!

Awake, my friends! Wake-up and *see* the climate change and collapse around the Globe. If not for the animals, or even your personal health, do it for the next generation, your children.

Say *no* to meat. *Any meat*. By the way, while we are on the subject of meat, remember that there is no such thing as a *vegetarian* egg. An egg is an ovum or an undeveloped chick. If it is fertilized, it is a chick embryo, the equivalent of a fetus. If it is unfertilized, it is a menstrual product of the hen, her ovum. Either way, it is gross, and it is horrible. Therefore, there is no such nonsense as a *vegetarian* egg!

Man *must* take responsibility for the ultimate legacy he lives behind. But then again, he may be long gone, the way of the dinosaurs, wiped out from the face of the earth, and so it won't matter. Whereas dinosaurs were eliminated by nature, man just might be foolish or arrogant enough to do it to himself.

Is man *really* that unintelligent?

Awake, my friends! Say no to meat, then, and make a difference, one person and one family at a time. Stuff that belongs in a graveyard should really go *there*, not in our digestive tracts to rot, ferment and sicken us!

Wake up to the fact that the human body is a priceless treasure achieved after many, many life-forms. It has most certainly been a hard-fought battle through the *circle of life* to attain it. The human body is a shrine in which both the *aatma* and the *Paramaatma* reside. This temple is to be used for a higher purpose and spiritual elevation. Do not make it a graveyard or a rubbish can!

By design, and by intention, the human body is unique and special. It is the only temple on this planet where two eternal and divine *chetnas* reside. Treat it with the respect it deserves, and it will serve you well; So well, in fact, that you may even be able to achieve the ultimate goal of human existence!

Well, what's going on *your* plate and into *your temple*?

11.4: Organic Farming: Not Just a New Craze

Nowadays, we hear more and more about 'new' organic farming and its benefits. Is organic farming for real is it just a passing fad or craze?

Actually, 'organic' farming is nothing new. The *kisaans*, the local and traditional farmers in Bhaarat, have been practicing it for centuries. Only recently has mechanized farming, the introduction of pesticides and fertilizers and such dangerous chemicals changed all this, this true and tried proven formula of 'organic' farming.

Modern mechanized farming is considered to be high-tech and extremely profitable, whereas 'organic' farming is considered low-tech or primitive, and marginally profitable at best. A modern farmer stands tall and proud atop his huge mechanized monsters, while a traditional farmer literally drags behind on his ox-plow. Although a lot of differences separate the two farmers, only a few are necessary to illustrate some major issues.

Lets look at each type of farmer just briefly.

We will start with an 'organic' traditional farmer. A kisaan generally knows when to plant the seed, he may use a hull or an ox plow to prepare the land, and he uses *gober,* or cow manure to both fertilize the soil *and* repel pests. He then either uses irrigation from ox-dug wells, or times it perfectly and allows the rains to water the crop, which is *what* we eventually eat. What you see is, in effect, what you eat and taste. For example, apples look like apples, taste like apples and nourish like apples. Though not this simple, this highlights the main processes of a traditional kisaan that are radically simple and yet exquisitely effective.

Let us know consider a 'modern' farmer. He uses mechanized means to prepare the land and plant his seed, a method more brutal to the worms and other macrobiotic life in the soil. He then sprays or dusts with chemical fertilizer, which may engorge the plant product without really nutritionally enriching it any way. This means you get more 'stuff' and less nutrition per bite. He then dusts the crop several times with poisons called pesticides. These are actually absorbed and adsorbed onto the plant products, so they *will* eventually end up inside of you. These 'pesticides' also kill the worms, the macrobiotic life as well as the micro-biotic life in the soil eventually turning that very once-productive soil lifeless, unproductive and now poisoned. By the way, the *Kalki Puran* has several references to 'sterile' and non-productive land, so we are definitely on our way to a devastating future if this 'bhoomi apraadh' continues by poisoning the land.

To get back to our highly commercial and modern mechanized farmer, he may irrigate the crops, but since mechanized farms are larger, he will dig or use wells that are significantly deeper than ox-dug wells. Or, he may simply use locally stored water supplies, such as city water. Either way, this will contribute to depletion of deep water tables and future water shortages in the region. Next, the excess run-off from his irrigation will poison everything it runs across, and eventually poison the wells and rivers that other humans depend on far away from the original farm, the original source of this contamination. Eventually, the toxins from pesticides and fertilizers also seep deeper into the soil and find their way into underground streams and water channels, further poisoning all creatures (including humans) that use these water sources.

The crop is mechanically harvested and will have everything on and in it, from chemical fertilizers to pesticides to even diesel fuel. Then, before it hits the shelves in your local food store, it will have been waxed over (another petroleum product?) to make it appear shiny and glossy. The final product, though is deceptive, for what you see is *not* what you eat. You are now consuming a product that may be genetically altered and manipulated, is mostly nutrient poor, but is poison-rich, is more 'stuff' and thus more space-occupying and hence you will be able to eat less of it. Using the prior example, the apples look bigger and shinier than the original. They, however, have a different taste, almost apple-like but without the tanginess or bitterness, and marginally worse than the original in terms of 'healthy' nutrition.

So, in summary, what you are eating from a modern farmer is a bigger and better looking apple that *almost* tastes like one but not quite, is marginally nutritional, and also delivers an 'acceptable' dose (to the modern farmer, his vendors, his corporate and banking sponsors, and to his government buddies overseeing the appropriation of his subsidies) of wax, pesticide and chemical fertilizer to boot. *Yummy!*

Awake, my friends! If you really understood what you just read, you should not only be shocked but outraged! I know I am! Wake up and smell the poison in your food and your children's! Be very outraged! Act! Act Now!

But what can *you* do? How can *you* make a difference?

Well, really by doing the same thing as eating vegetarian. Vote with your wallet! One person, one family, and one community at a time.

Do not buy the fake, artificial and poisoned food from your local 'food' stores that do not offer authentic organic produce. Let the mechanized monsters and the greedy chemical farmers, who only care about padding their wallets, go the way of the dinosaurs. Let them die a natural *financial* death on their own. When nobody buys the poisoned junk they peddle, they will go elsewhere. Force them out of *your* community by hurting them financially and making it thus impossible to stay in business. If enough communities join in, these farmers will have to change their ways for the better, change trades, or go elsewhere to poison another unsuspecting community.

Education of the local community is key to its health and prosperity. Nowhere else is this more true than nutrition. Progress and prosperity are founded on the physical and mental health of its members, the citizens comprising a community. It all starts with nutrition, and that starts with *your decision* of what it is that you put in your tummy and that of your family.

Awake, my friends! Support your local kisaans, your local farmer that respects the *bhoomi*, mother earth, rather than poisoning her. Band together as family units and buy only from the local kisaans. If enough people do this, the local kisaans will prosper again and return *us* to good health by providing us *real food,* not genetically mutilated, waxed and poisoned crap!

Awake, my Hindu friends! Your local traditional kisaan has always been an organic farmer *and* your's and your child's best friend.

You just didn't know it!

11.5: Maximize Your Legacy, Not Your Footprint: Be Eco-Sensitive!

A sore subject with most people today is the environment and the concept of global responsibility. Well, it really shouldn't be, and it is easy to make a *huge* difference. Wait, don't pass on this – read on and see how *easy* it really is. It is extremely important.

It is truly easy to be *eco-sensitive*, meaning minimizing your footprint on the environment. And it starts with *you*. Obviously we all have to live and thrive, so we must take from the environment. That is necessary and obvious. However, we must take as little as we can and as little as we *need* without being wasteful. You must do your part. You can make a difference! And it all adds up. You want to leave a legacy of responsibility and achievement behind, not one of destruction, plundering and waste. Okay, so how and where do we start?

Easy! Start with the everyday choices we all make routinely. And if sounds mundane and unimportant, it isn't!

We will illustrate with a few choices and examples, and you follow through with some real thought every-time you do anything at all.

For starters, waste not a drop or a morsel.

This relates to all resources, food, energy, water, and so on. So, start with the morning. For instance, when you brush your teeth or shower or bathe, use the water necessary for getting the job done, and have the water at a correct temperature. Actively try not to be wasteful. Turn the water down or even off frequently when lathering or washing, for example. Set the water temperature towards cool rather than warm or piping hot! Colder showers are more invigorating and have a smaller energy impact than hot ones. Also, get out of the shower just a little earlier by actively paying attention to the task at hand. Sing if you wish, but get your thinking done outside of the shower. Multiply the savings in water and heating by everyone engaged in this simple implementation, and the communal and global savings can be tremendous!

Remember, we said waste not a drop. The problem that is imminent is that water supplies are 'peaking' and that we face water shortages in the near future. In fact, parts of the world are already experiencing the effects of drought and dwindling water supplies. Alas, water shortages in the future may be an even bigger threat than dwindling 'fossil fuel' supplies.

The same consideration and thinking attitude goes towards food. Eat what you need, but do not be extravagant. In fact, eating slightly less than 'full' is healthier and preferable to over-eating and feeling stuffed! Waste not a morsel! Finish everything on your plate, and only put on it what you *can* comfortably finish. Choose what goes on your plate wisely. That, too, impacts not just the environment but your health as well.

Okay, appropriate and sensible water and food utilization is good for you and the environment. What else can you do? Energy consumption, or more correctly its unintentional or overlooked wastage, is another big one. Pay particular attention also to the energy impact that you have on your environment by making *active* decisions rather than just *passive* automatic ones.

For example, turn on lights only *where* you need them and only *when* you need them, and remember to turn them off when you exit. We all know someone who never bothers to turn lights off, right? Well, you really should! Whether you can afford it is not the issue here. Why leave the lights on when you don't need, them only to waste energy? Walking out of an office or a room in a hurry is the usual cause for forgetting to turn the lights off *as you exit.* Well, simply by making an active decision to turn the lights off *every time* you exit makes a huge difference on energy consumption. If you do this regularly, it becomes second nature, and becomes an automatic activity. Easy to do, right?

The other thing to consider is *task lighting* as opposed to diffuse or *general lighting*. For example, using fluorescent desk lamps is more cost-effective, more energy efficient, more productive, and better for your eyes than incandescent or even halogen lighting that is general or ceiling mounted, which is less efficient, more glare-producing to the eyes, more heat-producing, and less efficient. Simply *choosing task lighting* makes a great difference all around.

The same careful attention should be given to energy-consuming appliances and devices as well, such as radios, televisions, fans, computers, printers, and so on. Even the so-called 'green' and smart devices such as computers and monitors that go into a low-power 'stand-by' mode consume some energy, no matter how small it may seem. When you factor in thousands of such 'green' devices it adds up exponentially and quickly, and you really should see 'red' and do something about it! Therefore, turn off all non-essential electrical devices before you exit. The use of power strips or centralized switches makes it a snap to turn off all non-essentials daily or when unnecessary. Also, in the warmer places, add fans to your cooling regimen, and raise the temperatures of automatic air-conditioning units by a couple of degrees. This minor change will probably not even be perceptible to you, but can create a huge positive impact when you factor in more people doing the exact same thing.

Energy conservation is not just limited to the home environment but should really carry through in everything you do and everywhere you go, whether at work or even on a vacation where you may not be directly paying for it. The overall impact to the environment would be stunning. The real goal of reducing the so-called 'green-house gases' will thus become more easily achievable with such easy decisions and their implementation.

Use your discretion when you decide on your mode of transport as well. Again, it is not a matter of whether you can afford it or not. Plan ahead on your trips to minimize the number of stops and the number of trips when using motorized vehicles. This will make your commute or journey shorter and will allow for more efficient use of your time, leaving you extra time for play or leisure. Use your most fuel-efficient vehicles most of the time, and use the least-efficient ones the least possible. Fill-up completely, and make less frequent fuel stops. Drive sensibly, not aggressively. Burning gas and generating more brake-dust is foolish *not* fuelish!

Another big problem that we are facing is alarmingly rapid deforestation and the re-arranging of our vegetation around us. Deforestation is also tragic not just from the climatic point of view, but from an ecological viewpoint as well. Numerous species of creatures small and large alike are on the endangered speicies lists or are facing imminent extinction. This is yet another truly terrible and horrendous man-made tragedy in the making.

Deforestation and re-arrangement of vegetation are, however, really two separate issues, so let us deal with them separately.

The first is deforestation, which most of us feel there is little we can do about. Maybe, and maybe not. Though there are many reasons contributing to deforestation, let us see how we can keep from contributing to it. Let us consider simple and easily applicable everyday issues again.

Let's start with paper, an important natural product that we use an incredible amount of daily. Do not waste it! Use only the paper you need, and use both sides when possible. Do not discard paper, but re-cycle it.

Buy re-cycled paper whenever possible, and buy the better qualities of paper only if absolutely necessary. Obviously, paper and paper goods come from trees, so use these products wisely, and remember to re-cycle. The same goes for other wood products and remember to re-cycle when possible. Next, plant trees whenever and wherever possible, but with consideration to another important point.

This brings us to the next issue, the *rearrangement* of our vegetation.

When considering landscaping, one should plant native vegetation whenever possible, rather than planting vegetation that is not native to the region. There is definitely a good reason why different types of vegetation grow in different places. Staying with native and naturally occurring vegetation ensures that it will thrive without requiring additional resources such as irrigation, fertilization, and so on. This allows better utilization of natural resources, primarily water.

The other 'hidden' issue is that all vegetation is a natural, integral part of the local ecosystem, and 'everything' works in nature based on the simple fact of each component being present in the first place. Therefore, if you remove naturally occurring vegetation and supplant that with 'imported' varieties or varieties not native to that locality, you have just destroyed an integral part of the local ecosystem that *will* impact local population of insects, birds, small animals, soil conditions, and indeed other animals and vegetation that relied on that native vegetation in the first place. Hence, careful attention must be paid to 'landscaping' new or existing projects to avoid loss of entire micro-ecosystems.

Clothing is next. Although cotton is a cash-crop, it also has other useful benefits in addition to cotton fiber and textile, such as oil. Synthetic materials tend to require more resources in manufacturing and also may have a greater environmental impact, so stick to cotton. It breathes better, usually is better for your skin, better for the economy, and is natural. Avoid polyesters and silks. Silk production is especially cruel, and if you choose silk, *you* propagate a cruel industry. Choose wisely, and buy what is flexible and necessary. Do not buy clothing extravagantly, for that is arrogant and wasteful.

And absolutely refuse to wear *dead animals* as coats or adornments of any kinds! Consider the fact that ivory trade and the lust for rhino horns have driven these animals to near extinction! Fur coats from exotic animals have resulted in similar tragic outcomes. The list of such human arrogance and indifference is long, and continues to grow. It never ceases to amaze me how low we as humans can go, and how brutal and *inhumane* we humans can really be!

Another big issue is energy production in the first place. The continued use of pollution and cancer causing and toxic fuels without the integration of other enovironmentally friendly fuels is unsustainable and foolish. The use of 'fossil' fuels, nuclear fuel, and coal are examples of this.

Nuclear energy is the most foolish and dangerous notion for mass energy consumption. It takes a lot of energy to mine for, extract and refine uranium, the fuel source for nuclear energy, making it a poor choice over even fossil fuel and other energy sources. Add to this the problem of highly toxic nuclear waste storage, and suddenly, nuclear energy sinks to the bottom as it really is the worst energy choice.

Hydroelectric power is another source of energy that is projected as 'clean' by its proponents. While that may be true to an extent, the environmental impact is tremendous. Harnessing the power of flowing waters or large pools of water, such as rivers, by damming them, is what generates hydroelectric power. Natural river flows, however, take multitudes of centuries to develop, and entire local ecosystems change and adapt gradually. Damming a river alters drastically the entire local ecosystem 'instantly' without allowing for adaptation. This usually results in *considerable* local destruction of plant and animal life surrounding the project. Not only that, these projects are also generally harmful to the communities around them, and even those much further downstream are affected by the damming of a river. Therefore, hydroelectric power is not a very good option either. Remember, we only create misery when we go against nature.

At all cost avoid utilizing or buying into the concept of 'fuel' from grains or produce, such as 'corn fuel' or 'biodiesel' as these products have low 'burn' efficiencies meaning it takes more to do less. Additionally, the modified production of such grains would serve better for human consumption and ending world hunger than wasting time and resources on the *inefficient* burning of it. Using 'bio-fuels' is foolish and harmful in every way imaginable, and ends up hurting the farmer, the economy and the environment in the long run!

Explore the feasibility of solar and wind power in your community. These are non-depleteable and readily available sources of energy that are literally 'wasted' by not harnessing their power. Again, no matter how small the initial utilization is, the communal and global impact over time can be tremendous not just in reducing the greenhouse gases but by reducing air and environmental pollution as well. Therefore, the use of solar and wind power must be integrated into everyday use immediately. More focus should be given to these immediately in making them more efficient and easier to integrate into everyday life. For example, the use of solar panels on rooftops of houses for the production of adjunct electricity is completely feasible and ready to use now. Their use on top of buses, trucks, and possibly even trains and other large commercial vehicles to provide additional power in an adjunctive or 'hybrid' mode with diesel fuel is another possibility. *Genuine* and determined research must be directed to other energy sources such as wind, solar, hydrogen power, and on improved efficiency and utilization of all existing energy sources and their utilization, not just for vehicles, but for industrial applications as well. Large production facilities or warehouses could easily house huge solar panels and windmill turbines, producing power that could be self-utilized or even put back on the 'energy grid' to be sold and utilized elsewhere. The possibilities are endless. There is really no shortage of imagination and creativity – just a shortage of willpower, desire and resources, and an abundance of greed by those who benefit at the expense of all else.

The ideal energy sources are the utilization of sun, wind and hydrogen. Solar and wind energy should be used to generate hydrogen. If the use of solar, wind and hydrogen energy was to be implemented, the overall negative impact on the environment would lessen dramatically, the health and wealth of the communities affected would increase dramatically, dependency on foreign imports would decrease, and entire countries, their people and their economies would strengthen significantly.

These are not Utopian or foolish notions but are carefully thought-through statements that will stand the tests of economists and time. Wise leaders and wiser communities would do well to heed these warnings and thoughts!

We have seen from the preceding discussion with just a few simple examples (you investigate and implement in other aspects of your life) that making just a few wise choices during the course of your everyday life can start to have a significant impact on you, your pocket-book, your family and community, and indeed the world. And the great thing is that as a Hindu, you are already doing this! The concept of simple living, that is, and minimizing your footprint on the environment. And it isn't really difficult at all, is it?

Start with *you,* and watch it spread. The benefits are universal!

Yes, it really *is* that simple!

11.6: Thirty-Three Cror Devta! How in the world do we worship them all?

Hindu mythology has thirty-three *cror* devta. How in the world can we be expected to worship them all? This is absurd, right?

It *is*, and it really *isn't*.

Let us explore the *true* meaning and significance of this *apparently* ludicrous statement.

First, there is no such thing as thirty-three cror devta as separate and worshipable deities! We have already reviewed briefly the true divine avataars and other shaktis that are not avataars. Therefore, we do not really have to worship thirty-three cror devta. That would be absurd indeed!

The *true* meaning of the statement, though, is beautiful and meaningful, and captures the very essence and wisdom of Hindu Ideology if one allows it too.

What we do know from our shastra is that there were about thirty-three cror aatmas or jiv-aatmas floating around then. Following Goswami Tulsidas and his true darshan, all these thirty-three cror jiv-aatma are *aunshi* of the One and Only Paramaatma. As such, with this darshan in mind and in our heart, each and every Jiv-aatma is divine, representing the Supreme in a small but significant way. Hence, each such jiv is a Devi shakti, and therefore a dev. When one can apply the true knowledge of the scriptures, every living creature is divine; that is the ultimate significance of what Goswami Tulsidas teaches us. Hence the wonderful concept of thirty-three cror devta!

How is that for *divine darshan* and *summ-bhav*?

Only in the *vishaal* and expansive great heart of Hinduism!

11.7: Ganpati Visarjan: Dev *Puja* or Dev *Apraadh*?

This is a festival that has originated from southern India. It is a ten day long festival in which Lord Ganesh is decorated and ceremoniously worshipped for this period, and at the conclusion of the festivities, is cast into the ocean.

The meaning behind this important festival is highly significant, but the way it is carried out is apraadh! Awake, my Hindu friends! First realize why it is that we devote these ten wonderful days to worshipping Ganesh, and why it is that He is cast into the ocean. Do not participate in apraadh! Dev Apraadh!

The reason why we worship Ganesh for this period is that He is the ideal son and protector of His mother, Parvati. Parvati had asked Ganpati to stand guard while She went for a bath. She asked Him not to let anyone through until She returned. We know that Lord Shiv returned home after many years from His Samadhi, and went to Parvati. Shiv had not seen Ganesh, and Ganesh didn't know His father, Lord Shiv. Therefore, mindful and respectful of His mother Parvati's instructions, Ganesh stopped His father Shiv at the door and would not let Him proceed inside. Ganesh did not know Shiv was indeed His father. Shiv, angered, beheaded Ganesh and proceeded to Parvati. We know that Shiv bestowed an elephant head on Ganpati's body once He realized what had happened. Shiv also gave the vardaan that Ganpati would be worshipped first in any puja at all for that puja to be successful.

Ganpati is worshipped for a ten-day period, then, because He sacrificed Himself in obeying His mother's instruction. He was an obedient son and protector that paid with His life in fulfilling His mother's instructions. This makes Ganesh worthy of worship for ten glorious days. But not the elephant-headed Ganesh! He only became elephant-headed afterwards.

So, why worship Him and caste Him into the ocean? That is indeed Dev Apraadh! So what is the significance here, and how did it get so distorted? Let's go back to the original story.

When Shiv beheaded Ganpati, Ganesh's head actually fell on Chandra Lok. Such was the might of Shiv's blow! Ganesh's lifeless head lay in Chandra Lok, while His body eventually gained a new head, that of an elephant. The question then arises, what became of the original *lifeless* head?

Well, my Hindu friends, the *lifeless head* is really what we should cast into the ocean, for that is what befits a Dev's body. We do *not* cast the final beautiful elephant-headed form of Ganesh in the ocean! That is Dev Apraadh!

We worship the *dutiful Ganesh*, son of Parvati, for a period of ten days in honor of His sacrifice for His mother. This form of Ganpati must be the original human-headed Ganesh. Then, we respectfully and ceremoniously, with *solemn* pomp and honor befitting a fallen hero, cast His body signifying His lifeless head in Chandra Lok, into the ocean. That is befitting a fallen Dev!

Therefore, in the Final Analysis, to merely worship the elephant-headed Ganpati for ten days and caste Him into the ocean is ignorant, mindless, meaningless and Dev-Apraadh!

Awake, my Hindu friends! We must worship the *human-headed* Ganpati for ten days, caste *Him* into the ocean, and restore His glory by then finishing the festival with the restoring of the elephant-headed Ganpati back in our hearts, our homes and our temples.

11.8: Hinduism: The Magnificent Culture, The Magnificent People

First off, ask yourself: Hindustaan has 'Hindu' in it; do *you* have Hindustaan in *you*?

Consider the fact that Hinduism is *decaying* at an *alarming* rate. It is literally being shredded apart while Hindus either ignore this or allow this. Our samaaj, our sanskriti, our vichaar, our culture, our religion and everything we stand for is being either carefully and deliberately destroyed, or is decaying and rotting from within. Please read this carefully, for these are carefully chosen words. We will elaborate on this observation in *The Current Predicament* in the next chapter, so please *do* read it.

So, Hinduism worldwide, and everything it stands for such as morality, peace, integrity, harmony, tolerance, 'tradititional' family values, multi-generational homes and respect for women and elders, ahinsa and so on, is losing ground at an alarming rate. Hindus either choose to ignore this, or are participants to a varying degree in it.

If we stand aside and choose to do nothing while Hinduism gets torn down, then we are *napunsak* or impotent and deserve to be slaughtered like we surely will be. We deserve to fall from Grace, like Krishna tells Arjun, and lose everything including our very identity.

On the other hand, if we willingly allow ourselves to be drawn to the flash and fireworks show, a *mirage*, that is put up by non-Hindus, we most certainly shall lose our identity and then, too, deserve to be slaughtered.

According to Krishna, not taking sides in such a core and fundamental debate on one side or another is impotency and stupidity, as well as a being a sin. By default, when you do nothing, and take no responsibility, you are a loser and deserve to fall from Grace like Krishna says you surely will.

How can we Hindus allow this? Do you not recall all the sacrifices great people have made for Hindustan? Were they in vain? Are you willing to step aside while our children's books get changed, the stories of our true heroes get distorted, turned upside down, or even completely eliminated? Or are you willing to see our temples, one mandir at a time get torn, polluted and so on? Or that we lose important political seats and lose the ability to be governed *by Hindus*? Will such political agendas and legislation not be able to tear down the Hindu samaaj within a mere generation? What is even more frightening is that this is *already* happening in Hindustaan today! It is happening while the meek and impotent Hindus either do nothing or worse join them! Why does your aatma not shriek at you! Or are you just too deaf to hear it screaming at you! This should sicken you to your core, yet you *meekly* let it happen! Enough! Awake! Awake, my Hindu friends! Awake before it's too late!

Or are you afraid? If you carefully look around the world today, and study the history of the world as well, you come to a startling conclusion:

It is the five percent of the people on the planet
that are making or have made
ninety five percent of the people suffer!

That has to be the height of stupidity! The sad fact is that the ninety five percent of us that allow the five arrogant and greedy percent to unleash this on us are the *real* culprits. Think about that for a moment! We, the ninety five percent, let it happen so we are *really* the ultimate cause of the damage that ultimately befalls us!

Let us look at it from yet another perspective. Let me illustrate with a simple example.

In Africa, lions on the open plains hunt wild water buffalo as a potential prey. The herds of buffalo can number anywhere from thirty or so on up to hundreds. The pride of lions is usually five to ten, with usually just three or four lionesses on the hunt. The hunt is organized skillfully by the lions with the aim of dividing the herd and revealing the weak, the young and the old, and splitting them off from the rest of the herd. At the beginning of the hunt, the lions split up, and fan out. One or two then begin the attack causing instant panic and causing a stampede in the herd. As the hunt progresses, the strong buffalo surge ahead, and weak are divided and split off. The lions join up against the one main target thus selected, attack and bring it down, while the rest of the herd stops a short distance further up and look on. The victim is then devoured by the whole pride. This is the typical scene.

However, this is not *always* the case. Water buffalo can be very unpredictable. Every once in a while, for reasons known only to the water buffalo, as the hunt starts to progress, three or four buffalo will turn around, circle rump to rump, and face the lions head-on with lion-killing horns aimed straight at the hunter. When this happens, the lions back off slowly and retreat! If the lions do not retreat and attempt to attack, the buffalo will stand their ground, and drive their sharp horns into the belly of the hunter, thus vanquishing the hunter. This scene, though not typical, happens consistently enough, and lions can and do get killed by the water buffalo.

Remember, it was not the buffalo that attacked. The lions did. The buffalo merely stood their ground. How about making this a learning experience for us?

Make the water buffalo our guru and learn from it. For it can change not just our life, but the life of generations to come. If only three or four buffalo stand rump to rump and stave off the determined lions, why can't we do the same? If the entire buffalo herd, or even the majority of them stand together, can they not wipe out lions entirely rather than facing them down? It is the ninety five percent of us with the foolish and typical panicked buffalo herd mentality that allow the five percent of the vicious and the insane to divide us, rule over us and change us!

If we can only learn from the buffalo, stand rump to rump, there is nothing the secular militants can do, especially if we are determined to drive our dharmic horns into their belly once and for all!

Let us unite and stand Hindu rump to Hindu rump with our *dharmic* horns, our duty-bound horns, aimed at the very heart of the non-Hindus that would seek to divide or corrupt us. Like the water buffalo, we *will* stand our ground and vanquish those that wish to divide us Hindus.

Let us earnestly and sincerely begin a grass-roots movement to *peacefully* but with *great determination* take back Hindustaan peace-loving bhaaratwasis. Let us teach *bhaaratia sanskriti* in *our* schools to *our* children once again. Let us sing *Vande Mataram* proudly and loudly again! Let us not be afraid to tell *true* stories in our schools of how non-Hindu invaders were repelled and how Hindus have never stepped back from making the ultimate sacrifice. Let us teach that "G" is for Ganpati, and not for "Gadheda" or the such!

Begin with yourself. Make a difference, one child, one person, one family at a time. The emphasis remains firmly and solidly on family values and God, for the family unit is the smallest building block of society and indeed the nation.

And what is a 'Hindu' family?

It is a family that is founded on firm spiritual beliefs and values *with implementation* into daily life, which is the rightful fruit of that spiritual foundation. It is a family that not only preserves but actually *cherishes* the sanctity of marriage, having *both parents* raising the children responsibly, and having wise grandparents to guide and steer them through as-yet uncharted waters. It is a family that lives not just *to*gether, but *for* each other. A family that not only eats together, but helps cook and clean lovingly *for* each other. A family that not only practices gender appropriateness but actually cherishes and respects their women without being archaic or fanatical, and women who in turn prize their *laaj-sharam*, their modesty and humility. And most certainly, it is a family that not only prays together, but *for* each other, their nation and the rest of creation as well. And finally, it is a family that stands firmly enough on their beliefs to protect, nurture and nourish their elderly, the bona-fide repositories of priceless social and spiritual knowledge, that will help steer not just the family but indeed their nation to not only prosperity in this life, but the attainment of the *true* goal of human life and existence in the very first place – the Lotus feet of Radhe Shyam.

Let us do this one school, one politician, one mandir, one village, and one city at a time. You will be amazed at what one person can achieve. Remember a humble little five-foot Indian? How about two? Fear not, then, for *You* are in great company! Make the world a nobler and more peaceful place. Bhaaratia vichaar *is* noble and admirable, and second to none. It only fosters peace, haromony and prosperity by ferreting out the evil within, and always leading by example, never by force and brutality. But it takes a brave man to make a stand. Remember a brave tiny Hindu who brought a massive colonial empire to its knees?

And what is Hinduism? What ultimately starts to characterize and define what is really at the foundation of Hinduism?

Hinduism is *the* all-encompassing platform from which one can *soar* to Krishna. It is really and truly the best and most noble one. One that lives *and* let lives. Proud but never arrogant, unassuming yet noble, gentle but never feeble, even uneducated perhaps but never ignorant, but most of all, like Shri Vishnu Himself, a rose in one hand and sudarshan chakra in the other. Hindus Awake! Look at and study form of Shri Vishnu. Carefully study it, and realize that you are from him, a part of him, and very dear to him!

Like the water buffalo of Africa, let us unite and stand Hindu-rump to Hindu-rump in a circle with our children and elders well protected in the center. Only then can we call the shots. All non-Hindus trying to tear

Hinduism down take note: Would you prefer the rose, or the *sudarshan chakra*? It is your choice! Shri Vishnu gave us both, and Shri Krishna directs us! We will drive our dharmic horns deep in your heart and use our sudarshan chakra forces for whatever it takes to defend *our* dharam, *our* Hindustaan, *our* bhoomi, *our* seema, *our* sanskriti, *our* shastra, *our* mandirs, *our* peaceful and noble culture, *our* elders and *our* little ones, *our* women, and *our* vichaar!

And so, I ask once more. Hindustaan has 'Hindu' in it; do *you* have Hindustaan in *you*? *Truly and sincerely?*

Remember, dharam does *not* defend us, *we* defend *our* dharam! Simply *chanting* His holy name defends *no*t our dharam!

Awake my Hindu friends! We need more Sardar Patels, more Bhagat Singhs, more Lal Bahadur Shastris, more Subhash-jis, more Guru Govind Singhs, more Shiva-jis, more Swami Dayanand-jis, and we need them to Awake now for Bhaarat!

We need to proclaim loudly and boldly *Vande Mataram* once again! *Jaago!* Awake! Hindus Awake! The time for action is *now!*

Jai Hind!

11.9: What's in a Dress & Your Appearance?

This is an easy and interesting discussion. It gets back to the ABCD or OBCD we discussed in the *Preface* portion of this discussion.

So what's in a dress and your appearance? Everything! We are not talking about a particular dress, but rather a dress code. It's called Hindu Pride. Or, put another way, pride in the fact that you *are* a Hindu. Let's elaborate, shall we, and get to the point?

How you dress is important in many ways. Let us look at some.

Of probably the most importance, you need to realize that how you dress affects you *and* the observer, *not* just the observer. Please understand this simple point. We usually dress based on what the projected or perceived judgement would by an observor. For example, if you go to a family picnic, you would not want to wear a suit, right? This is because it is very likely everyone would be dressed in a casual manner, and you would stick out noticeably like a sore thumb. You would also be the 'differrent' one, and that is likely to make you feel uncomfortable or unwelcome or even both. Conversely, if you were invited to a state house for a formal occasion, you would not want to wear shorts and a t-shirt or jeans, right? Well, part of this equation is psychological. We humans need to 'belong' and not stand out. In the preceeding example, you would have dressed according to how you thought others would judge or perceive you. Hence, we dress more to impress an observer, rather than how we really may want to, the main reason being we wish to 'fit in' and not stick out. But the problem is that this very psychological issue also ends up affecting *us*, not just an observer.

Usually, how we decide to dress is predicated on what we do, where we work and so on. These things will certainly influence our decision, but they are not ultimately responsible for it – You are! For example, unless you work in an environment that requires a uniform, such as a nurse, a crew-member of a uniformed organization, or so on, you have the flexibility to decide within reason what you will wear. If you work in a library, a school, a non-uniformed governmental agency and so on, *you do* have a choice in what you wear as long as it is appropriate. This primarily applies to the work week.

How about how you dress on your time off, or weekends and such? You obviously have all the flexibility you need to decide on what you wear, right?

Let us forget about the observer for the moment, let's focus on *you* and look at it from the *reverse* perspective – yours! Really, though, this is the *correct* perspective. Let us illustrate.

On the days that you dress in rags, or very casual, you will notice that your mood roughly follows that, you will also feel laid-back, mentally relaxed, and you may get a few things done, but not significantly so. Your overall self-esteem will be down a notch or two, but if you are going to stay home, that would not necessarily present a problem.

At the other end of the spectrum, what happens when you put on a sharp, crisp business suit and go out, whether for business or pleasure? Your self-esteem will be up a few notches, your mental attitude and aptitude will follow, your thoughts will be focused and crisp, and you will be efficient for the most part in whatever you do for the day. You will get a significant amount of work done, and you will be more relaxed and satisfied at the end of the day, rather than through the day, for having achieved something meaningful.

Okay, so where are we going with this, you ask? What is the *real* point that we are trying to make? Well, let me clue you in. It is elegantly simple but oh, so important. If you *dress* like a Hindu, you will *feel* like one, *act* like one, *eat* like one, *think* like one, and *behave* like one! It really is that simple *and* that important! But the impact it has *on you* is tremendous and long lasting.

As to the specifics of our dress code, there is not a particular type that we call 'Hindu' because we have a rich and colorful diversity, but we do have some common elements. I am not asking you to wear full traditional Indian dress to work, but I am asking you to preserve some elements of it, and especially on weekends or holidays when not at work. For example, for women, the bindi or chandlo, bangles, and most importantly their modesty, are subtle but unique and important identifiers of our Hindu culture and identity. It is their beauty and their shringar that is a proclamation of the fact that they are proud to be a Hindu. Heck, even non-Hindus are wearing bangles and bindis! And *that* is the way to influence others. In a *positive* manner!

It is not enough to say don't be the crowd but stand out from it. That is just too *blazee*. Awake! Don't just stand *out* from the crowd, my Hindu friend, stand head and shoulders above the crowd! Be recognized! Be respected! Why blend in? That is simply boring and mundane. Where is the uniqueness in it? What is so special about that? *But to be a Hindu!* Wow! The wonderful and peaceful connotations, the connotation of silent strength, the will and the power to induce *change* from even great empires! Now *that* is something worthwhile! Let that be the beacon for the world. You may have heard the old adage – lead, follow or get out of the way, right? Well, my friends, why follow? In fact, why even lead? Heck, beat your own path, if that is what your dharam and your heart tells you is right!

Ultimately, what *should* matter to you is not what the observer thinks, but what you think. If all that matters is what an observer would think than you have more issues than we can deal with here! Anyway, what should matter is what *you* think, and how *you* feel. *That* should influence your decision. You should have the integrity and the self-esteem to do what you want as long as it is reasonable and prudent. Therefore, *you* should decide what you are going to wear. You should influence others, and not the other way around! You let whoever wishes to follow.

Hence, if you are a Hindu, dress like one! If you dress like a Hindu, you will feel like one, act like one and behave like one! That is the point! Hindus really are second to none, and you should be proud to dress, act and behave like one. You should be proud to be a Hindu, and that pride should carry over to everything you do. The rewards and returns are truly amazing. You are who you are, and you should be proud of it. You cannot and should not pretend to be someone or something that you are not.

Honesty and integrity should be in everything including how you dress. The bigger picture of this is that ultimately how you dress will most definitely influence you and those around you, your life, and yes, your spiritual and after-life too.

But wait! It doesn't just stop there even. What about the next generation? How will you influence them? Will it be by hiding behind an assumed name, or will it be by giving them the gift of our rich and meaningful culture that can change even great empires peacefully? And don't forget the most important gift of all – the ability to be a devotee and return home to our maker.

Do you want to take away that priceless treasure that took an eternity of generations to build from the next generation – *your* children?

Awake, my Hindu friends! Are you going to stand tall and and be respected for who you are, a proud and great Hindu with the connotation of silent strength, the will and the power to change even great empires, or are you going to be a 'me too' blend-in, a nobody and lose your identity, your dignity, and ultimately, even your liberation?

Awake, my Hindu friends! Dress like a Hindu and do it with pride! Then and only then will you think like a Hindu, feel like a Hindu, act like a Hindu, behave like a Hindu, be noble and compassionate like a Hindu and, most significantly, worship the Supreme like a Hindu for the attainment of the real purpose of human life in the first place!

For your generation's sake *and* the next, and for real progress toward the ultimate goal of human life, *dress for the occasion!*

11.10: What's In a Name?

We discussed outward appearance in the preceding section in the form of attire and dress. You should realize that how you dress is important, both to the observer and to you. Now let us take this two steps upstream and apply it more broadly. Even then, realize that the broad application will ultimately result in more focused and personal results.

Let us look at two issues that deal with names.

One is the name 'India' and the second is the culture and the 'religion' that is termed 'Hinduism.' Not that there is anything wrong with either. In fact, both are great! But we are on a mission. We have to strive to be right first, and then allow everything else to fall into place. Since one is tied to the other, we will deliberate both issues simultaneously.

The *Veds* are the original ancient scriptures of the Hindus. The religion that would follow should correctly be called '*Vedic Dharam*' or '*Sanatan Dharam*' rather than '*Hinduism*.' We noted this point at the beginning, and we shall make it one last time as we conclude our initial discussion. It is worthwhile noting here again that the term '*Sanatan*' really means 'eternal' and hence always existent. One must understand fundamentally, then, that the term *sanatan* denotes a process that has no beginning and no end. It is, therefore, truly timeless. This process has *always* existed, and there was *never* a time when it did *not* exist. Time, then, is essentially taken out of the equation. Therefore, '*Sanatan* dharam' has no beginning and no end.

In spoken terms, however, the *connotation* may be used differently, if incorrectly. Sanatan dharam is also sometimes interchangeably used for 'Hinduism' or 'Hindu religion,' but there technically *is* a difference. The word *Hindu* is derived from the word *Hind*, referring to the motherland. The colonialists probably derogatorily referred to us as *Hindus*, the ones from the land of *Sindhu*, or the river Sindhu. The colonials also probably had a hard time pronouncing the word *Sindh*, hence the word 'India' given by the colonialists. This reasoning would also apply to city names, such as Bombay when it really should have been Mumbai, and so on. Other theories and suppositions have been advanced. Who really knows and, for that matter, who *really* cares? The terms 'Hindu,' 'Hinduism' and 'Hindustaan' have now come to imply and stand for something very special and deeply meaningful, and rightfully so, and that is perfectly acceptable regardless of their origin. It is the *now*, the vartamaan that matters, so debating the origin and its appropriateness, as some of my learned Hindu friends are inclined, is really pointless, foolish and divisive!

The word 'Bhaarat' also refers to India, and was *supposedly* derived from the namc of King Bharat who was a supremely powerful king in olden India and who was credited with many difficult achievements. However, more correctly, when Shri Krishna addresses Arjun as *Bhaarat* in the *Bhagwat Gita*, His implication is that Arjun has the *proper attitude and aptitude* for knowledge. Therefore, according to this interpretation, Shri Krishna defines 'bhaarat' as one who is *fit to receive the correct knowledge* that He was about to deliver.

Therefore, according to this last interpretation, the term *Bhaarat* is also used to describe *one that is fit* to receive this *vidya*, or *correct* knowledge. Hence, the use of the word *Bhaarat* or *Hindustaan* to refer to *India* is very meaningful because it is auspicious, sentimental, historic in context, highly patriotic, but most importantly, means a land where *the people* are *fit* to receive *the* correct knowledge of the Supreme. Very cool indeed! The Bhaaratia people worldwide should then be thought of as those 'fit' to receive this proper knowledge *if* they follow the teachings of Shri Krishna.

Sanatan dharam is also mistakenly viewed by some to mean all-encompassing, meaning broadly embracing the worship of all gods and seeing God in all of them. To this group, *sanatan dharam* means that worshiping Vishnu, Krishna, Shiv, Lakshmi, etc is equally correct since all such forms represent one God. A noble approach, but one that still represents an incorrect use of the term *sanatan*, for sanatan really means eternal and timeless.

In The Final Analysis, the common understanding, then, is that although technically *incorrect*, the terms *Hinduism*, *Vedic Dharam*, and *Sanatan dharam* are okay to be used inter-changeably, but the terms *Vedic Dharam* and *Sanatan Dharam* are more correct and definitely much more meaningful when referring to our dharam, and we are *Bhaaratia* people in the land of Bhaarat, where we are fit to receive the correct knowledge of the Supreme.

However, regardless of technical issues, suffice it to note and proclaim that we *are* proud Hindus, we are Hindustaani, the national language is Hindi, and Hinduism is the most peaceful, the oldest and greatest religion, dharam, culture and people on the face of the planet! Hindus have contributed to the world extremely important things but, more importantly, a Hindu remains the shining beacon to the rest of the world for peace, strength, family values and unity, patriotism, and list continues *ad-infinitum*.

Regardless of *where* a Hindu lives in the world today, he should be a great asset to his family, his community and most importantly his nation, leading *by example* of what is achievable. Hindus are constantly the envy of even the *devtas*, and with a good reason!

Hindu Pride Rules!

Vande Mataram!

Jai Hind!

11.11: Ahinsa, Not Inaction

Understand this! Ahinsa makes sense, but that it does *not* mean inaction or tolerance of evil on any front whatsoever.

Lord Krishna makes this abundantly clear to Arjun, who had put forth a good argument wanting to retire rather than fight and kill his distant family. It is really Lord Krishna who first initiated the concept of ahinsa[27], who was the final *shanti doot*, the final messenger of peace, and yet who was *also* the One to finally direct Arjun to *annihilate* the enemy or to die trying.

This is not a contradiction as some fools may argue, although *apparent* contradictions with Shri Krishna's *avataar* abound. It plainly and firmly emphasizes that *ahinsa* does *not* mean *inaction*. Read that last phrase *again*, as it is one worth committing to *firm* and *immediate* action.

Consequently, Shri Krishna at first *did* attempt a peaceful resolution. When one was not forthcoming, the *Pandavs,* and not Shri Krishna, decided finally that war it had to be. When Arjun was anguished and bewildered on the battlefield by seeing his extended family, those whom he loved and adored, lost his resolve to fight and thought that simply putting down his Gandiv and retiring to the jungle to live life as a sanyasi was more appropriate. Krishna then delivered the correct *vidya*, the correct knowledge, that we now treasure as the *Bhagwat Gita*, that showed Arjun and *us* that abandoning our prescribed duty even to worship God is never acceptable and in fact is a sin! He showed Arjun that in fact Bhishma, Drona, and so on were already dead even before the start of the battle! Arjun would simply be the *nimit karan*, fulfill his responsibility and obligation as a Kshatriya, serve the samaaj by making it more noble, get the glory of doing his dharam, his duty, and be relieved of sinning!

Hence, one must never abandon his prescribed duties, responsibilities, and obligations to one's family, society, community and indeed the nation and ultimately the world. However, these responsibilities and actions then must be carried out according to *Krishna's* instructions and teachings, and not merely on one's unguided notions and whims. The priciples of truth, honesty, sincerety, dharam, and so on.

Having thus refocused our mind and thoughts, one needs to realize *without hesitation* or a doubt that Ahinsa never equals inaction!

Let us look at an extremely foolish and ridiculous notion that keeps Hindus vulnerable to non-Hindu intervention and subsequent conquest.

Remember, Krishna is a cowherd, not a cow. Most Hindus foolishly act like *cows* rather than like *cowherds*. Like foolish people, we wait for someone or something divine to help us with the solution to our problem because we are too lazy, too ambivalent, too scared or too stupid to lift a finger for ourselves. We forget to act like cowherds. We speak of Krishna, yet don't follow His lead or direction.

For example, as Hinduism rapidly continues to be eroded from within *and* from without, the Hindu society, *acting like cows*, simply tolerates it waiting for some divine interaction. It lifts not a finger to getting us back in the right direction. The rishis, gurus, honest politicians, and Hindus all wait. And wait. And wait! Waiting for what? Do something first! We must be willing to take the first step so Krishna can take nine! How is He going to help if we are too ignorant, too lazy, or simply too docile to even *start* to do the right thing? Does a cowherd wait while a *hinsac prani*, a lion, a tiger, etc attacks his flock? Obviously not – the cowherds band together and repel the attacker, right? And, with Krishna on your side, you would prevail. Why the madness, then, in simply waiting like the cows at the slaughterhouse? You *will* get slaughtered! Think about that!

How about another illustration? Want lunch? Lets try chanting *roti, dal, chawal*. Let's chant till lunch appears courtesy Krishna's mercy, right? Right! You could chant till you literally dropped dead from hunger and food would not appear! Man, the odesity and the stupidity! The *cow* mentality instead of the *cowherd* mentality.

Let's elaborate a little more. Let's take *roti*. Lord Krishna grew into a crop the seed that *we* planted. He supplied that seed, by the way. He provides the nourishment, the air, and *everything* for the plants to grow and produce the seed, wheat. Does that wheat simply fly onto our plate as roti? Or do *we* first pick it, mill it, make the dough, roll it, bake it and then put it onto our plate? Krishna helped by providing the plant that provided the seed, *we* picked and milled it, added water and other stuff He provided and made it into dough. Then *we* rolled it, and baked it with fire He provides, and put ghee on it from milk and cows that He provided again. Get it yet? It is called teamwork! We only have to do an extremely small task, the proverbial one step, and He does everything else that we call the remaining nine steps.

So why wait as our Hindu samaaj and vichaar is torn down bit by pretentious bit, one child, one school textbook, one politician and one temple at a time? Are you really that dumb as to believe that mere chanting will cause Krishna to magically appear and reinstate the correct Hindu texts, and so on? Or are you simply too lazy to get off your couch to do anything? Or, do you simply not care? Well, if you are, or you don't, then you deserve to get slaughtered like the cow you choose to be!

Fools tell us that Gandhiji followed a path of non-violence and so we should set aside or criticize Lord Krishna's teachings or Gandhiji, or both. However, this criticism stems from a lack of knowledge, a lack of understanding, and an utter lack of intelligence.

Gandhiji shows us by example. He *acted*, but walked a tight-rope between action and violence. He did *not* stand aside or retire. He followed Lord Krishna's instruction *to act*. However, he chose a path of non-violence. Remember Shri Krishna Himself advocates ahinsa.

Let's examine *why* he chose this path.

Gandhiji was not a Kshatriya to start with. He was a lawyer by training, and a very intelligent one. Therefore, he could size up the situation his beloved country was in. Out-gunned at every point and every turn. To face the then brutal British head-on would mean wholesale death of his beloved countrymen, and no purpose would be served in the end. Violence only begets violence, that is the nature of the beast.

Even *shaastra* says that in sizing up the enemy, one must weigh the two armies, and if your side comes up lighter, one needs to walk away to do battle another day. Gandhiji did not want wholesale slaughter of his fellow men and indeed even of his adversary, so he explored other options.

The winning strategy he came up with was brilliant and simple, which would spare lives, both Indian *and* British. Immobilize and cripple the British government in India, and cause them more trouble than it was worth. India had the power of numbers if not the number of guns. Therefore, act to cripple the whole infrastructure, rather than to kill and destroy. This method would be longer and harsher to him personally, but the wholesale slaughter of his nation would be spared, and durable peace through establishment of higher moral principles could be achieved.

Consequently, critics who rush to judge Gandhi as a hypocrite when it comes to Lord Krishna's teachings in the *Gita* are mere fools. To the contrary, Gandhiji proved to be its best modern disciple! This is why a re-definition of an old adage is necessary. It is not really true that "Knowledge is Power", but rather "*Applied* Knowledge is *True* Power!" Those who understand the laws of physics can relate to this in a simple example, that it is not the static energy that is the most useful in the actual process of work but rather, it is kinetic energy.

Therefore, as we said before, realize that Ahinsa *always* makes sense, but it *never* means inaction!

This final thought is worth repeating. Ahinsa *always* makes sense, but it *never* means inaction! When you turn the other cheek and sit down and *do nothing*, you do this at yours *and* your nation's peril!

Are you listening Bhaarat? Are you listening, my Bhaaratia friends?

Hindus **Awake!**

Jai Hind!

11.12: Religion and Clannism in Hinduism; What is the Point?

Now for the final siddhant, which is the most important one. It is the one that deals with dharam, individually and collectively, and its *true* and *intended* purpose.

The first thing we need to do is make a simple statement that *everyone* needs to understand, and do so with firm and unyielding conviction,

True dharam founded on vidya, the correct knowledge, always unites. It is only avidya, the lack of this proper knowledge, confounded by arrogance that divides.

The true *sadhak*, one that *really* has the *desire* and the *longing* for the Supreme in his heart never splits hairs over *what* form that Supreme takes. He, in fact, derives great pleasure and pride in *all* of His forms *regardless* of what form! Only fools that have yet to conquer their *avidya* and ignorance divide over His countless and beautiful forms.

This, sadly, is the case today, for there are sects and sampradays that are cultish, clannish and highly divisive, splitting hairs and nit-picking *dharam* in the guise of 'religion' to the detriment of Hindustaan and indeed *all* Hindus worldwide. The old adage of divide and conquer is true, and yet we foolishly fight each other! What chance do we have of seeing light if we keep up this nonsense? We are *all* Hindus, and that should be enough!

You can elect to call the Supreme by whatever name you choose if you wish, for in the end all paths lead to *and* end in the one Supreme.

Some paths may be longer, some fraught with danger, some with obstacles, and so on, but as long as you are on a mission to seek the ultimate truth, all paths will end up in the same direction. As long as we as humans comprehend the concept that there *is* a Supreme personality, one that we bow to, it matters not *what* you call Him as long as you follow His wishes and observe His rules and teachings.

If, however, we look at the *saar*, the cream, the ultimate abstraction, the very essence of what all the Hindu scriptures tell us, the one name, the culmination of all paths, yogs, thoughts and efforts stands out. Let us examine this *essence* briefly.

The one name that *is* the source of all names according to all scriptures is the one that is also the most attractive, the most captivating, the

Supreme, the King of all Kings, the Judge of all Judges, the Source of all Sources, the Creator of all Creations, the very Life of all life, and ultimately and eternally, the God of all Gods – *Krishna.*

Throughout our discussion, we have pointed out that the Supreme, the PurnaPurshottam Bhagvan, the *adi Purush*, the one to be known by the Veds *is* Shri Krishna and none other. Shri Krishna *is* the source of simply everything, of all creation, and all avataars, all manifestations.

The *Shrimad Bhagwat* reveals,

... Krishna tu bhagvan svayam ...[28]

The author of the *Veds*, Bhagvan VedaVyas, in this line from the verse from the *Shrimad Bhagwat,* confirms and ascertains that Shri Krishna *is* indeed *svayam bhagvan*, the Supreme Himself, and *not* an avataar or manifestation.

The same verse, complete, reveals,

Ete camas kalah pumsah
Krishna tu bhagvan svayam
indrari vyakulam lokath
mrdanyanti yuge yuge[29]

This verse from the *Shrimad Bhagwat* describes that *all* other forms are incarnations or expansions of the Supreme, Shri Krishna, and it is indeed *He* who manifests in one form or another in the different Loks in different Yugs as needed.

If one accepts the authority of the Veds, then one also positively and without a doubt also affirms this final and ultimate truth from the same source and authority. Period.

In the *Bhagwat Gita*, Krishna proclaims that it is indeed *He* that is the 'Brahman,' the Supreme personality, who is to be known by the *Veds*, and proclaims *eko Hum, dvitiya nasti,* meaning the *one* Supreme Himself, Krishna, without another. Indeed, Shri Krishna Himself says that *He* is the compiler of the Vedant[30].

Shri Krishna says in the *Gita*,

Yasmat ksaram atito ham
Aksarad api ca uttamah

Ato smi loke vede ca
Prathitah purshottamah[31]

Shri Krishna establishes that *He* is the greatest, beyond Kshar and Akshar, and is recognized by the *Veds* as the *Purshottamah*, the Supreme.

Therefore, Shri Krishna is indeed *Advait*, One without another, from whom simply *everything* originates. Krishna is the source of everything, seen and unseen, realized and unrealized, perceived and imperceptible.

Hence, when one *applies* true vidya, the *gnan* or knowledge, one gains true *bhakti* with which one can begin the joyous journey culminating at the Lotus feet of Shri Krishna. Indeed, dry theological knowledge without proper implementation and subsequent *bhakti* and *prem* leads *only* to *mooddhta*, *jaddhta*, and arrogance!

If we now proceed further, any 'religion' ultimately serves one purpose and one purpose only: To get you to your final and correct *spiritual* destination. When one is eventually able to reach at the lotus feet of Shri Krishna, one will have had to shed *everything*, including *all religion* and *religious labels*. Only after shedding all kinds of baggage, including religion, and thereby becoming completely free can you reach Krishna.[32]

In *The Final Analysis*, only *Sanatan* dharam is left, for only *it* is eternal. Realize *eternal* or *sanatan* means timeless and forever. Recognize also that time is only applicable to us in creation, and is not even a factor pertinent in the Creator's abode.

Therefore *sanatan dharam* is timeless, ageless, eternal, and universal.

And *it* does *not* belong to any one caste or nation or indeed even people. Its' eternal existence is demonstrated by Shri Krishna Himself who says in the Gita that *He* returns *periodically* to re-establish *this* Sanatan and eternal dharam:

yada yada hi dharmasya
glanir bhavati bharata
abhyutthanam dharmasya
tadatmanam srjamyaham

paritranaya sadhu nam
vinasaya ca duskrtam
dharma-sanstharpanathaya
sambhavami yuge yuge[33]

Nowhere in the Gita does Krishna say "*Hindus*" or reference them in any way whatsoever. Nor does He mention a particular religion, sampraday, sect or cult!

To the contrary, Krishna asks us to *tyaag everything* and surrender completely (sharnaagati) unto Him and *only* Him in complete devotion: [34]

sarva dharmanp parityajya
mam ekam saranam vraja
aham tvam sarva papebhyo
moksha isyami masucha[35]

Presented with such truth straight from the Supreme, one quickly realizes that bickering about names of *avataars* aside or even the teachings of various *sampradays*, only *bhakti and surrender* to the Supreme *really* matter.

And, *Shri Brahma Samhita* proclaims that although Shri Krishna, the Supreme and Original Purush, is difficult to achieve by the *Veds*, He is easily attained by true devotion.

Therefore, regardless of the *name* used in achieving Him, the *only* vehicle is *true bhakti*, the rightful fruit of *complete sharnagati*. The rest is utterly trivial, foolish, arrogant, divisive and, indeed, completely immaterial. If one is able to realize this, one will have achieved his ultimate position at Krishna's lotus feet. If Meera, Nursey, and Paan Bai are indeed such examples then, having achieved His Lotus feet, you will not for a *kshan* be able to remain without singing and chanting about Him and His Glory!

Re-stating what has already been said, man is so caught up with his materialistic life that he has little time to even realize that when he finally falls off the hamster mill as one day he will, he needs only a two-by-six pier or casket! Everything he spent valuable time aimlessly amassing will sit there and mock him as he draws his final breath, for he would have simply wasted this God-given human form of his if all he used it for was the endless and completely useless material quest.

The only *real* tangible is here and now! *Vartman*, the Present! That *is* under your control! Life is truly worth living and most certainly worth enjoying to the fullest. And Hari-bhajan *is* what makes it all worthwhile.

Live life to the fullest, *but* within the constraints set by our wise and selfless rishis. Enjoy life, but always with Hari on your mind and in your heart. Your body is the soul's chariot, and its senses the horses. Hand over the reigns to your chariot and its horses to the *only* sarathi that you can trust with your soul. For *He* will never lead you astray, only to victory – back home to Him.

So, Awake, my dear Hindu friends! Chant! Chant His Holy Name with pure devotion! By *whatever* Name that pleases you, be it Krishna, Vishnu, Mahavir, Buddh, Swaminarayan, Ram, Shiv, Sai, or any of His glorious avataars. For in the end, it matters not *what* name you called Him by – only that you *did,* sincerely and with devotion.

In Kal Yug, life is short, *and* life is extremely busy. Therefore, waste not a *kshan*, not a precious moment of this human life. Live in the *vartaman kaal*, live every moment fully, and live life *for* Krishna, and *with* Krishna in it. For that, my Hindu friends, is the only true *dharam* for each of us - to live for Shri Krishna. And that, my Hindu friends, is not a religion. It is our duty, our goal, and ultimately our purpose in this side of Creation.

Ultimately, *that* is also the final *reality* and the *true definition* of sanatan dharam - a life lived joyously for Krishna and with Krishna in it, while faithfully maintaining one's duties and responsibilities to one's family, community and nation.

Then, *and only then*, will life have been worth living as a Hindu and a human being.

Jai Shri Krishna!

CHAPTER 12

Current Observations on Hinduism:

The Vital and Urgent Need to Return to the Basics

Dharam does not defend us, We defend our dharam!
Jaago! Awake, my fellow Hindus!

12.1: Hinduism - The Present Predicament facing the Hindu Society as a whole

The observations presented here deal with two broad and *extremely* serious issues *urgently* facing Hindus today irrespective of their position in society or where they live on the globe. These are the current generation decaying from within, and the future generation being systematically and methodically corroded and corrupted from without.

This treatise is short and brutally candid.

There is no mincing or sugarcoating of words. If you *feel* that this commentary is addressing you, it probably is. If you are offended by these observations, my apologies, but then it means a nerve has been touched.

On the other hand, if you *are* offended, maybe it's time to do some heartfelt and perhaps even long overdue soul searching and apologizing or making-up of your own.

After reading this short section, ponder the following *as* a Hindu:

> If you feel offended, do something!
>
> If you do not feel offended, please do something *more*!
>
> If you do not care either way *and* you are a Hindu,
>
> you should *Awake*!

The Present Generation's Predicament

Hindus are shedding fundamental Hindu principles such as non-alcoholism, vegetarianism, marital sanctity, celibacy, *puja*, *bhajan*, *kirtan* and *satsang* as easily as shedding clothes at the end of the day.

There is a ubiquitous affliction of "I " and "me" verses the age-old Hindu "family" and "us." They indulge themselves in the moment, and live solely for the moment. Family members are looked upon as cumbersome, 'needy' or 'whiny,' or 'uncool' whereas 'friends' and in-laws are perceived as much 'cooler' and easier to hang out with. Older family members, such as grandparents, parents, or older siblings swallow their pride despite abuses, carrying on with their 'duties' to snobbish, arrogant or perhaps even abusive younger members.

The grass certainly *appears* greener on the other side to these hypocritical, feeble-minded and lobotomized Hindus. They want their material desires and wants satisfied immediately, and will step on or over family members to achieve this in the quickest way possible. Money becomes the goal rather than the vehicle.

Yes, these materialistically driven Hindus have certainly achieved. But *what* have they *really* achieved? Take a closer peek, draw back the veil of flash and glitter, and the deeper truth of what they have really achieved is repulsive.

They may have nice houses but not homes. Their possessions may have multiplied, but their values and their families have divided. Incomes may have grown, but scruples and ethics have shrunk. They wish to fit in even if principles are compromised, rather than stand out for their morals and principles. This unbelievably also includes the *atrocious* business of *dealing* with, or worse yet, even *consuming and eating*, animal products. Even the sacred cow is no longer off-limits!

Yuva balaks and *balikas* (teenage children) pretentiously congregating in clubs, bars and discos, drinking, dancing and writhing life *aimlessly* away, while homes and *mandirs* (temples) stay *shaant,* or forlorn. All in the name and pretext of having a 'good' time. Unwanted pregnancies, undesired or rushed marriages, broken homes and hearts are the usual and consistant outcomes of such jaunts. And later, much later, it is all regretted if not verbalized, but it is awfully late by then.

Grehast, or married, couples exchanging partners on weekends or 'working' vacation jaunts with sickening impunity, rationalizing and giving in to their basic *vaasnas,* or desires, as readily as animals do! And with no apparent regrets! Morbid? Absolutely! Upset? You *should* be!

These 'progressive' Hindus, the young and the not-so-young alike, forget their *sanskaar*, principles of upbringing, their spouses, parents and grandparents and brothers and sisters who lovingly and without hesitation sacrificed whatever was necessary for them. And these same children as adults banish them to nursing homes and institutions or place them with hired 'help' under the guise of making a difficult choice in their loved one's best interests! They do this with utter and blatant disregard for previous, current or future generations.

Shameful, abhorrent and sacrilegious do not even *begin* to describe this rampant de-humanizing and de-Hindu-nizing behaviour!

Instead of taking an older partially disabled and perhaps even a little childish parent by hand and leading them to evening puja and aarti at the temple, they are shoved into institutions under some pretext. Then, its "out of sight and out of mind," and the parties begin. How can a Hindu do this to someone who led them to school by the hand so lovingly day in and day out? How is this conceivable? How can we sit at a bar chugging a "cold one" when our parents have tears in their eyes?

Hindus are losing compassion, *laaj and sharam*, humility and shame, self-respect, social or samaaj-respect, respect for their elders and colleagues, and such core values in brazen ways. They are turning into hypocrites and aggressive and unethical business people, putting greed and desire above all else. This is true of even Hindus that are in places of great responsibility such as the various branches of government, Temples of worship, and yes, even those that worship the deities, the sacred *pujaris*, or priests, are reaping great material rewards by turning *darshan-lalsa* (desire of the *darshan* of the deities) of the innocent public into a booming business of *darshan-laalach!* Talk about hypocrisy at its worst!

How can one imagine this of a people that Swami Vivekanand proudly proclaimed light little *deeps* in their temples (and hearts) with their families in the evening when the rest of the world lights up at pubs? How is this possible? Can it be because we no longer remember our Hindu principles and teachings? Are we so far gone that Lord Ram's and Lord Krishna's teachings fall on blind eyes and deaf ears? Have we completely forgotten the great Chaanakia? Did great people like Swami Vivekanand make such proclamations too early or perhaps even falsely?

While we, the present population ignorantly or feeble-mindedly turn our attention to the immediate satisfaction of our whims and *vaasnas*, setting an atrocious example for our children and our future leaders, let us examine an even more serious problem of *erosion of Hinduism* that will seal our fate as a by-gone Hindu nation and a by-gone Hindu people *if* we let it.

The Future Generation's Predicament

The other particularly serious and pressing issue facing the Hindu society and the Hindu nation is that our very foundation, our religion and culture, is being methodically, carefully and deliberately destroyed from right under our feet. There are many examples of this, and we will illustrate with merely a few.

Let's take our future leaders, our children, who are being systematically brainwashed starting at an early age right in our own schools. Texts and study material are being modified so that the *heroes* who had died for a Hindu cause are either eliminated entirely, or their tales methodically distorted.

We are allowing legislation whereby non-Hindus are granted political seats and granted government subsidies on religious pilgrimages. It has gotten so ludicrous that the mighty Hindu nation is having to *beg* for what is rightfully theirs even within its remaining borders in Ayodhya and Mathura, what to speak of what is being lost in Kashmir and Maansarovar!

Why is the mighty Hindu nation afraid to proclaim *Vande Mataram* or *Jai Hind* in schools, over loudspeakers or even in the streets, while non-Hindus within the mighty Hindu nation show no such cowardice? Why do we have to revise *our texts* for *our children* from "*G*" for "*Ganpati*" to "*G*" for the "*Gaddheda*" or the donkey that we really are becoming?!

Why are we so afraid to teach *our* sacred scriptures in *our own schools* to *our own children* like the *Ramayan*, the *Shrimad Bhagwat* or the *Shrimad Bhagwat Gita* in our own country while the Quran and the Bible continue to be taught in Muslim and Christian schools within the borders of the mighty Hindu nation without any such parallel fear or cowardice? Freedom of religion should be applicable across the board, right? Why then do Hindus fear to teach alongside other religions?

Let's look at some *guesstimated* 'statistics' for those who would like to look at the world through rose-colored glasses. I include in this category naïve, foolish and impotent Hindus that preach peace and meditation as the *only* answer to all Hindus' problems completely forgetting, or worse overlooking or ignoring, the lessons Shri Krishna taught Arjun when faced with a similar decay of values and traditions that comprised the noble Hindu *samaaj*.

Examine the Hindu *and* Muslim population statistics in Hindustaan today compared to the time of partition, and then do the same for the former East and West Pakistan. See some alarming trends? Why does the mighty Hindu nation tolerate such gross and malicious trends? It has to be *the* height of idiocy and insanity!

The mighty Hindu nation is being impotent and tolerant to the point of its own detriment, much like allowing a disease or cancer to remain unattended to that is *only* easily dealt with in its initial stages. It is more difficult if not impossible to deal with cancer once it spreads and takes root. Did *mahaan* or great people like Bhagat Singh, Lal Bahadur Shastri, Subhash-ji, Swami Dayanand-ji, Sardar Patel, and so on die in vain? I pray not!

Do not take me wrong, my Hindu and non-Hindu friends. This is not meant to be anti-anyone or anti-anyfaith. Do not attempt to misconstrue this in any way unfairly or unjustly. I am merely illuminating a point that is obvious and self-explanatory. It is all about the *balance* of peace and harmony. What, do you think, would happen if the roles or sides were reversed? In fact, it has already happened worldwide! Not even for a moment would a Hindu anything be tolerated or even entertained!

Remember, this is most definitely *not* a call to violence! Violence only begets violence, and *must* be avoided at any cost! We must learn the lessons great thinkers and leaders like Mahatma Gandhi and Dr. Martin Luther King have sacrified lives tragically for.

This *is* definitely a call for a peaceful and deliberate grassroots movement based upon understanding our riches as Hindus, and the realization of not just the tragedy but the *atrocity* it would be for the future generations of Hindus to be deprived of their rightful and rich heritage and inheritance. A Hindu, every Hindu, is entrusted to be the keeper of the elegantly peaceful yet mighty and noble concept of 'dharam' and to pass this on to the future up and coming generations.

I am not anti-anything or anti-anyone, just a Hindu that says enough is enough! We need to be fair to ourselves as Hindus *as well!* I am proud to be a Hindu and would like for my kids and their kids to have the opportunity and the chance to enjoy that very same privilege. I want them to enjoy that privilege *side-by-side* with all my non-Hindu friends who rightfully enjoy theirs in the free world! We wish to stand as equals, proud and free, and not as a subverted, sub-serviant, coerced, afraid or meek people.

Yes, it may be true that it is far easier to blend in with the crowd then to stick out. Yes, it is easier to ignore the little voice inside than to follow it. But, that does not make it right. We need to *not* shun what we intuitively know to be correct. It is always more difficult but ultimately more rewarding to do what you know to be right. *Listen to that little voice.* It is the *Hindu* voice telling you to *Awake!* Slumber not, my Hindu friends, for you have slumbered enough. It is time to take stock and take responsibility. It is time to re-take your life, that of your entire family, and that of the generations yet to come.

A local community of strong, spiritual, and caring families makes for a productive and strong regional community with integrity and honesty. This leads to social and financial prosperity and strength, which then makes ultimately for a strong and prosperous nation. To maintain world peace, there must be a *balance of power* without greed, and a country founded on strong families will definitely wield an equally strong military presence. The best deterrent to crime and invasion, whether personal or global, is always a great defense that can not only withstand any foreseeable onslaught but also easily repel it. A country that merely believes in peace, chanting, and 'world peace' through a 'borderless world' without having the perceived and real power of dissuation ultimately falls victim and prey to other predatory nations and neighbours.

Remember a frail little five-foot Indian with a radiant smile with the power to melt even great empires? Although he has made several mistakes, we must learn from history and apply that knowledge. We must act! Ahinsa, but never inaction, remember? It is amazing what can be achieved with just *one little Indian* brave enough to take that first step in the difficult but right direction!

The principles of Hinduism and their defense is a noble and worthwile cause. Hinduism teaches family value, spiritual value, social value and national value *above* selfish and momentary personal value. It is one that teaches peace and harmony with *all* of creation. God's creation. Not a secular one, but a universal one. A 'balanced' one where even a strong nation refrains from turning into a predatory nation. An eternal one. A *sanatan* one. One that is timeless and has no beginning and no end. One established by Lord Shri Krishna Himself. The prayers recited only by Hindus have this spirit of well-being for all of creation when we pray daily, *Aum Sarve Bhavantu Sukhina, Sarve Santu Niramaya, ...* .In essence, we pray for *all* of Creation to be happy, healthy, see good, and not be afflicted by misery. Only in Hinduism can you find such *sam-bhav,* equality, for all created beings, not only just Hindu or not, but also human and otherwise!Hindustaan once again must be a shining beacon for peace *and* might, a source of inspiration for Hindus worldwide to do what is right, and ultimately a source for every human on the planet to follow.

Chanting in temples and humbly asking for what is rightfully ours is only the *first* step. But don't stop there! Shri Krishna went to ask, too, as Yudhistir's *shanti doot*, or messenger of peace, but He did not stop there. Why should we forget what He teaches us? Why should Hindus have to beg for what is rightfully theirs in their *own* once-mighty nation? *How shameful and astoundingly preposterous is that?*

Hindus Awake! It is time for action, my Hindu friends! Education for our future leaders, our children, is *the* key. *Avidya,* or false knowledge, must be banished and replaced with *vidya* and patriotism. The once mighty, noble and *parakrami* Hindu nation is crumbling. A nation that is the progeny of rulers and heroes like Bhagirath, Raghu, Shivaji, Jahnsi ki Raani, Bhagat Singh, Lal Bahadur Shastri, Swami Dayanandji, and so on is collapsing!

Our once mighty and invincible Hindu nation needs to step up to the plate and do what is right one family, one child, one school, one politician, and one city at a time. But we must do so *now*.

Urgently, and as a matter of top priority. Now! Before it's too little too late! Awake! Hindus Awake!

Jai Hind!

12.2: The Need in this Age of Kali

Let us now stop and change gears. Take stock of the times we live in. This is the age of Kali, or *Kal-Yug*, the yug or era of progressive and rapid degeneration of moral and ethical values. It is the era of ignorance, the era of darkness. The shortest of the four yugs, it is also purported to be the moral worst.

It is the era where "good" is in short supply, and there seems to be an uninterruptible, bottomless supply of "bad" or evil. It is the age where "I" and "me" are paramount and all else takes second place. Self-satisfaction and self-gratification are the undisputed reigning champs of goals and desires, and all else seems irrelevant.

Money becomes the motive rather than the vehicle. Money becomes the object of envy and desire. Individual material goals and material desires *(vasnaas* and *kaamnas)* take precedence over family and interpersonal relationships, family goals, family desires and harmony, what to speak of society's or nation's needs.

Man is in spiritual free-fall because the senses, or *indriya*, reign supreme, and humans become their slaves rather than their masters. Man is in a constant rat-race, caught up in flash and one-upmanship. He forgets that for all its flash, a bungalow, a car, or a flat-screen plasma TV doesn't buy lasting happiness or true human companionship or relationship; nor will it do anything to elevate his conscious or conscience for this life or the next. It may buy him momentary glee or a fleeting sense of satisfaction, and it may even earn him more headaches by arousing the envy or jealousy of others.

Man has little time to even think or realize that when he finally falls off the rat or hamster mill as one day he certainly must, he needs only a two-by-six pier or casket! Everything he spent valuable time aimlessly amassing will sit there and mock him for having wasted this God-given human form of his. Literally, what a waste!

There is a lot to be said for the age-old Hindu philosophy of *simple living and high thinking*. Think about that!

Paradoxically, this is also a *wonderful* era to live in.

Yes, wonderful. Remember the age-old adage of the cup being half *empty*? Well, how about half *full* instead? Yup, in this *wonderful* age of Kali-Yug, it is not *all* bad, for there is a great positive aspect if one can see it. There is a *divine* "exemption" if you wish that is only available in this wonderful age. God is the most easily attainable in this age, which is why it happens to be the most *wonderful* of all ages *despite* all of its shortcomings.

The all-knowing knows that man will sink to the lowest of consciousness in Kali Yug. He will be busy chasing money, a mate, a neighbor's wife, his tail, or whatever else happens to catch his fancy, thus leaving him very little or no time for spiritual and mental elevation. Hence, with all the flash, glamour and distractions abounding, there will be little time for *puja* and *kirtan*, let alone austerities and *yagnas*.

Therefore, God in His grace and mercy, has allowed for a *divine exemption* where *He* can be attained by *bhakti* and devotion alone without the necessity of performance of severe austerities and the like.

This, my learned friends, is what makes our *Mrityu-Lok* (planet of mortals, the earth) and Kali-Yug the envy of even the *devtas*. The only requirement is that it be true devotion to Krishna. The practice of daily mala-jap for the show of it (*dhambh*) without true devotion is foolish and self-deceptive, for example. One must be doing what one does sincerely and straight from the heart. Remember, not a step towards Krishna is wasted. But that step towards Him must be with genuine faith and devotion.

Though Krishna controls all, he gave us a mind and a heart. If we turn our will to *truly* attaining Krishna, we *shall*. Recall that this is a promise He makes in His *Gita*.

He also says that *not a drop* of devotion shall go unaccounted for. Therefore, any moment in His thought shall bear the *correct* fruit leading to His eventual attainment. Whether you start in the womb, like Shukhdevji or Prahaladji, or start at 70, all steps taken toward Him *shall* count.

And these steps count the most in Kali-Yug, for *it* has the shortest path of all Yugs that lead to Krishna.

How cool is that?

Awake! Hindus Awake! Seize this opportunity, for life is short, and great opportunities like these extremely rare!

Get off the hamster mill, and learn to live life *with Krishna* in it!

12.3: The Socio-Political Need

There is an additional and *parallel* purpose, though. In these turbulent and ever-shifting times, it is important to *maintain* and advance Bhaaratia Sanskriti and Hinduism, along with its attendant culture, vegetarianism, religion and peace. We must not be divided and conquered. We must stop the internal bickering and pettiness forthwith. Bhaaratia vichaar is noble, and second to none.

We must unite under *one Bhaaratia* sanskriti. There must always be freedom of expression and religion in Bhaarat. But it *is,* after-all, Bhaarat and Hindustaan. A sovereign nation that holds *Hindu* ideals above all else.

Let us *learn* from the *Gita.* We must act. Inaction is impotency, and an impotent nation shall perish and lose its sovereignty and, ultimately, *everything.* This is stated by Lord Krishna Himself at the initiation of the great battle at Kurukshetra, where He delivers His Gita to Arjun. We must not be the aggressors. Lord Krishna Himself was King Yudhishtir's shanti doot. He sought to avoid bloodshed at any cost including relegating Himself to the position of the peace messenger. Therefore, aggression must never be initiated, but it must also never be tolerated whether physical, political, educational, or otherwise if sovereignty is to be retained.

However, let us remember a modern-day scholar of the *Gita.* A great statesman of a tiny physique, brilliant smile, and wonderful philosophy. Yes, the great Gandhiji. You should not *initiate* physical aggression. But you cannot simply stand by as your ideology and *samaaj* is torn down bit by tiny bit. Inaction or passiveness by those in a position of power with authority to act is considered *paap* by Lord Krishna. One must stand up for the Truth, the Culture, the religion, and self-government.

Shame on you if you choose to jump ship out of lobotomized or materialistic thinking. Freedom of thought, religion, speech and expression must always exist, and must always be cherished. These are cornerstone to Hinduism. Ultimately, these priciples are what *every* human in all of creation truly seeks – the dream to break free from the self-inflicted bondage to Maya. How can a human even think about *ultimate* liberation if even *worldly* liberation is quashed or subdued?

Hinduism *demands* freedom of thought, speech and religion. Therefore, if and when the attempts occur to try and snuff out these magnificient principles, such attackers must be repelled and vanquished decisively and swiftly.

In other words, do not be aggressors, but do not be conquered either, especially by non-Hindus in our own Hindustaan, whether in society, politics, literature, customs or government. Inaction *is* impotency, says Lord Krishna. Bhaarat, do not be impotent, do not be benevolent. Do not let mundane material greed and wants get in the way of your true ideals and those of your society, people and nation.

Jawaharlal Nehru unfortunately did exactly what he should *not* have done. He foolishly relied on corrupt and greedy assistants when he became the first Prime Minister of free India. He allowed his desire to cloud his judgment and prove in the end that morals and ideals of even a potentially great statesman can easily fall prey to whims and desires of a greedy or misguided assistant.

Current politicians need to *stop* being 'politicians' and become *patriotic statesmen* again! Isn't it interesting to note that the term 'statesman' is hardly used anymore? Perhaps the one screamingly obvious reason is that there are few dignitaries worth referring to by this meaningful connotation anymore! Politicians can *never* be great statesmen without first becoming patriotic. Herein lies the key to greatness - *patriotism.* Awake, my Hindu rulers in power, and stop being politicians! Become patriotic statesmen again, and illuminate Bhaaratia vichaar and sanskriti for the entire Universe to benefit from!

Listen up! Those of you Hindus in *any* responsible governmental position anywhere on the face of this planet. Lead the way by example! *Talk is cheap*, as everyone knows. Show me! Better yet, show yourself first! Prove to yourself and your family and community that you are even worthy of their trust. Be a true leader, a genuine statesman, and bring 'nobility' back to those in power anywhere rather than contempt and disgust. Do what is right for the people and for the nation. You can prosper, and you should prosper, but only with integrity and honor.

Pujya Gandhiji, though having taught the world what substance Indians are made of and showing us the path of non-violence, was forced aside and had to go along with putting a good politician but with corrupt and traitorous assistants at the head of Independent and free India at the moment of victory, casting the great Sardar aside. Having fought a difficult fight resulting in a colonial empire sinking to its knees, why cave in to the whims, tantrums and desires of a wannabe statesman? And at what great cost to the Hindu nation? Should Nehru have been allowed to be the prime minister at all? Remember, it is the ninety-five percent majority that let such foolish whims and desires bear horrible fruit we all have to eat.

Therefore, do not cave in to corruption, greed or politics. It is not the time to be ambivalent or passive.

Hindustaan must have *Hindu* put back *fully* into its *entire* fabric. Awake, my Hindu friends! Do not be the aggressors, but do not be passive! Awake, Hindustaan! Awake Bhaarat! Awake all Hindus! For you have slumbered way too long already! Awake Now! Before Hindustaan has to change its name or be divided and redrawn yet again!! The call to literary and philosophical battle is now!

Remember, it is *not* a call to violence! We must learn from Gandhiji! Violence shall shame us all. And, as Gandhiji so aptly put it: an eye for an eye will *certainly* make the whole world blind!

Gandhiji said that the real devils that we needed to fight resided in our hearts and that is where the battles must be fought and won. He did not toil in vain. It must be back to the basics, the fundamentals, the very essence and core of Hinduism. Yes, including the economic lessons of home-grown consumption and the power of masses, and everything else he taught us well. His principals are still very much applicable today. Yes, start with cotton. Educate the young.

These principals are applicable worldwide to peacefully advancing *bhaaratia sanskar* and *vichaar* to make the world nobler and less violent.

Awake! *Jaago!* I implore you again and again! Awake, my Hindu rulers in positions of power anywhere, and stop being politicians! Become the great patriotic statesmen again that our *poojnia bhoomi* is so *prakhyat* at producing, and illuminate Bhaaratia vichaar and sanskriti for the entire Universe to benefit from!

12.4: The Need to Unite

Let us examine another huge parallel and foundational issue that nobody wants to address. At least not by the horns, anyway.

We have a big, no a huge, nay a *monumental* problem with so-called 'religious differences' traceable to exactly *what name* to call the Supreme by! This is the most ludicrous, most childish and baseless issue to ever divide a people! Talk about dumb and dumbfounding! So great is the problem that it is tearing at and shredding the very fabric of Hinduism.

End the internal religious bickering henceforth! If you are truly a *genuine* believer in the Supreme Personality, how can you not see Ram in Krishna, or Shiv in Ram, or Shiv in Sai? How can you not see Krishna in Mahavir, or Swaminarayan in Krishna?

Only *fools* and *arrogant vidvans* and theologians distinguish between God and His glorious manifestations or avataars and divide over it! Why sink to such pettiness, only to expose to yourself if not the rest of the world that *you* have learned really *nothing at all* from the very Scriptures you quote?

Understand this concept completely. This will be repeated later, but make note of this fundamental idea that is allowing us to be divided and vanquished like the petty *fools* we really and so apparently are: It is pointless, meaningless, divisive and disruptive to split hairs and get polarized on opposing views of the ultimate truth, or someone's version of it. For, has anyone ever come back from the dead to tell you what *the* truth is? There is a reason, then, why it is called Faith. Yes, FAITH!

Is that really so hard to understand? The concept of Faith? *He* will help show you the correct way to Him *if* you have devotion and desire in your heart to know and attain him.

Call the God, the Supreme Personality, by whatever avataar or manifestation that pleases you, be it Krishna, Vishnu, Shiv, Ram, Mahavir, Bhuddh, or Swaminarayan, or any of His other countless and glorious names. The condition *must* be that you worship and follow the glory of the manifestation not only *without* degrading *His* other manifestations but also by duly respecting them as *His*! Why is this so difficult to understand? Does a modern day global businessman only accept dollars but refuse to accept sterling pounds? Then why the folly and atrocities with His avataars? Why the idiocies such as we only follow Mahavir but not Krishna and so on? Such thoughts and vocalizations, my Hindu friends are *the* height of stupidity and ignorance! Not only that, these are highly arrogant and divisive by their very nature. They eat at and tear at the very fabric uniting Hindus, much as a cancer spreads and rots the host from within. No wonder we Hindus can almost never act in unison!

Therefore, HINDUS AWAKE! Follow *His* rules. Sing His glory at the top of your lungs from the highest mountain in *whatever* name that pleases your aatma. But realize that His glory is present in every one of His avataars!

Most of all, *AWAKE*! Awake and unite, my Hindu friends, *before* our culture and religion are relegated to the depths of history books, and Hindu self-rule becomes a mirage, what to speak of mukti and moksh for not only us but for the generations yet to come! Awake, and unite under one Bhaaratia vichaar.

Therefore, I implore *you all*. Every Hindu on this wonderful planet! Jaago! Hindus Awake! Put aside the utter pettiness that will ultimately cost us *everything*, from our very identity to our great and once-mighty Hindu nation and people, if we let it. Slowly but surely it will happen.

Shame on us if it does! Jai Hind!

Remember, dharam does *not* defend us,
***We* defend *our* dharam!**
Simply *chanting* His holy name defends
***not* our dharam!**
Jaago!
***Awake*, my fellow Hindus!**
Our treasure is starting to slip away
One person, One family
and One generation at a time.
***Act Now*!**
The Sands of Time
And the doot of Yam
Wait for No-One.
The Time to Act is Now!
***hindus* Awake!**

**When It's all said and done,
The Final Choice is Yours.**

Your Move!

*T*o Continue Exploring our Magnificent, Phenomenal
And truly amazing Culture, Religion & Philosophy,
As well as build on *The Foundation*
we have started to lay,
In an 'out of the box' and highly simplified approach
In the same bold and even controversial style
That explores not *'what'* but more importantly *'why'*
Written in the same simple, fun and
easy to understand language,

Look for

hindus

Awake!

Book 2

By

Deepak N. Kotecha, O.D.,
&
Smita D. Kotecha, R.Ph.

Coming Soon!

CHAPTER 13

Recommended Reading

The Short but *Complete* List:

1. Ramayan
2. Shrimad Bhagwat
3. Shrimad Bhagwat Gita

CHAPTER 14

Bibliography

References

1. *Bhagavad-Gita As It Is,* Second Edition, by His Divine Grace A. C. Bhaktivedanta Swami Praphupad, Bhaktivedanta Book Trust, 1989, 9.17
2. *The Rig Veda,* translated by Griffith, Ralph T.H., 1896, 1.22.20
3. *Bhagavad-Gita As It Is,* Second Edition, by His Divine Grace A. C. Bhaktivedanta Swami Praphupad, Bhaktivedanta Book Trust, 1989, 15.13
4. *The Mundaka Upanishad,* Internet Edition, by Swami Krishnananda, The Divine Life Society, Sivananda Ashram, Rishikesh, India, 1951, 1.7
5. *Srimad Bhagavatam,* by His Divine Grace A. C. Bhaktivedanta Swami Praphupad, Bhaktivedanta Book Trust, 1987, 3.21.19
6. *Bhagavad-Gita As It Is,* Second Edition, by His Divine Grace A. C. Bhaktivedanta Swami Praphupad, Bhaktivedanta Book Trust, 1989, 9.8
7. *Bhagavad-Gita As It Is,* Second Edition, by His Divine Grace A. C. Bhaktivedanta Swami Praphupad, Bhaktivedanta Book Trust, 1989, 10.39
8. *Bhagavad-Gita As It Is,* Second Edition, by His Divine Grace A. C. Bhaktivedanta Swami Praphupad, Bhaktivedanta Book Trust, 1989, 7.6
9. *Bhagavad-Gita As It Is,* Second Edition, by His Divine Grace A. C. Bhaktivedanta Swami Praphupad, Bhaktivedanta Book Trust, 1989, 7.7

10. *Bhagavad-Gita As It Is,* Second Edition, by His Divine Grace A. C. Bhaktivedanta Swami Praphupad, Bhaktivedanta Book Trust, 1989, 9.5
11. *Bhagavad-Gita As It Is,* Second Edition, by His Divine Grace A. C. Bhaktivedanta Swami Praphupad, Bhaktivedanta Book Trust, 1989, 4.7,8
12. *Manu Smriti – Laws of Manu,* Bharatdesam, http://www.bharatadesam.com/spiritual/manu_smriti/manu_smriti.php, V.5
13. *The Chhandogya Upanishad,* Internet Edition, by Swami Krishnananda, The Divine Life Society, Sivananda Ashram, Rishikesh, India, 1984, Part V, 5,1-3
14. *Bhagavad-Gita As It Is,* Second Edition, by His Divine Grace A. C. Bhaktivedanta Swami Praphupad, Bhaktivedanta Book Trust, 1989, 3.6
15. *Bhagavad-Gita As It Is,* Second Edition, by His Divine Grace A. C. Bhaktivedanta Swami Praphupad, Bhaktivedanta Book Trust, 1989, 9.17
16. *The Rig Veda,* translated by Griffith, Ralph T.H., 1896, 1.22.20

17. *Srimad Bhagavatam,* by His Divine Grace A. C. Bhaktivedanta Swami Praphupad, Bhaktivedanta Book Trust, 1987, 1.3.28
18. *Bhagavad-Gita As It Is,* Second Edition, by His Divine Grace A. C. Bhaktivedanta Swami Praphupad, Bhaktivedanta Book Trust, 1989, 2.56
19.. *Bhagavad-Gita As It Is,* Second Edition, by His Divine Grace A. C. Bhaktivedanta Swami Praphupad, Bhaktivedanta Book Trust, 1989, 9.17
20. *Bhagavad-Gita As It Is,* Second Edition, by His Divine Grace A. C. Bhaktivedanta Swami Praphupad, Bhaktivedanta Book Trust, 1989, 9.17
21. *Bhagavad-Gita As It Is,* Second Edition, by His Divine Grace A. C. Bhaktivedanta Swami Praphupad, Bhaktivedanta Book Trust, 1989, 1.19
22. *Bhagavad-Gita As It Is,* Second Edition, by His Divine Grace A. C. Bhaktivedanta Swami Praphupad, Bhaktivedanta Book Trust, 1989, 9.17
23. *Bhagavad-Gita As It Is,* Second Edition, by His Divine Grace A. C. Bhaktivedanta Swami Praphupad, Bhaktivedanta Book Trust, 1989, 15.15

24. Bhagavad-Gita As It Is, Second Edition, by His Divine Grace A. C. Bhaktivedanta Swami Praphupad, Bhaktivedanta Book Trust, 1989, 15.19

25. Bhagavad-Gita As It Is, Second Edition, by His Divine Grace A. C. Bhaktivedanta Swami Praphupad, Bhaktivedanta Book Trust, 1989, 15.20

27. Bhagavad-Gita As It Is, Second Edition, by His Divine Grace A. C. Bhaktivedanta Swami Praphupad, Bhaktivedanta Book Trust, 1989, 9.21

28. Bhagavad-Gita As It Is, Second Edition, by His Divine Grace A. C. Bhaktivedanta Swami Praphupad, Bhaktivedanta Book Trust, 1989, 17.14

29. Srimad Bhagavatam, by His Divine Grace A. C. Bhaktivedanta Swami Praphupad, Bhaktivedanta Book Trust, 1989, 1.3.28
Srimad Bhagavatam, by His Divine Grace A. C. Bhaktivedanta Swami Praphupad, Bhaktivedanta Book Trust, 1987, 1.3.28

30. Bhagavad-Gita As It Is, Second Edition, by His Divine Grace A. C. Bhaktivedanta Swami Praphupad, Bhaktivedanta Book Trust, 1989, 15.14

31. *Bhagavad-Gita As It Is,* Second Edition, by His Divine Grace A. C. Bhaktivedanta Swami Praphupad, Bhaktivedanta Book Trust, 1989, 15.18

32. Bhagavad-Gita As It Is, Second Edition, by His Divine Grace A. C. Bhaktivedanta Swami Praphupad, Bhaktivedanta Book Trust, 1989, 18.66

33. Bhagavad-Gita As It Is, Second Edition, by His Divine Grace A. C. Bhaktivedanta Swami Praphupad, Bhaktivedanta Book Trust, 1989, 4.7,8

34. Bhagavad-Gita As It Is, Second Edition, by His Divine Grace A. C. Bhaktivedanta Swami Praphupad, Bhaktivedanta Book Trust, 1989, 9.27

35. Bhagavad-Gita As It Is, Second Edition, by His Divine Grace A. C. Bhaktivedanta Swami Praphupad, Bhaktivedanta Book Trust, 1989, 18.66